TUNES FOR 'TOONS

TUNES FOR 'TOONS

MUSIC AND THE HOLLYWOOD CARTOON

DANIEL GOLDMARK

UNIVERSITY OF CALIFORNIA PRESS
Berkeley · Los Angeles · London

The publisher gratefully acknowledges the generous
contribution to this book provided by the Music in America
Endowment Fund of the University of California Press
Associates, which is supported by a major gift from Sukey
and Gil Garcetti, Michael Roth, and the Roth Family
Foundation.

University of California Press
Berkeley and Los Angeles, California

University of California Press, Ltd.
London, England

Library of Congress Cataloging-in-Publication Data

Goldmark, Daniel.
    Tunes for 'toons : music and the Hollywood
cartoon / Daniel Goldmark.
       p.   cm.
    Includes bibliographical references and index.
    ISBN 0-520-23617-3 (cloth : alk. paper)
     1. Animated film music—History and
criticism. I. Title.

ML2075.G65   2005
781.5'42—dc22   2004025268

Manufactured in the United States of America

14 13 12 11 10 09 08 07 06 05
10 9 8 7 6 5 4 3 2 1

This book is printed on Natures Book, which contains 50% post-consumer waste and meets the
minimum requirements of ANSI/NISO Z39.48-1992
(R 1997) (Permanence of Paper).

For Cyleste Collins

and Philip Brett

CONTENTS

List of Illustrations and Tables   *ix*

List of Music Examples   *xiii*

Acknowledgments   *xv*

Introduction: Why Cartoon Music?   *1*

1. CARL STALLING AND POPULAR MUSIC IN THE
   WARNER BROS. CARTOONS   *10*

2. "YOU REALLY DO BEAT THE SHIT OUT OF THAT CAT":
   SCOTT BRADLEY'S (VIOLENT) MUSIC FOR MGM   *44*

3. *JUNGLE JIVE:* ANIMATION, JAZZ MUSIC,
   AND SWING CULTURE   *77*

4. CORNY CONCERTOS AND SILLY SYMPHONIES:
   CLASSICAL MUSIC AND CARTOONS   *107*

5. *WHAT'S OPERA, DOC?* AND CARTOON OPERA   *132*

A Brief Conclusion   *161*

Appendix 1: Carl Stalling Documents   *165*

Appendix 2: Scott Bradley Documents   *167*

Notes   *171*

Bibliography   *199*

Index   *213*

ILLUSTRATIONS AND TABLES

FIGURES

1. Carl Stalling   11
2. The cloverleaf in *Fast and Furryous*   27
3. *The Swooner Crooner*   29
4. *The Fifth-Column Mouse*   34
5. *Mouse Warming*   37
6. *Bugs Bunny Rides Again*   42
7. Dancing in *Bugs Bunny Rides Again*   42
8. Getting out of town in *Bugs Bunny Rides Again*   42
9. Scott Bradley at Harman-Ising in the late 1930s   46
10. The flower and the weed in *Dance of the Weed*   56
11. Out the window, in *Solid Serenade*   65
12. Heading for the sink in *Solid Serenade*   66
13. Tom's disguise in *Puttin' on the Dog*   70
14. The dog's head gets around in *Puttin' on the Dog*   71
15. Paul Whiteman crowned king in production sketches for *King of Jazz*   82
16. Cannibals/natives dancing in production sketches for *King of Jazz*   83
17. Louis Armstrong and the band playing in *I'll Be Glad When You're Dead, You Rascal You*   86
18. A native becomes Armstrong in *I'll Be Glad When You're Dead*   88

19. A jungle drummer becomes Tubby Hall in *I'll Be
    Glad When You're Dead*   89
20. Bubbles and animal skins in *A Rhapsody in Black
    and Blue*   91
21. *The Isle of Pingo-Pongo*   92
22. Stepin Fechit in *Clean Pastures*   95
23. Jazz greats appeal to the head angel in *Clean
    Pastures*   95
24. Cab Calloway and his band and Louis Armstrong
    in *Clean Pastures*   95
25. Satan comes calling in *Clean Pastures*   97
26. *Tin Pan Alley Cats*   98
27. *Three Little Bops*   105
28. *Rhapsody in Rivets*   112
29. *Rhapsody Rabbit*   112
30. Bugs versus Giovanni Jones, round 1, in *Long-
    Haired Hare*   115
31. Bobby-soxer Bugs in *Long-Haired Hare*   118
32. The Hollywood Bowl in *Tom and Jerry in the
    Hollywood Bowl*   119
33. The musicians in *Baton Bunny*   120
34. Bugs takes charge as Stokowski in *Long-Haired
    Hare*   122
35. Depictions of Leopold Stokowski in *Hollywood
    Canine Canteen* and *Hollywood Steps Out*   124
36. Magic runs amok in *Magical Maestro*   126
37. *Jump Start*   133
38. Title card of *What's Opera, Doc?*   137
39. Elmer, the mighty hunter, in *What's Opera, Doc?*   137
40. Elmer in a rage in *What's Opera, Doc?*   138
41. Love duet and ballet in *What's Opera, Doc?*   139
42. Elmer mad and then sad in *What's Opera, Doc?*   140
43. Bugs meets Hermann Göring in *Herr Meets Hare*   144
44. Dramatic action and heavy breathing in *What's
    Opera, Doc?*   149
45. Bugs as Brünnhilde in *What's Opera, Doc?*   152
46. The world comes crashing down in *What's
    Opera, Doc?*   156
47. The disdainful steed in *What's Opera, Doc?*   157

TABLES

1. *Mouse Warming* cue sheet   38
2. *Bugs Bunny Rides Again* cue sheet   40
3. Music in *What's Opera, Doc?*   147

MUSIC EXAMPLES

1. W. A. Mozart, sonata in C major for piano,
   K. 545   2
2. Raymond Scott, melody for "Powerhouse"   28
3. Sigmund Mogulesko, "Khosn, Kale Mazl Tov"   33
4. Scott Bradley, themes for the weed and flower from
   Dance of the Weed   57
5. Twelve-tone scale in *Puttin' on the Dog*   71
6. Alphons Czibulka, "Wintermärchen"   109
7. Franz Liszt, Hungarian Rhapsody no. 2 in C-sharp
   minor   111
8. Melody for "Be vewy quiet—I'm hunting wabbits!"   137
9. Melody for "Oh Bwunhilda, you're so lovely"   139
10. Melody for "Kill the wabbit"   153

ACKNOWLEDGMENTS

In tracing the history and development of this project, I am reminded that it spans close to twenty-five years, and involves many, many people—so many that I'm certain I will forget to thank or acknowledge *someone* (who I hope will forgive my poor memory).

My piano teacher, the late Blanche Nissim, convinced me it was not enough to just hear the Mozart that inspired this study, but to play it in the hopes of beginning to fully understand it. Ron Perry helped further this affection for music with a great deal of encouragement during high school.

I was a new music major at the University of California, Riverside, when I first realized my affinity for and interest in cartoon music; the faculty of the Department of Music encouraged me to continue asking questions. They included Barbara Bennett, who generously hosted in her home my first attempt at empirical research: a gathering of music students playing "name that tune" with cartoon soundtracks. Edward Clinkscale first planted the seed of the notion that music history might be a rewarding field. Philip Brett and Byron Adams gave me a remarkable amount of guidance and support at a time when I found "musicology" an unfamiliar term; these three men ultimately inspired me to become a musicologist myself.

While at UCR I took a class taught by a visiting professor, Irene Alm, a UCLA graduate student. On hearing of my proposed project, she insisted I contact her UCLA colleague Jim Westby, who guided me through many of the thorny issues I first faced with my research, and has remained a good friend and an unrelenting critic.

I could not have made a better decision than choosing to pursue graduate work at UCLA, where the faculty and my colleagues shared my excitement about new and interesting topics. David Ake was the first graduate student I met on my arrival, and my respect for him as a colleague and my affection for him as a friend continues to grow. Within my first quarter of graduate school I gave my first "real" paper on cartoon music at a meeting of the Royal Music Association at Royal Holloway, University of London, where I met a future colleague and close friend, Mai Kawabata. Durrell Bowman was my *Simpsons* co-conspirator; I could always count on him and Louis Niebur to join me for a meal or a drink when we had to stop work. Charles Garrett came to the program just as I began to slip into the haze of late-night writing, but fortunately I got to know him well enough to find in him a stimulating colleague with an especially fine wit.

While the entire faculty of the Department of Musicology saw my work at one time or another, Robert Walser, Mitchell Morris, and in particular Susan McClary helped me see this project to its completion. Susan taught me how to formulate questions that I could often barely articulate, and then showed me how to tear those questions apart to develop new ones. Her love for teaching and her unmatched abilities as a writer and editor made her the ideal mentor, both then and now.

Other friends and colleagues in academia have encouraged me by vetting drafts and providing useful feedback. Jeff Smith and Tim Anderson, from the world of film and media studies, have been wonderful advocates for my work. Neil Lerner has been encouraging me and my research practically from the day this project began. Marty Marks's scholarship in film music gives me a goal for which I can continue to strive. And Claudia Gorbman's remarkable grasp of issues regarding film *and* music continues to inspire me.

The animation community (that part consisting of animation historians in particular) is remarkably small and close-knit, and I feel especially fortunate to count many of these people as friends. They have supported my work and this project for many years.

My first contact with the archival side of Warner Bros. cartoons came through the very helpful folks at the USC Cinema-Television Library, including over the years Stuart Ng, Bill Whittington, Noelle Carter, Leith Adams (at the Warner Bros. Corporate Archive), and the ever-present and indomitable Ned Comstock.

Jerry Beck's love for animation is infectious. He has provided me with introductions to dozens of people, has made himself available for questions and requests, and has supported this work without fail. Michael Barrier, Greg Ford, and Mark Kausler have been generous to a fault in sharing their time and considerable resources with me. The knowledge possessed by these three about popular culture and specifically about animation always keeps me on my toes.

Alf Clausen, Steve and Julie Bernstein, and the late Richard Stone shared their experiences as cartoon composers with me. I was thrilled to find in Rich Stone someone who obsessed on Carl Stalling as much as I, and was glad to have the chance to get to know him before his much too early death in 2001.

Other people in animation who contributed to this project include Leonard Maltin, Mark Langer, Ray Pointer, Will Ryan, Linda Simensky, Steve Schneider, Keith Scott, David Gerstein, J. B. Kaufman, Rob Clampett, and Howard Green. Chuck Jones gracefully granted me several interviews in the early 1990s.

I also received encouragement, help, or inspiration in various ways from Yuval Taylor, Chris Ware, Irwin Chusid, Robb Armstrong, Richard Leppert, Ivan Raykoff, Gordon Haramaki, Rudy Behlmer, Meg Wilson, Phil Brophy, Todd Doogan, and Neal Flum.

My time as a librarian and archivist at Spümcø animation gave me an invaluable chance to work in the animation industry and meet dozens of creative folks who simply love cartoons. I learned a great deal from working with John Kricfalusi, who has a passion for classic cartoons unmatched by anyone I've ever met, while Vincent Waller became a wonderful mentor for many years.

For all but four months of my time in graduate school I had the incredibly good fortune to work, first freelance and eventually full-time, at Rhino Entertainment in West Los Angeles. Besides being a truly "great place to work," it enabled me to meet many talented writers, artists, and self-professed music geeks. My co-workers in editorial taught me a completely new approach to writing (and critiquing writing) about music, and have permanently changed my approach to writing and teaching for the better. They include Julee Stover, Vanessa Atkins, and Steven Chean. Among other Rhinos (and friends) who helped this project in its development are Rick Brodey, Dee Murphy, Bob Carlton, and Thane Tierney. Thane in particular has been utterly selfless, spending hours discussing everything from cartoons to folk rock, and made the ultimate commitment by reading this book in manuscript and deftly guiding me through some tricky issues.

I did not know what to expect when I moved to Tuscaloosa to take a job at the University of Alabama. I certainly had no idea I would meet such welcoming, stimulating, and simply wonderful colleagues in the School of Music and throughout the university. Jerry Rosiek, Jeremy Butler, Kurtis Schaeffer, Joshua Rothman, Jessica Lacher-Feldman, Utz McKnight, and Harry Price are all, in part, responsible for helping me craft this book in its final stages. Special thanks are owed to Jerry Rosiek and the entire Interdisciplinary and Interpretive Research Writing Group, who make editing one's own work invigorating and enjoyable. The community at Alabama that welcomed us in has made the experience so positive that I still can't convince my friends around the country that such an environment exists anywhere.

A minigrant from UC Riverside helped fund my initial research on classical music in cartoons, while a generous travel grant from the American Heritage Center at the University of Wyoming allowed me to spend several days looking through Carl Stalling's music library, as well as other useful documents.

Of course, I must thank my exceedingly patient editor, Mary Francis, as well as the anonymous readers of this manuscript for their many useful and insightful observations and suggestions.

My family has known about my idée fixe for years and has unstintingly encouraged my studies. My grandparents urged me my entire life to "keep my head on my shoulders"; I'm sorry they can't see this. My parents, Larry and Carol, supported this project literally from its moment of inception—the day I asked for piano lessons. They and my brother, Josh, have provided moral, financial, spiritual, and comestible sustenance. My extended family—the Collinses, the Prystowskys, and the Mileses—have all played a part in this, most of all by supporting my life with Cyleste Collins, my dear friend and now my dear spouse.

Before we met, Cyleste had only seen *The Simpsons* a few times—now she gets the jokes faster than I do. She has been subjected to more information about cartoons than anyone would ever imagine. She has read far too many versions of this manuscript and has always been able to help me see things differently. Her support, patience, and love make this book what it is.

And just as I began to dig in to this project in earnest, we had an addition to our family unit—Maggie, a twenty-one-pound so-called Wheaten Terrier Mix. Amazingly, she has been content to just hang out under the desk in my office (at home, school, or work) while I hack away at my prose. Maggie's unabashed affection gives both Cyleste and me perspective on our busy lives.

WHY CARTOON MUSIC?

Around age five, I had my first encounter with what Germans call an *ohrwurm,* or earworm: I had a tune stuck in my head. I had no idea where or when I had heard it. With the help of a piano teacher, my mother and I finally identified the piece as Mozart's piano sonata in C major, K. 545. The tune I was stuck on was the opening melody (see music example 1). I took piano lessons for four years, and during that time I learned to play the piece. My interest in the piano faded and I moved on to other instruments, although the Mozart stayed with me as something of an idée fixe. In my early twenties, I got stuck on another tune during a class on Romantic music: Schubert's "Die Erlkönig," with which I felt a strange familiarity—particularly the opening melody in the piano's lower register. Not long after that class, I realized that I had learned both the Schubert and the Mozart from a cartoon, or, more accurately, from many cartoons.

Mozart's C major sonata, the so-called facile sonata (presumably because of its relative technical simplicity and simple melody), appears in more than a dozen Warner Bros. cartoons. The revelation that I had learned this melody from cartoons came as a shock. At the time of my epiphany, however, I did not recognize that most of the references to the tune were actually a jazz combo arrangement of the song written by the composer and bandleader Raymond Scott, titled "In an Eighteenth Century Drawing Room." This later discovery confirmed my suspicions

EXAMPLE 1 W. A. Mozart, sonata in C major for piano, K. 545.

that not only had I gleaned knowledge of classical music (Rossini, Liszt, Brahms, von Suppé, and others) from watching cartoons on Saturday mornings, but I had learned other styles of music as well. I soon realized I had a working familiarity with songs from no less than a dozen genres or traditions, among them classical, jazz, Tin Pan Alley, Hollywood film musicals, folk songs from America and around the world, Viennese opera, and nineteenth-century American parlor songs, particularly the work of Stephen Foster. This project thus began as I tried to satisfy my curiosity about how much music I had learned from cartoons; it quickly blossomed into a full-scale investigation of music's role in animated cartoons, with a special emphasis on how cartoon music could embody cultural meanings. I decided to focus initially on what is often called the Golden Age of Hollywood cartoons (those shorts produced by animation studios for theatrical release from the early 1930s to the mid-1950s), because these cartoons had given me such a broad and eclectic introduction to music; I later expanded my scope to include all forms of animation.

Having an interest in cartoon music by no means leads directly to an actual study of that music. For most of their existence, animated shorts and animation in general have typically been viewed as devoid of any intellectual import whatsoever. The close relationship between comic strips and cartoons, and the frequency—observed by the film historian Kristin Thompson—with which "animated film narratives . . . drew upon fantasy, magic and traditional stories as a motivation for stylization," encouraged film critics in the 1920s and '30s to see animation as directed solely at children and led to "a trivialisation of the medium."[1]

Cartoons are also typically lumped together as a self-contained genre because they happen to have been created through the same process: animation. Yet even if we narrow our focus to just the output of the most prominent animation studios from the 1930s to the 1960s, we find a tremendous variety of output: animated shorts, two-reelers, and features fulfilling the requirements of every imaginable Hollywood genre, including westerns, mysteries, dramas, musicals, and documentaries, as well as comedies of every conceivable style—romantic, slapstick, chase, black, and musical. Animation is *not* a genre; it is a technological process that creates a particular (highly idiosyncratic) means of visual representation. The question then becomes, how did animation get pigeonholed into comedy? Thompson posits that because "animation could do things live-action could not, and hence it came to be assumed that it *should* do only these things," and because of the tradition that "all cartoons were supposed to be comic," a new ideology subsumed cartoons, one that allowed only these seemingly "appropriate" narratives to be used.[2] Thompson also shows that when television became the dominant source of visual entertainment, animation producers no longer counted adults as part of their ideal demographic; as they began to concentrate exclusively on children, they targeted their humor at a far less sophisticated viewer.

Fortunately, this trend has shifted in the last decade. A wealth of new animated television series have reinvigorated the public's interest in animation, in no small part thanks to the remarkable success and longevity of *The Simpsons*. *Ren & Stimpy, Animaniacs, King of the Hill, Powerpuff Girls, Dexter's Laboratory, SpongeBob SquarePants, Futurama, Fairly OddParents*, and numerous other shows have brought back the idea that animation appeals to people of all ages. The growing popularity of anime in the United States has also helped animation's credibility. True, a great many cartoons still pander to children, feature poor writing, and function as little more than animated toy commercials. But there are just as many stimulating shows appearing each year. As a result, animation studies has grown into a formidable discourse.

Soon after beginning my research I became frustrated by the lack of critical work on cartoon music, which convinced me that others found it insignificant. Until very recently, neither film studies nor musicology afforded film music any credence as an important topic; and film historians, as already noted, seldom gave more than a cursory glance toward animation, particularly Hollywood cartoons. I should not have been surprised that so little research had been done on the intersection of two already marginalized areas. This picture has changed considerably, however: film music criticism has burgeoned with the acceptance in the academy of general media studies, and critical investigations of animation have also expanded (although not to the same extent as those of film music).[3] But no matter who considers the topic, the resulting criticism never seems to exceed the bounds of the author's discipline. The film studies–based writings take little account of any actual music, and the few musicological essays seldom offer more than simple biographies enlivened by some musical examples. Neither approach considers much of the history of the animation industry or examines its production methods.

A telltale sign that cartoon music is seen as a poor relation to film music is the application of film music terminology to cartoons. Such dichotomies as source/underscore, diegetic/nondiegetic, and iconic/isomorphic can be very useful in discussions of the music in live-action films. They all in some way gauge the degree to which music stays within the traditional bounds of the narrative. That is, the audience usually knows whether or not the music is coming from within the story or diegesis (thus, nondiegetic music is perceptible not to the characters on screen but only to the audience). Occasionally these terms can be helpful for analyzing particular situations in cartoons, but they fail to take into account that music is far more integral to the construction of cartoons than of live-action films because the two forms are created in completely different ways. I therefore find such terms of limited utility.

Surviving evidence regarding music in films made before synchronized sound was developed indicates that cartoons received much less attention than features. Cue sheets and specially created scores—today of great interest to film music scholars—were created for cartoons only under the most extraordinary circumstances, and we thus have few substantial clues about how cartoons might have been accompanied. In his 1920s handbook, *How to Play the Cinema Organ,* George Tootell includes "'Cartoon' comedies, such as those of the famous Felix, though in these more opportunity is offered for the exercise of the musician's wit. The organist is recommended to extemporise accompaniments to cartoon comedies, which are always short and concise, and offer scope for witty extemporisation; it is not too much to say that a skillfully accompanied cartoon can often be the most popular item in the programme."[4] Tootell focuses on cartoons as occasions to display wit and perhaps skill, rather than discussing how music in them might be used to establish mood or define character. Edith Lang and George West's accompaniment guide of the same era offers similar advice, although it devotes an entire chapter to music for live-action comedies and animated cartoons.[5] The connection between cartoons and comedies is borne out in Erno Rapée's *Encyclopedia of Music for Pictures* (1925), which contains lists of appropriate songs for use in hundreds of situations. The sole entry relating specifically to cartoons is "Aesop's Fables," which contains a cross-reference to the more general category of "Comedy Pictures."[6]

Two years before Rapée's book was published, the earliest indication of an original musical arrangement for a cartoon appeared. On 2 June 1923, the periodical *Motion Picture News* printed

JAZZ AND "AESOP'S FILM FABLES" GOOD MIXERS

Jazz music goes well with "Aesop's Film Fables." That's the conclusion reached after a number of tests, and consequently hereafter Pathé, the distributor of these subjects, will furnish musical effect sheets to each distributor booking one of these cartoons, declares a statement from the Pathé home-office. At the New York Capitol this week "Spooks" was presented with a musical jazz accompaniment, and at the Strand "The Mouse Catcher" was similarly presented.[7]

Clearly some cartoons, like most early feature films, were distributed to theaters with "special scores." Though none of these has survived, other tangible examples of early cartoon music exist: for example, *PianOrgan Film Books of Incidental Music, Extracted from the World Famous "Berg" and "Cinema" Incidental Series,* comprising seven volumes in the 1920s, included five pieces under the heading "Animated Cartoonix." In 1926 the Cleveland-based music publisher Sam Fox printed *Loose Leaf Collection of Ring-Hager Novelties for Orchestra.* The second of ten pieces in the collection, "Funny Faces," bears the subtitle "A Comedy Sketch (For Animated Cartoons, Eccentric and Acrobatic Dancing, Etc.)." These same pieces were included in Sam Fox's classified catalogue three years later; a four-volume collection of music from the same company in 1931 bore the title *Incidental Music for News Reels, Cartoons, Pictorial Reviews, Scenics, Travelogues, etc.* and contained works by Edward Kilenyi, L. E. DeFrancesco, J. S. Zamecnik, Harry Read, and several others.[8] Cartoons in this period certainly were accompanied by music, but the form was not yet taken seriously. Indeed, the perception of cartoons solely as comedies limited their scores' potential before it even had a chance to develop.

Most books and manuals from the 1930s on film music make some mention of animated cartoons, still grouped with comedies and other short subjects. Walt Disney's cartoons are most frequently used to exemplify "good" scores, no doubt in part because the association of the Disney name with animation had become so ubiquitous. This international fame explains why, for instance, in *Film Music* (1936) Kurt London discusses only Disney's music in the section "Sound Cartoon Films" before moving on to European animation directors.[9] During this era the music in Disney's cartoons also gave rise to a term: "mickey-mousing," the exact synchronization of music and action. It was supposedly coined by David O. Selznick, who was derisively likening a Max Steiner score to the music of a Mickey Mouse cartoon. The phrase implies not only that the music in question is simplistic, or "mickey mouse," but also that it is telegraphing to the audience too much information: that is, the music is calling attention to itself as it describes what is happening on screen.[10] I'll address the usefulness of this term more fully in chapter 2.

As the animation industry reached a productive peak in the 1940s and '50s, coverage of cartoon music somewhat increased in various literary or professional journals, particularly *Film Music Notes*. Because *Film Music Notes* always tried to provide biographical as well as professional information on composers working in Hollywood in the 1940s, biographies of cartoon composers appeared sporadically. Once again, the predominance of the Disney studio in Hollywood ensured that their composers were the most frequently featured, with the sole exception of Scott Bradley. Darrell Calker, James Dietrich, Joe de Nat, Dave and Lou Fleischer, Eddie Kilfeather, Frank Marsales, Winston Sharples, Sammy Timberg, Arthur Turkisher, Clarence Wheeler, Eugene Poddany, Philip Scheib, Hoyt Curtin, David Raksin, Gail Kubik, Eugene Rodemich, Bernard Brown, Carl Stalling, Milt Franklyn, William Lava, and others writing music for cartoons received little or no attention.[11]

By the time critical examination of cartoon music began appearing in the late 1970s, the Hollywood studios producing theatrical shorts had all closed or ceased producing shorts. Roy Prendergast spends an entire chapter of *Film Music: A Neglected Art* (1977), "Music in the Cartoon and Experimental Animated Film," looking back at what was already a bygone era. He mainly explores Scott Bradley's music (relying in part on Bradley's numerous *Film Music Notes* articles) and the sound-on-film experiments of John Whitney and Norman McLaren. Just three years later, Jon Newsom provided an in-depth examination of the history of cartoon music in the *Quarterly Journal of the Library of Congress*.[12] His discussion centers largely on Disney, MGM (Bradley again), and the music for the UPA shorts of the 1950s. The subjects chosen by both Prendergast and Newsom reflected the information available. For instance, because practically nothing on the Warner Bros. composer Carl Stalling existed then (or now), he is barely mentioned at all; his influence on the rest of the industry had yet to be widely acknowledged. Since that time, a handful of other articles on cartoon music have appeared, treating topics that range from the application of Sergei Eisenstein's theories of sound to Disney cartoons to how the technological limitations of early sound affected the cartoons' music in the early 1930s.[13]

In many ways the responsibilities of cartoon music resemble those taken on by traditional film scores: establishing the setting, drawing the audience into the story, providing the viewer with additional information about a scene, telling the viewer how to feel at any given moment, and vitalizing the "lifeless" pictures of the film. This last point is particularly important for animated drawings, whose figures—unlike those in live-action films—were never alive to begin with. The medium of animation requires that music for cartoons be conceived and constructed differently than traditional feature film music. We can best see these differences by examining two issues: who helped to establish the paradigmatic sound of Hollywood cartoons, and how music was used to enhance and intensify cartoons as a whole.

Tunes for 'Toons thus presents a set of case studies rather than an all-encompassing history of cartoon music. And my key questions lead me to focus on two broad ideas: genre and compositional style. I discuss the methods of Carl Stalling and Scott Bradley, in my opinion the two most influential composers of music for theatrical cartoons, at the one studio where each had the most historical significance. For Bradley, that studio is necessarily MGM; for Stalling, a choice is possible. While some, with reason, might select Disney, arguing that his work there in 1928 and 1929 defined the entire field for years to come, I concentrate on Warner Bros., where he came into his own as a composer and where he wrote close to one new score every week for more than twenty years.

Carl Stalling's extraordinary influence on cartoon music as a whole suggests a host of possible avenues to explore, including his relation to mickey-mousing; the original music he wrote for each score that succeeds in mickey-mousing the action with its unexpected and unique melodic lines and instrumental choices; his collaboration with his arranger (and eventual successor), Milt Franklyn; and the role played by his experiences with Disney and Iwerks in preparing him for Warner Bros. Here I take up the most pressing topic, particularly in the eyes of his critics: Stalling's employment of popular songs in his scores. I thus examine why their use was so frequent if not pervasive, how those songs became a musical language through which Stalling could tell stories, and how his particular style colors our understanding of the Warner Bros. cartoons.

Scott Bradley, whose approach was diametrically opposed to Stalling's, provides the ideal foil. Bradley's formal training in composition and his love for contemporary classical or concert hall music explain why he avoided popular songs in his scores and why he constantly sought to raise the public's awareness of the quality of music in animated cartoons. He pays careful attention in his music to the action of each cartoon. I discuss the modernist techniques Bradley used both to elevate his scores aesthetically and to give them a unique musical "signature"—a compositional style distinct from that of any other studio composer for cartoons, most of all Stalling (who once said that his idea of a modernist composing style was the use of augmented intervals).[14]

The comparison of jazz and swing music with classical music and opera is not only natural, it has been made repeatedly in films and cartoons themselves. I therefore examine how the various studios made use of such culturally charged music in the cartoon narrative, gauging the success of composers at either integrating stylistic elements of these forms or completely appropriating them into their scores. To be sure, the most significant portion of existing scholarship on music and cartoons is devoted to the role of jazz and swing, but it has typically focused on representations of black jazz musicians. Equally important in these cartoons is what the very different approaches to jazz tell us about the public's view of the genre and its creators when these shorts were produced. Moreover, the look of jazz does not tell the whole story: the songs chosen, the personalities represented, and the specific styles appropriated in each short show how pervasive an element of popular culture jazz had become. Numerous forms of it—swing, bop, Dixieland, vocalese, boogie woogie, big band, and even free jazz—surfaced in cartoon scores or stories during the Hollywood studio era.

The natural complement to a study of jazz is a study of classical music. If we are to believe the oppositions set up in cartoons and films of the 1930s, '40s, and '50s, these two genres are cultural and aesthetic antagonists, constantly jockeying for social preeminence. The increasingly highbrow aura surrounding classical music and its practitioners provided cartoon directors with an endless supply of jokes at the expense of concert hall culture. After looking at *many* of these cartoons, we see that certain topics (the appearance and actions of the conductor, the attitudes of singers, and so on) and specific pieces (Rossini's *William Tell* overture and Liszt's Second Hungarian Rhapsody, for instance) seem perpetually ripe for ridicule. What makes the comparison of classical music and jazz so rewarding is that they actually have a great deal in common, especially in how they were used. Popular culture, expressed in animation, took the most recognizable bits of both as fodder for social commentary.

Tunes for 'Toons is far from objective or definitive: I have a very specific and relatively narrow agenda in mind. I focus on Carl Stalling and Scott Bradley because I believe that they helped establish the public's notion of what cartoon scores should sound like. Both men had well-defined ideas about what they wanted their music to convey, yet this desire for self-expression constantly pitted them against the Hollywood production system. Their chief obstacle was their limited opportunities (if any) to create a dialogue between the music and the visual components of the film. Stalling overcame this hurdle by using popular music to comment on the scores, while Bradley wrote music so specific to the animation that the cartoons often seemed to become animated ballets. Stalling and Bradley provide the most compelling case studies for this book, in part because of their musical influences and opposed approaches to scoring. My discussion of classical music and jazz also reflects my interest in these genres, and my particular fondness for cartoons that are scored exclusively within them. Any apparent neglect of other studios—Disney, Lantz, UPA, and Fleischer, among others—by no means implies that I think them unworthy of discussion. I know that I am only scratching the surface of what remains to be investigated, and I hope that the reader will take away from this book a sense of the endless possibilities for future research. No matter which cartoons we choose to look at, the significance of the music in those cartoons has changed—not only because audiences have changed but also because animation and our culture more generally have evolved and been transformed over the past fifty years. The music in the cartoons still provides meaning, but we must repeatedly rediscover what that meaning is.

Carl Stalling and Popular Music in the Warner Bros. Cartoons

The name Carl Stalling has appeared on movie and television screens for more than seventy-five years. His work as a composer for Hollywood cartoons was apparently headed for the same fate as practically all film music: heard but never widely recognized for its creativity and originality. That changed two decades after his death in 1972, when Greg Ford and Hal Willner produced *The Carl Stalling Project* (1990–95), two CDs of Stalling's music taken from his time at Warner Bros. (1936 to 1958). The discs sold surprisingly well for a niche release; the first of the two discs actually appeared briefly on the *Billboard* album chart.[1] As a result, a new interest in cartoon music began to emerge in the early 1990s. Through the CDs, Stalling (see figure 1) suddenly became visible to animation fans who had never before thought about him or his work for the cartoons. More important, people began to realize how much contemporary cartoon music—on television, in theaters, and online—models itself on the sound of the Warner Bros. cartoons (which has indeed become the standard in the field), a sound that Stalling developed and systematized. As a musical director for cartoons produced by Walt Disney, Ub Iwerks, and Warner Bros., Stalling had years to develop and eventually perfect his approach to relating music to what he saw taking place in each cartoon he scored. It seems sensible to begin my discussion of Hollywood cartoon scores by looking at the career and composing style of the one person who had the greatest impact on the field.

The most characteristic feature of Stalling's cartoon music is his heavy reliance on popular songs. As a film accompanist he learned to use songs to amplify the on-screen story; he carried this approach with him into

FIGURE 1 Carl Stalling. Photo courtesy Michael Barrier.

the animation world, where he combined short original cues with songs arranged for whatever instruments the studio could afford. The vast collection of popular songs Warner Bros. owned offered him more musical options than he would have at any other time in his career. But not everyone agreed with his style; the Warner Bros. director Chuck Jones once remarked that "Stalling was good at writing his own music, but he seldom did."[2] Several of Stalling's colleagues saw him as a talented composer who relied too much on the stories evoked by the titles of popular songs to help him formulate scores for cartoons. Yet it was these songs that enabled Stalling to illustrate the on-screen humor on an entirely separate narrative level from the actual animation, and his strategies eventually became identified with the Warner Bros. style. This chapter examines how the two sides of Stalling's personality as a composer—the humorous side and the practical side—came together in each score through his use of popular or precomposed music.

STALLING'S FIRST YEARS

We can better understand how Stalling incorporated film-accompanying techniques into his cartoon-scoring methods by looking first at his early experiences as an accompanist. In an interview conducted in 1969, he recalled his first professional job as a musician:

> I played the piano at a theater about a block from former President Truman's home in Independence, Missouri, around 1910. That was my first job in the Kansas City area, but I'd played the piano in 1904 at Lexington, where I was born. Lexington is forty miles east of Independence. In those days, they just wanted a piano going while the operator was changing reels. In the cities, they had two machines, so you didn't have to wait for the next reel, but in little towns like Lexington they hadn't gotten that far yet.

The year before taking that job in Lexington, Stalling had seen *The Great Train Robbery* (1903) and decided he had to be "connected with the movies in some way."[3] He worked at the Isis Theatre in Kansas City, Missouri, in the mid-1920s, playing afternoons and evenings and conducting the orchestra from either the piano or the organ. As the orchestra leader, Stalling chose music to accompany the features; for shorter films, including newsreels and short comedies, he would improvise at the keyboard.[4] If we can judge from the advertisements printed in the *Kansas City Star* for the Isis (often referred to in the ads as "Isis the Irresistible"), Stalling had extensive experience playing for cartoons in the theater. Each ad highlighted the feature film showing that week in large type, while smaller letters at the bottom listed other "Added Attractions"; these regularly included "Carl Stallings *[sic]* at the Hope Jones organ," playing for, among other items, "Felix, Comical Cat," (Aesop's) "Fables," "Our Gang Comedy," and even "Alice Comedy"—a reference to the "Alice in Cartoonland" series created and produced by a young filmmaker from the Kansas City area, Walt Disney.[5]

Stalling met and befriended Disney in the early 1920s, when Disney was producing short animated commercials for the Newman Theatre. Disney had moved to California in 1923 to produce animated cartoons, but he stopped in Kansas City in 1928 with finished prints of two Mickey Mouse cartoons, *Plane Crazy* and *Gallopin' Gaucho,* which he left with Stalling to score. (Contrary to popular belief, Stalling did not score *Steamboat Willie,* the first cartoon Disney produced and released with synchronized sound that same year.)[6] Stalling proceeded to write the music for nineteen more cartoons for Disney until early 1930, when he left the studio at the same time as Ub Iwerks, Disney's collaborator and primary animator in his studio's early years.[7] Stalling worked for a short time at the Van Beuren animation studio in New York, where, he recalled, they "didn't have anything for me to do"; he left the same year to join Iwerks at his new animation studio in California. He was with Iwerks on and off for six years, occasionally going back to Disney as an arranger and a pianist; he played the piano for Practical Pig in *Three Little Pigs* (Disney; Gillett, 1933) and arranged the scores for numerous other shorts.[8] After Ben "Bugs" Hardaway, another Iwerks alum, recommended Stalling to the producer Leon Schlesinger, in 1936 Stalling moved to his new job at Warner Bros.; he worked there until his retirement in 1958.[9] Before he began working for Warner Bros., his experiences as a composer working in Kansas City had already informed his idiosyncratic method of scoring sound cartoons.

MUSIC AND COMEDY, SILENT STYLE

> Medleys of old time hits can supply valuable material for the scoring of comedies.
>
> Erno Rapée, *Encyclopedia of Music for Pictures* ([1925] 1970)

Insight into how Stalling (or any accompanist) might have approached silent cartoons and live-action comic films in the 1920s is offered by contemporaneous film music manuals, particularly Edith Lang and George West's *Musical Accompaniment of Moving Pictures*. In the section "Animated Cartoons and Slap-Stick Comedy," Lang and West recommend that

> The player should learn to recognize, and be able personally to enjoy, the fun of the comic situations depicted on screen. Nothing is more calamitous than to see "Mutt and Jeff" disport themselves in their inimitable antics and to have a "Brother Gloom" at the organ who gives vent to his perennial grouch in sadly sentimental or funereal strains. . . . If the "point" of the joke be missed, if the player lag behind with his effect, all will be lost, and the audience cheated out of its rightful share of joy.[10]

In this advice, the authors spell out one of the most basic duties of accompanists as storytellers: they must not only know where and when the comedic moments will occur within a picture, they also must cue the audience to those incidents. Any competent film accompanist would be expected to know enough to draw the audience's attention to important moments in the story. Every film genre requires its own approach;

for comedy scores, Lang and West rather appropriately suggested a sense of humor.

Regardless of genre, what musical vocabulary should be used to enhance the story of a film? Many collections of music for film accompanying that were published in the 1910s and '20s worked on a system of reducing each scene in a film to a one- or two-word description, which would suggest a variety of musical analogues to accompany the scene. If the titles of these pieces—such as "Hurry No. 2," "Indian Dawn," and "In the Stirrups"—did not indicate their purpose clearly enough, then the brief characterizations beneath their titles would reassure any skeptical musicians that they had chosen an appropriate piece.

One handbook developed later in the silent era by Erno Rapée worked on the principle of the signifying possibilities of a single descriptive phrase: *Motion Picture Moods for Pianists and Organists* offered accompanists hundreds of familiar melodies in a volume indexed under headings of mood or subject matter, including "Wedding," "Hurry," and "Fire-fighting." A properly trained accompanist, as the media historian Tim Anderson points out, needed at any given moment to quickly present an appropriate musical analogue for the emotion or "adjective" on screen; Rapée's volume and others like it made such connections between the drama and its score almost immediate. But relying on an adjective created new problems, because the adjective, "like music, refers to no one specific thing."[11] Such simplified approaches had practical advantages, but they could also lead to scores consisting of only a few melodies. Lang and West advised accompanists against falling into the musical rut of using the same "lively tune that must serve all cartoons, comedies and jokes, invariably and indiscriminately," especially because "in the cartoons and in the comedies all sorts of other emotions, besides that of plain hilarity, may come into play; there may be sorrow, doubt, horror and even death."[12] A committed theater musician would be familiar with a wide spectrum of materials providing a wealth of musical options. Any accompanist interested in keeping the audience involved would certainly vary the melodies used throughout the afternoon or evening (not just in an individual picture), adding constantly to the musical and emotional range of the show.

While standard accompanying fare for movies included original music and arrangements of light classics, contemporary popular songs gave composers new and interesting tunes to work with. Popular music related to movies dates back to the late 1910s, when the "title song" was born. The licensing fees required by the American Society of Composers, Authors and Publishers prevented most theater musicians from using ASCAP-represented tunes (that is, until an agreement was finally reached in 1926), but it was clear that using popular music in films could be highly profitable for the publishers, the producers of the film, and the songwriters.[13] If a song were tied to a feature, as "Rosemary" was to the film *Abie's Irish Rose* (1928), the accompanist could play the theme song as the movie was shown, and perhaps the audience could even sing it before the screening began. Such promotion or plugging would drive up sheet music sales, increasing the song's popularity and encouraging other people to see the movie, which in turn would fuel more sheet music sales, and so on.

For the accompanist, using popular songs was a way to become known as a hip bandleader, as Lang and West note: "This part of the show [i.e., comedies] is admirably adapted to the introduction of all sorts of popular songs and dances. The player should keep in touch with the publications of popular music houses, since it will repay him to establish a reputation which will make the public say: 'Let's go to the Star Theatre—you always hear the latest tune there.'"[14] With both theaters and ASCAP blessing the presence of popular songs in film scores, accompanists like Stalling had few restraints on the music they used. The musical vocabulary as defined by Rapée's handbook (and by Lang and West, who had their own lists broken down by category) became far richer once current songs were added. Such an expansive musical palette enabled accompanists to create entertaining programs week after week. Anderson mentions that many composers would "create and play to the specific cultural needs and demands of the audience";[15] Stalling surely would have done the same.

Let's suppose, however, that Stalling, for the sake of a truly funny take on a film, purposely chose music that went against the grain. That is, what if the idea linking the music and the image led to its own gag, which itself relied on recognizing the song's words as inapposite in the context of that moment of the film? Stalling probably caught on to this practice early in his career, and it became his trademark as a composer. Such accompanists were called "film funners," and the film historian Charles Berg describes their "stock in trade": "a mischievous sense of humor which exploited practically all films for their comedic potential regardless of the film director's intentions. The film-funner would, for example, accompany a dramatic scene where burglars are craftily entering the heroine's home with the strains of the romantic love-song, 'Meet Me in the Shadows.'" Berg also notes, "While the practice was approved of because of the title's or lyric's relevance and the pleasure the audience derived from hearing old 'favorites,' film music advisors . . . cautioned against the excesses of 'film funners,'"[16] overdoing the comic effect or trying to create comedy where none was intended. When feature-length films and grand movie houses became the norm, film funners began using their musical clichés exclusively in comedies, where such behavior seemed appropriate.

If we consider the different functions of music in films, comedies or not, we quickly recognize that popular song references had to do much more than just plug a song. Though not every accompanist followed the lead of the film funner, composers increasingly realized that a few well-chosen songs could contribute to a film's narrative while also giving the audience something they might recognize, if only subliminally.[17] Stalling thus learned the power of music to shape, direct, and manipulate both the emotional level of the story and the feelings of the audience when he worked as an accompanist. He tried to tap into this power with each score he wrote, and these same experiences would eventually inform his sound cartoon scores. As he told his interviewers, "I really was used to composing for films before I started writing for cartoons. I just imagined myself playing for a cartoon in the theater, improvising, and it came easier."[18] We will see later just how rooted Stalling remained—for his entire career—in the practices of his first job as a musician.

THE PRACTICAL SIDE OF WARNER BROS. SCORES

The process of scoring and recording cartoon music begins with the cartoon's story. The animation historians Michael Barrier, Steve Schneider, and Hank Sartin have shown that music motivated the early Looney Tunes and Merrie Melodies (those produced from 1930 to 1936) more strongly than any other element of the narrative. Because these early Warner Bros. cartoons pay more attention to music and performance than to story development, some critics have found their story lines less than compelling.[19] Warner Bros. never exhibited much concern about narrative development; typically each short centers on a generic situation or set-up—Daffy in a western locale, Elmer chasing Bugs through the woods—that enables the characters to lead the story wherever they want. Instead of building a trajectory toward a traditional climax and dénouement, Warner Bros. cartoons constantly introduce new gags and shtick, equal in intensity, to move the story forward. Similarly, Stalling's scores have no emotional arc, instead carefully complementing and conveying whatever joke is being perpetrated at a given moment in the narrative.

Although Warner Bros. cartoons lacked plot lines that progressively raised the emotional stakes, the successive streams of gags and verbal jokes kept the emotional level high. When films at the turn of the twentieth century began to increase in length, short, mischief-driven gags that provided a quick payoff began to fall out of use; the short gags could not support the more extended narratives, such as chase scenes, that were being written. Mischief, as the film historian Tom Gunning points out, "works through interruption rather than development."[20] With this in mind, we might consider Stalling's preference for brief, rapidly changing musical cues: the short cues are consistent with the storytelling style prevalent at Warner Bros., which moved along from gag to gag. Stalling learned about writing music for comedies by accompanying gag-driven silent stories—Buster Keaton films, *Our Gang* shorts, and cartoons (including *Aesop's Fables, Felix,* and *Krazy Kat*). Their plots progressed in short spurts, and he wrote his music to match the intensity level of the narrative. As a result, Stalling took a building-block approach to his scores, treating them as individual segments; he devised cues that were brief and still packed a significant dramatic punch, telegraphing the moment's mood or idea before the next gag came along. This method also meant that his scores did not slowly crescendo into a violent episode, as did the scores of many of his colleagues (such as Scott Bradley).

The Warner Bros. cartoon division had an even more compelling reason for their elaborate scores: the original deal that the producer Leon Schlesinger made with Warner Bros. specified that music owned by Warner Bros. would feature in every cartoon created. Warner Bros. had a rich musical legacy, as it owned or had a controlling interest in more than a half-dozen large publishing houses, including DeSylva, Brown & Henderson; Remick; Advanced; Harms; T. B. Harms; and "the original Tin Pan Alley music house, formed in 1885," M. Witmark & Sons.[21] Schlesinger's original contract gave Frank Marsales, the composer for the Warner Bros. shorts from 1930 through 1933, "complete access to [Warner's] musical libraries" for the Looney Tunes.[22] The Merrie Melodies series, begun in 1931, required (by contract) a verse and chorus of the title song in each cartoon, a proviso that turned the Merrie Melodies into primordial music videos and forced the animation directors to delve more deeply into the Warner Bros. music catalogue.

The motives of Warner Bros. were clearly financial. Studios invested in sheet music in the 1920s to keep from spending exorbitant amounts of money to license songs. They also made money if they owned the copyrights on songs featured in their own films, profiting from the publishing, licensing, and sales of sheet music, performances and recordings, and radio airplay.[23] Schlesinger no doubt understood the money that could be made by exploiting the studio's song catalogue in new media forms, particularly those that, like cartoons, would emphasize the recent advances in sound. Warner Bros., at essence a producer of feature films, took an early step toward corporate synergy by integrating two of its secondary concerns: music publishing and short subjects.[24]

Practically all the cartoon directors had harsh words about the requirement to use the Warner music catalogue. Friz Freleng recognized the practical reasoning behind the plan: "We had to put two singing choruses in every cartoon, the idea being that if people heard something they liked in the theatres, maybe they'd go out afterward and buy the song sheets."[25] But the main flaw was obvious, as Bob Clampett pointed out as he recalled his early days creating Merrie Melodies: "We'd have a great story going along, but then we'd have to stop and have the singing chorus."[26] Tex Avery was far more blunt in his evaluation of the consequences: "We were forced to use a song, which would just ruin the cartoon. You'd try like a fool to get funny [during the song], but it was seldom you did. . . . Finally, when Schlesinger let us get by [without using the songs], the cartoons started picking up."[27] Perhaps Chuck Jones was the most succinct: "It was a pain in the ass."[28] Whatever their feelings about it, the "song per cartoon" rule ensured that the music was the star in the earliest Warner Bros. shorts, as each short featured an on-screen performance of a Warner-owned and -controlled tune.[29]

As the directors make clear, a song's appearance almost always meant a full-scale performance, bringing the story to an abrupt halt—especially if the song began in the middle of the cartoon. Showcasing the featured song in a musical number was an interruption that prevented the narrative from building toward a dramatic climax of any sort, as any dramatic tension that had developed would dissipate immediately. We cannot be sure exactly how much this mandated approach contributed to the emergent Warner Bros. style, but we can see that several of the directors adapted their gag writing to accommodate the policy, a shift that in turn affected how Stalling constructed his scores.

The Warner Bros. cartoon division underwent considerable internal upheaval in the mid-1930s. Hugh Harman and Rudy Ising, the two men who first brought animation to Warner Bros., parted ways with Schlesinger over a contract dispute in 1933, only to begin producing cartoons for MGM the following year. Most of Harman and Ising's creative staff of animators and writers (and their composer, Frank Marsales) stayed loyal to them at first; Schlesinger eventually hired many of them back to Warner Bros., one by one.[30] On the positive side, the departure of Warner Bros.' original animation crew led to promotions for those who stayed on, as well as some new hires to replace those who had left for good. This new regime was responsible for the second generation of Warner Bros. cartoons, including the development of characters such as Porky Pig, Daffy Duck, and eventually Bugs Bunny. Tex Avery and Frank Tashlin both began directing (although each was credited as "supervisor" on the actual title cards) in late 1935, and Bob Clampett and Charles "Chuck" Jones, originally animators in Avery's production unit, quickly moved on to directing: Clampett began in 1937, Jones a year later.

Each director that Stalling worked with at Warner Bros.—Chuck Jones, Friz Freleng, Bob Clampett, Tex Avery, Robert McKimson, Art Davis, Frank Tashlin, Norman McCabe, and the team of Ben Hardaway and Cal Dalton—had his own approach to storytelling. These differences in humor and style made it necessary for Stalling to vary his approach to scoring cartoons for each; his ability to adapt to their particular idiosyncrasies demonstrates both his skill and his creativity as a composer. The directors developed their own characters as well as dipping into a general pool of more renowned figures (e.g., Bugs and Daffy) that everyone used. Chuck Jones had the Road Runner and Coyote, Robert McKimson had Foghorn Leghorn, and Friz Freleng had his animated doppelgänger, Yosemite Sam, to name just a few.[31] Michael Maltese, who received a writer's credit on the first cartoon to feature Sam, *Hare Trigger* (1945), told Michael Barrier that he "based Sam, who was short, red haired, and wore a mustache, partly on Freleng himself, who was short, red haired, and wore a mustache."[32]

Carl Stalling came to Warner Bros. in 1936, in the midst of all this change, facing two challenges. The first, the need to feature a song in every Merrie Melodie, was in fact a welcome opportunity after his earlier experiences with Disney, where he typically had to use older songs to avoid stiff licensing fees. More critically, he had to show the directors and writers that the cartoons could feature such songs and still be interesting and funny. They had not been impressed by the efforts of Stalling's predecessor, Frank Marsales. Freleng once observed that Marsales's "music was like something you'd find in the street. It was absolutely lacking in anything you needed to make a picture good; he didn't synchronize. . . . Before Carl, the music was used only to set the tempo, which was usually impossibly slow, unless we picked it up for

something he'd understand, like a chase."[33] Stalling more than rose to
the challenge, serendipitously finding that his work at Warner Bros. could
not have better matched his abilities and past experiences as a composer
and accompanist.

Warner Bros. eventually became Stalling's ideal home. During Stalling's time at the early Disney studio, Walt Disney pioneered the use of
bar sheets—a notated blueprint of the music, dialogue, and animation
timing—which made possible very precise synchronization of the soundtrack and the action. While discussing the early attempts to match music to film, Stalling explained why they were necessary: "Perfect synchronization of music for cartoons was a problem, since there were so
many quick changes and actions that the music had to match."[34] A
method had to be devised to ensure the audiovisual simultaneity that animation could afford; once perfected, bar sheets became invaluable to
planning out any cartoon. When he arrived at Warner Bros., Stalling was
no doubt happy to discover that many of the directors there were also
using bar sheets, a process that had been imported by the former Disney
colleagues and employees Harman and Ising.

This synchronization of music and image became part of the implicit
musicality in the Warner Bros. cartoons, and it was another key component of Stalling's compositional style. According to Stalling, once the
basic story for a cartoon had been finalized in storyboard form (usually
300–400 key poses and drawings), he would meet with the cartoon's director and determine the various tempi for each scene. This mapping out
of the cartoon's action, known as "timing," enabled the directors to tell
their animators precisely how many frames per second each scene had.
It also enabled Stalling to compose the score without seeing the cartoon.
The director Friz Freleng, who had some musical background himself,
noted that Stalling

> never waited until the picture was done. Often he'd compose right from
> my bar sheets, writing music to the action I indicated. And later he might
> say, "Hey, could you make this bang (or whatever sound effect it was)
> come out on the beat?" And if it worked better musically that way, I'd
> change it. . . . I did everything in phrases of fours and twos, so Carl could
> follow it. If a character walked, I'd put down the steps, evenly, and he
> would write the music to those steps. I'd never leave him in the middle
> of a beat or the middle of a phrase. If I had a cat run across the room, I'd
> figure out how many steps that cat was going to use; I then set it up so that
> if the cat paused or some sound effect was needed, it happened on the beat.
> I didn't write any of the music, but I did write the phrases and the rhythm
> for Carl.

In the case of an on-screen performance, the music would be recorded first to provide the animators with a vocal track to which they could animate mouth movements. "Then Carl or Milt Franklyn would write [the prescored song] out on a music sheet," Freleng recalled, "which I'd use to direct the action."[35]

Stalling found Warner Bros.' library of popular music another advantage to his position at the studio: "My leaving turned out better for Walt and it turned out better for me. At Warner Brothers, I could use a lot more popular songs; they didn't mind paying for them, as they had their own music publishing firm." He elaborated, "At Warner's, I could use popular music. That opened up a new field so far as the kind of music we could use. At Disney's, we had to go back to the Nineteenth Century, to classical music, to 'My Old Kentucky Home.'"[36] By framing his discussion of composing in terms of the popular songs he could use, Stalling reveals how important such tunes were for his scores. As early as the mid-1930s, the directors began to shy away from featuring or integrating into their stories Warner Bros.–owned songs, but Stalling did not follow their lead. Instead of writing a higher proportion of original music, he began scouring the libraries of music at his disposal even more thoroughly. A contract between Schlesinger and Warner Bros., dated 1 September 1940, broadly lays out what musical materials the studio would provide the animation group.

SOUND RECORDING: Warner agrees during the period of this agreement [1940–45], without cost to Schlesinger, to furnish and supply Schlesinger with all music that is either in public domain or music owned by Warner or by any of the music publishing houses owned or controlled by Warner, musicians, singers, voices, talent, sound, sound equipment and recording crew used in the recording of the cartoons, and shall complete said cartoons so that they may be used for theatre exhibition purposes. All recording of music and sound effects shall be done under the supervision of a musician and of a technician employed by Schlesinger.[37]

Clearly, Warner-owned songs were to be made available to Schlesinger's group, even in 1940, when the explicit need to promote songs in the Merrie Melodies was significantly reduced. This agreement permitted Stalling to continue using the music that he had just begun to exploit four years earlier.

MUSICAL GAGS AND INSIDE JOKES

The production process at Warner Bros. gave Stalling time to devise or search for the appropriate music to use in a given short.[38] Knowing the story, its setting, and, most important, the gags involved, he could decide what songs might mesh well with the narrative. Not everyone at the studio approved of such a scoring style, however; several of the directors criticized Stalling's repeated use of certain songs for particular kinds of scenes. They also expressed concern that he depended heavily on popular songs rather than writing original music, choosing the tunes in what they saw as an uncreative and even clumsy attempt to make a connection between song and gag, and perhaps to engender some humor by juxtaposing the visuals and inappropriate music and thus create an entirely new gag (in the true "film-funner" fashion). Chuck Jones reminisced about Stalling:

> He was a brilliant musician. But the quickest way for him to write a musical score—and he did one six-minute score a week—was to simply look up some music that had the proper name. If there was a lady dressed in red, he'd always play "The Lady in Red." If somebody went into a cave, he'd play "Fingal's Cave." If we were doing anything about eating, he'd do "A Cup of Coffee, a Sandwich, and You." I had a bee one time, and my God if he didn't go and find a piece of music written in 1906 or something called "I'm a Busy Little Bumble Bee."[39]

David Weber, Friz Freleng's biographer, recounts that Stalling's reflexive use of such songs became a running joke between Jones and Freleng. He quotes the latter: "We both used to say we were afraid to use colored pencils, because whenever Carl saw a red pencil mark, he'd use 'Lady in Red,' and when he saw a blue pencil mark, 'Am I Blue.' Better to use gray and not risk it!"[40] Both Freleng and Jones found Stalling's literalism amusing but possibly limiting. The larger problem for Jones, who referred to Stalling's practice in numerous interviews, was his lack of certainty that people actually knew that Stalling was making a joke through the score.

The issue here is whether the success of a gag—be it visual, verbal, or musical—depends on its perceptibility. Jones faulted "Bumble Bee" for being "so obscure no one could make the connection."[41] Does the connection matter? The film scholar Jeff Smith addresses this very topic, noting that the words of a song typically do little to help the story or our understanding of it. In Jones's eyes, the music therefore supplied little humor; if no one got Stalling's joke, the musical selection itself had no value. But the music doesn't have to tie itself to the story to be funny. To explain how music can engender humor, Smith uses Arthur Koestler's concept of bisociation, in which humor "arises from the juxtaposition of two associative chains to create two incongruous ways of seeing something."

Precomposed or popular music, Smith explains, can create this effect by placing together the "original scenario" of the song used with the "immediate situation" occurring in the film. "These two frames of reference must be sufficiently different to create the incongruity upon which the pun is based. . . . [E]ach frame of reference must also be associatively elicited by some linguistic element of the title. . . . [T]he spectator must recognize the title's relevance to the narrative situation depicted in the film to activate the two interpretive possibilities presupposed by the pun's play of meaning."[42] The bisociative process here relies on the audience recognizing the lyrics of the song in question *and* connecting its use to that moment in the unfolding story for the joke to work. Most of the musical jokes "told" in Warner Bros. cartoons have no text to indicate the song's title and thus establish its connection to the story. For most of Stalling's twenty-two years at Warner Bros., characters sang because they had a reason to (and not, as had once been the case, to satisfy a contractual agreement); thus any featured songs would have been chosen to fulfill a specific dramatic need.

For example, in *The Fifth-Column Mouse* (Freleng, 1943), a house full of mice are resolved to rid their home of a hungry cat. They organize themselves into an efficient rodent army, singing the World War II song "We Did It Before (And We Can Do It Again)." The common struggle of cat and mouse (or mice, in this case), set against the significantly larger conflict between Hitler and the Allies, make up the dual "frames of reference" against which the mice perform the song. The "it" in "We Did It Before" constitutes the "linguistic element of the title" that links the two situations, thereby creating the musical pun by comparing the training sequence of the mice, set to this militaristic song, to the mobilization of the American armed forces following the attack on Pearl Harbor.[43] As the mice sing this song, with unaltered lyrics, no less, an audience in 1943 should make the connection—if they are listening and paying attention to the lyrics, and if they know the song well enough to recognize its words.

This formula may work perfectly well when lyrics are involved, but far more often Stalling's puns in cartoons relied solely on instrumental arrangements. In the absence of words, the composer cannot assume that the audience will know any more of the song than its title, and the joke ultimately depends entirely on their recollection of that. Under such circumstances, according to Smith, "viewers simply apply what they already know—a title or chorus—to the specific dramatic context that is depicted in the film. Thus one need not have a thorough understanding of the song's lyrics, but simply the minimal information supplied by the song's title. Not surprisingly, this system of musical allusions places a certain premium on well-known songs. After all, if the song is unfamiliar to the audience, then they will fail to grasp the specific way in which the song's title relates to the scene it accompanies."[44] This means of communicating with the audience through the music suited both Stalling's use of relatively short cues and the studio's preference for quick gags. The viewer has to recognize the music as something *not* original, and possibly related to the narrative on more than just a "meta" level; if he or she doesn't know the song at all, then the music simply illustrates the scene.

That Stalling composed *cartoon* music allowed him a great deal of creative freedom. One- or two-reel films, including cartoons, comedies, newsreels, and short musicals, were less prestigious than full-length features, in part because their brevity led to smaller production budgets. Because of their relatively low status, such films could freely play with the conventions of feature films; after all, shorts "were not necessarily governed by the same aesthetic roles and conventions" as features.[45] Tim Anderson points out that early film accompanists always had a choice between sticking with a film's "master narrative" and offering "narrative interruptions, disorder, and sidetracks that exhaustively investigate, discover, and create new meanings and spectacles."[46] That is, the real allure of accompanying was the film composer's freedom to tell a story. Stalling's willingness to push against the boundaries of comprehensible humor in his scores makes sense in this light. The Warner Bros. cartoons did all they could to stretch generic story lines (as exemplified by Disney) until all was topsy-turvy. Because Stalling had no particular reason to uphold a story's master narrative, he could create new meanings for the songs without worrying that they would detract from the cartoons.

In the notes to the first volume of *The Carl Stalling Project,* Will Friedwald remarks that audiences detect the musical puns Stalling sets up, even if the melodies have been reduced to a handful of notes, because they rely "on the collective unconscious which, after having followed enough of Bugs Bunny's episodic adventures, unknowingly makes the connection between the few bars of the motif Stalling sneaks by and the idea put across on screen."[47] Stalling may have relied heavily on favorite melodies, and he definitely used distinctive timbres for special scenes, but his music never stole attention from the visual action or the dialogue unless the story called for it. In the 1930s and 1940s, theater audiences (except at kiddie matinees) saw only one new Warner Bros. cartoon per week, and so few people would have noticed any continuity between the songs

Stalling cited and their corresponding gags. It thus seems unlikely that a "collective unconscious" played a significant role.

The most serious obstacle to appreciating Stalling's references is simply the passage of time. The cultural language he relied on has changed over the past sixty years, and melodies recognizable to some in the 1940s have been forgotten today. The availability of cartoons on home video and on the Cartoon Network enables children and adults alike to see a (limited) selection of Warner Bros. cartoons over and over again. Yet the repeated hearings of Stalling's stock melodies mean nothing if their historical significance has faded. I cannot help wondering if Stalling employed such songs to create yet another level of humor in the cartoons, to be understood and appreciated by the connoisseur of obscure music; as Smith says, such scores provide, for those who know the music, "a secondary frisson of pleasure in our recognition of its unexpected aptness to the scene it accompanies."[48] Stalling's frequent use of the song "A Cup of Coffee, a Sandwich, and You" would have had a humorous edge for those who recognized it. A secondary gag from the same song would surface when it appeared in contexts in which one character was trying to eat another (as in *Along Came Daffy;* Freleng, 1947): the title's implied "eating with you" becomes "eating you." If Stalling did make these musical gags for his own amusement, his attitude was remarkably similar to that of the Warner Bros. directors, many of whom claimed to have written their cartoons to please themselves. Chuck Jones, for instance, declared in 1988: "We never made films for adults, and we never made films for children. We made pictures for what I suppose you could call a minority. We made pictures for ourselves, and we were lucky because the producers never knew exactly what we were doing."[49]

The film critic John Tebbel raises yet another concern about Stalling's style: not that the musical pun could not be understood at all, but rather that people would misunderstand it. He argues, "A skewed link between the visual and the music can be a problem. In *Fast and Furryous* ('49), the first Road Runner and Coyote, the demon bird uses a free-way cloverleaf—a potent, fresh image of the time—to elude his pursuer. Stalling fields the chestnut 'I'm Looking Over a Four Leaf Clover.' While accurately paraphrasing the camera angle, the music's boisterous optimism contradicts the emotional content—bewilderment—of the scene."[50] Tebbel's interest in issues of postwar industrialism that appear in *Fast and Furryous* dominates his analysis of the scene. He takes quite seriously the content of the song, which works not as a comment on the scene's "emotional content" but rather as a quick gag about the highway cloverleaf. The setup to the gag confirms this: the Coyote has donned a pair of "Fleet Foot Jet Propelled Tennis Shoes" in order to chase the Road Runner at his own pace. Since both can now move with preternatural speed, Jones naturally takes the two onto the highway—an especially appropriate choice in the late 1940s, when interstate highways began to pop up around the country to the delight of those who relished a fast drive—where the Coyote can give chase at full speed. Stalling uses a minor theme in Smetana's "Dance of the Comedians" from *The Bartered Bride* for the freeway chase, a theme he used repeatedly to accompany the hyperspeed of the Road Runner. Jones shows the chase from a near side perspective for two seconds before switching to a far-off side view and then to an even more distant overhead shot, reducing the two animals to dots on the road (see figure 2). When they reach the freeway, the two animals are mere spots moving seemingly at random on a *three-leaf* cloverleaf.

This gag again illustrates the bisociative process that Smith describes. Two different references are made at once: as the characters race around the highway cloverleaf (with three loops), the song that refers to the four-leafed plant is heard. Because Jones's intended joke focuses on the highway, not the music, it loses nothing if no one recognizes Stalling's reference. Jones himself uses this joke in the 1952 cartoon *Operation: Rabbit.* Here, instead of chasing the Road Runner, the Coyote—"Wile E. Coyote, Genius"—must contend with Bugs Bunny's wise guy jokes and gags throughout the picture. At one point, after outsmarting Wile E.'s pressure-cooker-on-the-rabbit-hole plan, Bugs walks away, singing "I'm looking over a *three*-leaf clover that I overlooked be-*threee* . . ." Like the musical pun in *Fast and Furryous,* this play on words comes and goes in a moment; the audience's ability to grasp it depends on whether they are paying attention *and* whether they know the song.

These examples demonstrate that Stalling's sense of humor often determined what song he might use for a specific visual gag; frequently, he took advantage of a unique moment in a cartoon's plot to slip in a song whose title referred ironically to the narrative. The animator and historian Milt Gray asked him about this technique:

> *Gray:* Many times, you used the music to tell the story. In "Catch as Cats Can" (1947), Sylvester the cat swallowed a bar of soap and was hiccuping bubbles, and the music was "I'm Forever Blowing Bubbles." Did you make up those gags yourself, or did the directors help you with that?
>
> *Stalling:* It happened both ways.[51]

FIGURE 2 The cloverleaf in *Fast and Furryous* (Warner Bros.; Jones, 1949).

Similar jokes in this vein are legion, including in

Porky's Duck Hunt (Avery, 1936): "Listen to the Mocking Bird" is used when Porky is trying to shoot Daffy, and Daffy is teasing Porky instead of trying to escape

Angel Puss (Jones, 1944): "Angel in Disguise" is used as background music and music sung (appropriate for a cat dressing up as an angel)

Booby Hatched (Tashlin, 1944): "Am I Blue" is used in a scene showing a hen and her unborn chicks shivering in cold weather

Mouse Wreckers (Jones, 1949): "Sweet Dreams, Sweetheart" is used when Claude Cat is looking at a book about nightmares (by Freud!)

Mutiny on the Bunny (Freleng, 1950): "Put 'Em in a Box, Tie 'Em with a Ribbon (and Throw 'Em in the Deep Blue Sea)" when Sam the Pirate kidnaps Bugs to work on his pirate ship

Early to Bet (McKimson, 1951): "Blues in the Night" is used when the cat loses each card game (appropriate because we know he's going to be punished for each loss)

EXAMPLE 2 Raymond Scott, melody for "Powerhouse."

Little Red Rodent Hood (Freleng, 1952): "Angel in Disguise" is
used when Sylvester dresses up like an angel or fairy godmother

Hare We Go (Freleng, 1953): the Dutchman leitmotif from *The
Flying Dutchman* is used for Pirate (Yosemite) Sam's ship

Creating a gag with its melody was often only one of a song's uses in the
score. In most of the above examples, Stalling employed the melody for
more than just the five seconds needed to set up and execute a gag. By
choosing the proper meter, tempo, and orchestration, he could make a
song sound like anything from a dirge to a fox-trot, fitting the chosen
tune to the mood of the scene at hand.

For instance, in *High Diving Hare* (Freleng, 1949), Bugs is a carnival
barker trying to gather an audience to watch the spectacular diving of Fear-
less Freep. Yosemite Sam, a huge Freep fan, enters the carnival tent with
his guns blazing, yelling "Bring on Freep!" At that moment we hear a knock
on the stage door: it's a telegram from Freep, who has been delayed because of rain. As Bugs reads the telegram, Stalling uses the chorus to the
Tin Pan Alley song "April Showers," played on a solo trombone. Rather
than ending the tune there and moving on, Stalling includes most of the
song's chorus, switching to strings and winds. Even though the initial gag
has passed, the song can still underscore the scene, especially since little
action is occurring: Bugs is merely explaining to the audience that Freep
will not appear. Stalling lets the cue continue because Bugs's explanation
to the audience is an extension of the initial gag with the telegram. Only
when Sam barges onto the stage in anger does the music change.

Stalling did not always rely exclusively on the contemporary music that
Warner Bros. could provide him. He frequently drew on the music of the
bandleader Raymond Scott, especially for unusual tunes. Scott, who was
born Harry Warnow in 1909, began leading a small jazz ensemble (the

FIGURE 3   *The Swooner Crooner* (Warner Bros.; Tashlin, 1944).

Raymond Scott Quintette) in the mid-1930s. He appeared regularly on radio shows, including the very popular *Your Hit Parade* on CBS, where his brother, Mark Warnow, was the musical director. He and his group even appeared, playing their most famous tunes, in several Hollywood features (including, in 1938, *Rebecca of Sunnybrook Farm* and *Sally, Irene and Mary*). What made the group unique were Scott's instrumental compositions with titles that told the listener exactly what they were hearing: "New Year's Eve in a Haunted House," "Dinner Music for a Pack of Hungry Cannibals," "In an Eighteenth Century Drawing Room," "Reckless Night on Board an Ocean Liner," "Pre-Festival Music for the Coming Merger of Two Professional Marriage Brokers," and so on. Most of the recordings of the original Quintette were made between 1937 and 1939. At some point Scott's idiosyncratic melodies and titles came to Carl Stalling's attention, and when Scott sold the rights to his music to Warner Bros. in 1943, his songs became immediately available for Stalling's scores.[52]

The Scott piece that Stalling used more than any other is "Powerhouse," probably the bandleader's most famous composition (see music example 2).[53] The song's title gives us an inkling of the image Scott intended to depict: a source of energy for the industrial and technological boom before and during World War II. For Stalling, however, the melody's incessant progression, particularly in the second half of the song, represented more than just energy: it became a musical metaphor for progress. In *The Swooner Crooner* (Tashlin, 1944), Porky Pig runs a farm producing eggs for the war effort, with pullets that produce on a belt-driven assembly line (see figure 3). Stalling uses "Powerhouse" as the sound of industry, carefully synchronizing the contours of Scott's tune with each step of Porky's production as the movement of the hens visually matches the music's rhythm. The same tune can also portray the unstoppable progression of fate. In *Early to Bet* (McKimson, 1951), a cat bitten by the gambling bug repeatedly loses at cards to the farm bulldog and must pay the penalty after each loss. Stalling uses "Powerhouse" while the dog sets up each of the cat's elaborate penalties; in this case, the melody's inexorable forward motion signals the inescapability of the impending punishment (usually a beating). Scott's music enabled Stalling to go beyond the practice of choosing a song simply for its title. Given the highly descriptive nature of these tunes—we might even call them musical caricatures—Stalling did not have to depend on the viewer's preexisting knowledge. The tunes could (figuratively) speak for themselves.

GENERIC MUSIC AND MUSICAL STEREOTYPES

The film historian Tom Gunning has referred to early comic films from the turn of the twentieth century as examples of the "cinema of attractions," which, he argues, "addresses spectators with a visual display, rather than a developed narrative action."[54] The domination of gags over story development is only one of the similarities between such films and Warner Bros. cartoons. Another involves the use of generic story lines to create new plot situations, compelling the cartoon's director and writers to come up with gags specific to the stereotyped genre they were satirizing: western, vaudeville, romance, horror, and so on. As the film scholar Henry Jenkins has shown, an "economy" of representation is involved when a dramatic set piece is set up: "characters and situations needed to be immediately recognizable. An elaborate system of typage developed: exaggerated costumes, facial characteristics, phrases, and accents were meant to reflect general personality traits viewed as emblematic of a particular class, ethnic group, or gender. . . . Whatever its racist implications, such stereotyping was a necessary aspect of the highly economic style of vaudeville performance."[55]

These stereotypes played specifically to cultural expectations of appearance and sound; film accompanists learned very quickly that particular pieces could almost instantaneously evoke a response when used at appropriate times. In a study of narrative film music, Claudia Gorbman comments that the music in such situations focuses and telegraphs the "'correct' meaning" of the sequence on screen, while also deftly indicating to the audience aspects of "historical and geographical setting, and atmosphere, through the high degree of its cultural coding."[56] Stalling's musical process, directly tied to his own economy of description (his need to get his point across as quickly as possible),[57] involved using particular songs to signify whatever he found compelling in the images presented, whether they portrayed an ethnic or racial distinction, a geographical region, or even an inanimate object. Stalling identified the flavor of each new cartoon's plot and picked his music accordingly, often drawing on music he had used previously in certain generic situations.

Many of the songs he chose for these purposes came directly from his days as a film accompanist, when he and countless other organists used accompanying handbooks and various collections of original, copyright-free music that indicated which styles of music and tunes to use when and thus specified, by implication, what people expected to hear during particular scenes. For instance, Stalling inevitably used J. F. Barth's "Frat," Egbert Van Alstyne and Harry Williams's "Cheyenne," J. S. Zamecnik's "In the Stirrups," and Rossini's *William Tell* overture in westerns. Schubert's lied "Die Erlkönig"—listed in Rapée's *Motion Picture Moods* under the heading "Misterioso" and in his *Encyclopedia* under "Storm"—also appears in several westerns as the dramatic music for the villain (most often associated with Yosemite Sam).[58]

We can see the influence of Stalling's training as a film accompanist best in his method of establishing musical identities in cartoons by using generic melodies. When a cartoon uses stereotypes of race, gender, or nationality as the key to a gag, the joke can succeed only if the audience recognizes what marginalized group is being targeted. The exaggerated visual markers Jenkins alludes to (large nose on the Jewish car salesman, extra-high heels and lipstick on someone in drag, big lips and extra-dark skin on an African American) could be enhanced by the culturally mandated music for the "other" in question. Use of such music would ensure that the viewer was properly prepared for the ethnically, sexually, or racially inflected situation to follow.

Religion was not often a source for satire in cartoons, mainly because Hollywood's Production Code forbade such humor, especially when it was directed toward religious leaders. But such respect for the public's beliefs implicitly extended only to white Protestant America; members of all other groups could still receive "special" treatment, as long as the gibes weren't too extreme. For instance, Jewish characters or characterizations appear in cartoons from several studios, including *Laundry Blues* (Van Beuren; Davis and Foster, 1930), *Rodeo Dough* (Columbia, 1931), *Cubby's Picnic* (Van Beuren; Donnelly and Muffati, 1933), *Betty Boop's Big Boss* (Fleischer; Fleischer, 1933), *Three Little Pigs* (Disney; Gillett, 1933), *Bosko the Talk-Ink Kid* (1929—this is the pilot short that led to the first Warner Bros. cartoon series), *The Opry House* (Disney; Disney, 1929), and *The New Car* (Iwerks; Iwerks, 1931). The last two, scored by Stalling, both use the same melody for their "Jewish" gags: "Khosn, Kale Mazl Tov" ("Congratulations, Bride and Groom"), a song from the operetta *Blimele,* written (in America) by Sigmund Mogulesko and Joseph Lateiner in 1909. The song thus came into the hands of popular (and Yiddish) performers in the midst of vaudeville's heyday, a circumstance that may help explain its popularity; moreover, Yiddish popular music was then a thriving business. The klezmer scholar Henry Sapoznik has shown that "Khosn, Kale Mazl Tov" was a huge hit among the Jewish and gentile communities alike in New York, and before long it was known "as 'the' clearly identified Jewish tune."[59]

The song's easily recognizable melody (see music example 3) even showed up in semi-secular songs—as Sapoznik points out, Eddie Cantor's 1920 vocal version of an Original Dixieland Jazz Band hit, "(Lena Is the Queen of) Palesteena," featured "a four-bar paraphrase of Mogulesko's 'Khosn, Kale Mazl Tov' plopped into the middle of the arrangement" as a "Jewish mile-marker"; a reference to it also appears in the 1942 song "The Sheik of Araby" by Spike Jones and His City Slickers. The cartoons *Laundry Blues,* scored by Eugene Rodemich, and *Bosko the Talk-Ink Kid,* which has no composer credit, use "Khosn, Kale Mazl Tov" as well. The cue sheet for *Betty Boop's Big Boss* lists the song as "'Mazel Tov'—Traditional Jewish Melody" and states that the song is in the public domain. The song's popularity and strong association with the Jewish community probably led the cartoon's composer to believe that it was simply a traditional Jewish tune with no known provenance; as Sapoznik puts it, "'Khosn, Kale Mazl Tov' soon became one of several token Jewish tunes, and its authorship was quickly forgotten."[60] Perhaps the long-standing perception of Jews as an ethnic and not a religious group allowed them to be categorized by their strange and unusual music, much like peoples with roots in Africa, Asia, or any other ethnic background fertile for stereotyping.[61]

Race and gender also received special attention. A fairly limited number of songs served as the musical indicators of scenes or cartoons dealing with gender, mainly because comparatively few cartoons took on this issue. Throughout the Warner Bros. cartoons, the de facto gender is male, so any character resembling a female (in drag or in reality) receives special musical indication. "Oh, You Beautiful Doll," "It Had to Be You," or "The Lady in Red" all help identify a typically brief encounter with

EXAMPLE 3 Sigmund Mogulesko, "Khosn, Kale Mazl Tov."

such a character; it is also possible that with such tunes—unlike his use
of "An Angel in Disguise," a song employed in two different cartoons in
which characters dress up to resemble angels—Stalling might have been
trying to create irony in cross-dressing sequences.

Music for stereotypical black characters was usually drawn from jazz
tunes, or at least arranged in a jazz idiom. Such music reinforced the no-
tions of primitivism and hedonism that some then associated with the
African American population. Songs such as "Sweet Georgia Brown,"
"Swing for Sale," and "Nagasaki" appear often, performed by on-screen
jazz bands or underscoring a walk-on by an urban black character. For
a depiction of the Old South, plantation songs by Stephen Foster ("Old
Folks at Home," "De Camptown Races," and even "Massa's in de Cold,
Cold Ground") or Daniel Decatur Emmett's "Dixie" or Henry Clay
Work's "Jubilo (Kingdom Coming)" would suffice. Like other cartoon
stereotyping, the imagery that accompanied these songs gives them the
visual impact—and offensive overtones—that makes them especially
memorable. (We'll return to race in cartoons in chapter 3.)

Foreign nationalities were also identified with specific pop songs. Particularly during World War II, America's foreign friends and foes alike
had to be identified quickly by music in the numerous cartoons that dealt
with wartime topics. German and Japanese characters were subjected to
complete and utter humiliation as often as possible in Warner Bros. cartoons (and those of all other studios, for that matter). In scoring Japanese
soldiers or any aspect of Oriental culture, Stalling most often used stereotypical pentatonic melodies, and occasionally songs such as "Nagasaki"
and "Chinatown, My Chinatown."[62] In *The Fifth-Column Mouse,* a cap-
tive mouse brokers a deal with the resident house cat: the mouse's rodent brethren will wait on the cat hand and foot in return for his not eating them. As the cat explains this idea to the mouse, his speech becomes
unintelligible; we hear only a series of hard consonants meant to evoke
German. Immediately thereafter, the cat momentarily grows large buck-
teeth and speaks in Japanese-sounding pidgin English (see figure 4). During the brief German interlude, the bass instruments play a menacing chorus of "Ach du lieber Augustin," and Stalling scores the allusion to a

FIGURE 4   *The Fifth-Column Mouse* (Warner Bros.; Freleng, 1943).

stereotypical Japanese with the song "Japanese Sandman." By using his stock Axis music, Stalling tries to increase the likelihood that the audience will understand the reference to Germany and Japan.[63]

STALLING'S COMPOSITE SCORES

During his twenty-plus years at Warner Bros., Stalling's approach to scoring naturally evolved. He became accustomed to working with particular characters, he learned and exploited the strengths of the Warner Bros. orchestra, and he adapted to each director's different perspective on storytelling. Most important, Stalling's cue-by-cue (or song-by-song) scoring style came to mesh well with the absurd, nonlinear logic of the Warner Bros. universe.

The music cue sheets for the cartoons produced in his first three years at Warner Bros. (1936–38) clearly demonstrate the transformation and expansion of Stalling's musical repertoire. For *Porky's Poultry Plant* (Tashlin), *Toy Town Hall* (Freleng), *Milk and Money* (Avery), and *Porky's Moving Day* (King), all appearing in 1936, Stalling uses numerous selections from Sam Fox, a music publishing house that produced a great deal of music for silent film accompanists (including the works of the prolific silent film composer J. S. Zamecnik), but was not owned or controlled by Warner Bros.[64] The remaining music is chosen either from the public domain (Chopin, Franz von Suppé, Henry Rowley Bishop and John Howard Payne's "Home! Sweet Home!" etc.) or from among the older, more obscure titles of the Harms-Witmark-Remick catalogue. One such song that appears in *Toy Town Hall* is "Merrily We Roll Along" (Harms, 1935); within a month, it became Stalling's choice for the new theme song for the Merrie Melodies series, beginning with the cartoon *Boulevardier from the Bronx* (Freleng, 1936).

His first score for Warner Bros., *Porky's Poultry Plant* (which was Frank Tashlin's first director credit at Warner's as well), shows that Stalling adjusted quickly to having a large instrumental ensemble at his disposal.[65] He did not take advantage of the music his new position afforded him, however, as he used nothing from the Warner Bros. music catalogue. The score uses winds, brass, and strings; the instrumentation is particularly noticeable at the cartoon's climax, when Porky battles a group of buzzards for a hapless chick that the scavenging birds have stolen from Porky's chicken farm. Stalling uses a Zamecnik cue, "Furioso #2," to underscore an air-battle sequence clearly inspired by World War I dogfights.

By 1938 Stalling had full command of the music available to him through Warner's publishing concerns; for instance, *The Isle of Pingo-Pongo* (Avery, 1938) contains thirty-nine individual cues, which break down as follows:

Harms-Witmark-Remick song	18 cues
Public domain piece	10 cues
Original Stalling underscore	8 cues
Ad lib drumming	3 cues

From that time until his retirement, Stalling seldom wrote a score that totaled fewer than twelve cues of original and published music. Judging from the extant materials, Stalling apparently constructed a rough cue sheet for each score, listing the song's title and composer(s) and indicating whether the song was in the public domain; original cues would be labeled "Original A," "Original B," and so on. When the cue sheet was typed up, Stalling would add names for the original cues (usually indicative of the screen action), and he or someone else would look up and record the publishers of the other songs.[66]

Chuck Jones's cartoons for Warner Bros. often were inspired directly by music, whether Tin Pan Alley (*One Froggy Evening*, 1955), classical music (*Baton Bunny*, 1959), or opera (*What's Opera, Doc?*, 1957). One of Jones's trademarks as a storyteller is his fondness for pantomime, which can be traced back to his first days as an animator in the mid-1930s and which invites a highly interactive musical score. Admittedly influenced by Disney's character-driven shorts of the 1930s, Jones began directing cartoons for Warner Bros. with Sniffles, a super-cute mouse in the Disney style. Jones emphasized facial expressions and physical reactions as much as (if not more than) the dialogue. As he developed as a director, Jones became in effect a physiognomist, telling entire stories through the character's features and body language and eschewing dialogue. Years later, Jones described his method: "In principle, we usually tried to tell our stories through action rather than words. My first films as director were too wordy, but I learned not to use dialogue when actions would suffice."[67]

Many of Jones's shorts emphasize the story visually, drawing attention to facial expressions and reaction shots in place of dialogue. In cartoons that tend toward the pantomimic, the music can play an even more prominent role in telling a story. Stalling's music informs the audience about the action at hand, providing a functional replacement for the dialogue. The 1952 cartoon *Mouse Warming* perfectly exemplifies this technique. A boy and girl mouse, living in the same human house, try to get to know each other while simultaneously attempting to avoid Claude, the house cat.[68] The cartoon's opening sequence—in which the girl mouse and her parents move into their new home (see figure 5)—tells the story through the cues alone. The music cue sheet for *Mouse Warming* is given in table 1 (with my description of the screen action in the far right column). We can see that Stalling scores roughly the first minute of the cartoon mainly with songs whose titles describe the action. Since the cartoon has no dialogue, Stalling could freely tell the story however he liked through his musical choices, though the audience may or may not catch the allusions. His choice of songs sets up the love story; but once the cat interferes, Stalling can no longer rely just on song titles. He returns to "L'Amour Toujours L'Amour" as a love theme later in the cartoon as the two mice finally have their date (the boy mouse having disposed of the cat, with the help of the household dog).

Jones eventually solidified his preference for pantomime with the Coyote and Road Runner. This series, which began in 1949, came closer than any other Warner Bros. cartoons to delivering a recurring story line based solely on a chase, like that displayed in the Tom and Jerry series at MGM. Jones alone directed it until 1962. His chases were not only consistent, they were practically done by the numbers. The resemblances in Jones's cartoons go far beyond the recurring characters and the absence of dialogue. He proclaimed that "*all* comedians obey rules consistent with their own view of comedy." Thus, he developed strict rules to establish the boundaries in the Road Runner series: no dialogue (they are only animals, after all); all action must take place in the desert (the natural environ-

FIGURE 5 *Mouse Warming* (Warner Bros.; Jones, 1952).

ment of the animals in question); gravity is always the coyote's worst enemy; and "the road runner must stay on the road—otherwise, logically,
he would not be called road runner."[69]

The series consists mainly of "blackout" gags: that is, jokes that have
a fast set-up and punch line, followed by a quick blackout on screen before the next gag begins. For the Coyote, this means that each successive
ploy or contraption he devises inevitably disappoints him. Only rarely
will anything from early in the story come back to haunt the Coyote,
though such returns, when they occur—for example, a trap that the Coyote sets up in an early gag is not used then but later backfires on him—

Table 1. MOUSE WARMING CUE SHEET

Selection	Composer	Time (min.sec)	Action
1. Reckless Night on Board an Ocean Liner	Raymond Scott	0.32	Moving men unload furniture
2. In My Merry Oldsmobile	Gus Edwards, Vincent Bryan	0.08	Mouse family drives up
3. Sweet Georgia Brown	Kenneth Casey, Maceo Pinkard, Ben Bernie	0.05	Shot of little girl mouse carrying phonograph
4. Home! Sweet Home!	J. H. Payne, H. R. Bishop; arr. Carl Stalling	0.12	Shot of mouse hole with "Welcome" doormat
5. Ain't She Sweet	Milton Ager, Jack Yellen	0.05	Girl mouse peers out her window
6. Mouse-Warming	Carl Stalling	0.02	Recognition cue
7. Perpetual Motion	Unknown [J. Strauss]	0.10	Boy mouse in fast toy car
8. Trap	Carl Stalling	0.07	Girl mouse gazes out
9. L'Amour Toujours L'Amour	Rudolf Friml, Catherine Chisholm Cushing	0.08	Their eyes lock—it's love at first sight
10. Ain't She Sweet	Milton Ager, Jack Yellen	0.10	Boy hatches plan to meet girl mouse
11. Love-Sick	Carl Stalling	0.48	Cat swallows boy mouse

NOTE: The original cue sheet contained another column, "How Used"; all these selections are used as background instrumental cues.

enable Jones to give the narrative a sense of continuity. In the absence of an extended story arc, the musical score reflects the digestible chunks into which Jones breaks the story; the last fall or explosion suffered by the Coyote in the cartoon is always as humiliating and painful as the first. The use of recurring story lines, not just recurring characters, did not lead Stalling to develop specific themes he could repeat from episode to episode,[70] though he often relied on a theme from Smetana's *The Bartered Bride* that contained swift string passages to evoke a sense of the Road Runner's unreal speed. Yet chase sequences make up only a small portion of these cartoons, which are largely devoted to the Coyote's setting up and setting off various devices intended to capture or kill the Road Runner. These brief scenes (perhaps a dozen in a single eight-minute cartoon) seem to have provided little inspiration to Stalling, who mickey-mouses many of the Coyote's movements, using inventive stingers at each impact or explosion. Only in those moments when the Coyote gives chase could Stalling make use of popular or classical tunes.

In contrast to Jones's clear fondness for visual storytelling, Friz Freleng had a penchant for one gag after the next with almost no dramatic buildup.[71] Whereas Jones or Bob Clampett might drive toward a grand finish (not necessarily a pulling-out-all-the-stops finale every time, but something the audience would remember), Freleng's stories usually move along at a steady pace. Barrier remarks that "the gags in Freleng's cartoons tend to be of equal weight, so that a cartoon simply stops when its time is up."[72] Given such an even-handed approach to storytelling, the music had to follow the on-screen action carefully and not overpower it. Stalling treats these scores much as he would one for a silent comedy; as the story moves from one gag to the next, so too does the score. With short, self-contained cues, he could mirror each movement of the story, instead of coming up with an encompassing score with a clearly defined exposition, climax, and conclusion.

The 1948 cartoon *Bugs Bunny Rides Again* exemplifies Freleng's approach. The music in this cartoon (see the cue sheet in table 2), rather than telling the story through the song titles, evokes the mood of the old West. Because Freleng chose to spoof the classic western film, Stalling has an additional set of genre-based musical codes on which he can draw to manipulate the audience's expectations. Songs such as "Cheyenne," "Navajo," "My Little Buckaroo," and, of course, Rossini's *William Tell* overture all musically place the action in the old West—not because any of these pieces come from that time and place but because they either are meant to signify cowboys and cattle or have been culturally resignified (the Rossini is the obvious example of the latter). Because of their associations, the songs can either underscore the scene or play explicitly within the story. "Navajo," for instance, sets the western mood and serves as the appropriate music for the old saloon because Stalling plays it on a keyboard meant to sound like an old-time, out-of-tune piano. Some of the cues that don't have an explicitly western connotation—Rossini's

Table 2. BUGS BUNNY RIDES AGAIN CUE SHEET

Selection	Composer	Time (min.sec)	Action
1. William Tell Overture	Rossini; arr. Carl Stalling	0.12	Title music
2. Cheyenne	Egbert Van Alstyne, Harry Williams	0.14	Estab. shot of rip-roaring western town
3. Navajo	Egbert Van Alstyne Harry Williams	0.11	Estab. shot of saloon, shot of interior and drinking cowboys inside
4. The Erl King	Schubert; arr. Carl Stalling	0.20	Yosemite Sam enters
5. Yosemite Sam	Carl Stalling	0.24	Bugs emerges as the only one willing to fight Sam
6. Inflammatus	Rossini; arr. Carl Stalling	0.27	Bugs and Sam begin a duel
7. Sonata Pathetique	Beethoven; arr. Carl Stalling	0.44	Sam tells Bugs "This town ain't big enough for the two of us"
8. Bugs Bunny Rides Again	Carl Stalling	0.29	Sam challenges Bugs to dance; he does, and then turns it over to Sam, who takes up the dance
9. Wise Guy	Carl Stalling	0.17	Sam falls down mine shaft
10. Die Gotter-dämmerung	Wagner; arr. Carl Stalling	0.12	Sam mad at Bugs for getting him to fall down the shaft
11. Fighting Words	Carl Stalling	0.43	Bugs leads Sam out of town
12. William Tell Overture	Rossini	0.40	Sam and Bugs in a horse chase
13. The Loser	Carl Stalling	0.18	Sam and Bugs agree to play cards
14. My Little Buckaroo	Jack Scholl, M. K. Jerome	0.30	Sam and Bugs play; the loser must leave town

Selection	Composer	Time (min.sec)	Action
15. Cheyenne	Egbert Van Alstyne, Harry Williams	0.22	Bugs wins; he rushes Sam to the train station
16. Oh, You Beautiful Doll	Nat D. Ayer, Seymour Brown	0.05	Bugs and Sam see the bathing beauties in the train car
17. Miami Special	Carl Stalling	0.06	Bugs subdues Sam momentarily
18. Aloha Oe	Queen Liluokalani; arr. Carl Stalling	0.08	Bugs gets away in the train, leaving Sam behind

NOTE: The original cue sheet contained another column, "How Used"; all these selections are used as background instrumental cues.

"Inflammatus," the Schubert, and the Beethoven—function as generically dramatic music (or "agitato," as Rapée might classify them).

One of the more obviously generic western moments occurs when Bugs and Yosemite Sam ("the roughest, toughest, he-man hombre that's ever crossed the Rio Grande . . .") slowly pace toward each other, spurs jingling, and Bugs comments, "Huh—just like Gary Cooper!" (see figure 6). Stalling uses a dramatic section of a Rossini overture, rather than a piece that refers more explicitly to westerns, for the emotional coding it brings to the scene.[73] Stalling bases the original cue "Bugs Bunny Rides Again" not on the classic film-accompanying repertoire but on a vaudeville-style tune. Sam points his gun at Bugs and yells, "Dance!" Western film convention leads us to expect Bugs to begin hopping from one foot to the other to avoid Sam's bullets. Instead, he displays his vaudevillian roots with a tap-dance routine in the middle of the street to Stalling's original tune. When Bugs finishes his number, he yells, "Take it, Sam!" Momentarily forgetting himself, Yosemite Sam mimics Bugs's performance to the same music (see figure 7). In this environment, the dance music need not come from a specific source; it can simply appear at the appropriate moment. Even pieces that don't specifically evoke the old West help Stalling create the musical-narrative world that he wants.

The cartoon ends when Sam loses to Bugs in a card game and must leave town on the next train. When the two arrive at the station, they find a car full of bathing beauties, women in swimsuits on the Miami Special; the sight catches both the characters and the audience unawares

FIGURE 6 *Bugs Bunny Rides Again*
(Warner Bros.; Freleng, 1948).

FIGURE 7 Dancing in *Bugs Bunny Rides Again*.

FIGURE 8 Getting out of town in *Bugs Bunny Rides Again*.

(see figure 8). Stalling matches our surprise with a striptease version of "Oh, You Beautiful Doll," completely changing the tone of the previous scene. Here again we see the advantage of Stalling's cue-by-cue style, which enables him to easily follow the unexpected plot twists and gags in the cartoon narrative.

STALLING THE POSTMODERNIST

An analysis of two cartoons out of hundreds to choose from can only scratch the surface of Stalling's approach. His work for other directors, especially Tex Avery and Bob Clampett, is just as worthy of close readings. But even this brief survey reveals the versatility of Stalling's style, as he integrated popular songs and original cues to meet the demands put on him to fashion an appropriate musical foundation for the animated world created in each new cartoon. Much more can (and I hope will) be said about the specifics of Stalling's compositional style, the referential nature of his scores, the extraordinary breadth and range of songs he used, and the more unusual scores he wrote.

As he grew comfortable with the idea of matching an image with a song, each year Stalling added greater numbers of songs to his repertoire. The vast collection of popular music owned by the Warner Bros. publishing division ensured that he could draw on up-to-the-minute songs for his scores, giving them a popular air that was definitely not an element of his work at Disney or Iwerks. While not all the songs he used were current, his access to songs from the 1920s, '30s, and '40s enabled him to draw on several generations' worth of material. It is no wonder that people have claimed Stalling as an early postmodernist, who built a new system of musical meaning by taking apart an older system and rearranging its pieces.[74]

The jokes and gags in the Warner Bros. cartoons consistently allude to people, places, events, and ideas *outside* the context of the narrative world established in the short.[75] Intertextuality was a trademark of the Warner Bros. cartoons, as they repeatedly referred to all aspects of the real world, including themselves as cartoons. Cultural references can be found in each of the three main elements of a cartoon—visuals, dialogue, and music—creating a sum that definitely exceeds its parts. More than fifty years after their creation, these cartoons have become valuable historical documents that provide us with a unique view of popular culture and thought of the 1930s through the 1950s; they offered a place to comment on ideas and fads of the time and even an outlet for social critique. In this light, we can read Stalling's musical choices as his attempts to work with the cultural references the cartoons made. Perhaps such a reading helps explain why critics were so besotted with Stalling in the 1990s: the music of the Warner Bros. cartoons told the stories of modern society behind an animated visage.

"You Really Do Beat the Shit out of That Cat"

SCOTT BRADLEY'S (VIOLENT) MUSIC FOR MGM

Before interest in Carl Stalling's music surged in the late 1980s, most of the critical writing on music and cartoons focused on one composer: Scott Bradley.[1] The authors tended to revere Bradley's composing style, particularly his preference for writing original music, and thus implicitly praised his disdain for using popular music. Today, Bradley's name has joined those of long-forgotten film composers, while Carl Stalling has become the cartoon composer to be lauded and imitated.

Yet Bradley had held his position of prominence in the industry for decades. During his almost twenty-five years of composing cartoons for MGM (1934–57), Bradley not only made a name for himself as a composer but also developed a unique composing style that became highly influential in his own time and afterward. Though the stories of the MGM cartoons are often quite generic, they have a unique signature: violent action sequences combined with Bradley's illustrative approach to scoring. The penchant for extreme cartoon violence appears to have originated at the MGM studio during a time that America was involved in an unprecedented global conflict. As a result, Bradley developed a technique for musically describing and rendering violent physical action. Each formulaic story began to echo the last, but Bradley further adapted his style to complement the narrative and to hold the audience's attention while not resorting to music that somehow caricatured the action. In considering Bradley's music, we must examine how it confirmed or contradicted the audience's notions of the cartoon world. What did it contribute to the overall experience of watching a cartoon? Was Bradley able to warn us, through the music, of an impending collision before it happened?

BRADLEY'S BACKGROUND

Bradley recalled in an interview that he started his professional life as a musician working as a composer and conductor in a Houston theater, and then moved to Los Angeles in 1926 and "went into radio."[2] He began making a name for himself on the concert scene in Los Angeles in the early 1930s. His extant concert works from this period include "The Valley of the White Poppies" (1931); "The Headless Horseman" (1932), an "episode" for orchestra based on Washington Irving's "The Legend of Sleepy Hollow"; and "Thanatopsis," a cantata for soloists, chorus, and orchestra. Bradley conducted the Los Angeles Oratorio Society in the premiere of "Thanatopsis" at the Philharmonic Auditorium in Los Angeles on 17 March 1934.[3] The critic for *Pacific Coast Musician* compared "Thanatopsis" to Honegger's "King David" (the other work on the program) and wrote that it "is conservative enough to those who value musical beauty and comprehensibleness above a surfeit of dissonances, contrapuntal extravagances and effects."[4] In naming what Bradley appeared to be avoiding, this review makes a strangely accurate prediction of what his cartoon scores would become—highly dissonant, contrapuntally labyrinthine, and rife with special effects.

Fifteen years later, when the musicologist and composer Ingolf Dahl interviewed Bradley at MGM, Bradley devised an autobiographical "memo" for him:

> METRO GOLDWYN MAYER. INTER-OFFICE COMMUNICATION.
> TO: Dahl SUBJECT: Dis-a and dat-a FROM: Bradley. Born. . Russelville,
> Arkansas (but not an "Arkie" I hasten to add). . Studied piano, private
> instruction. . organ and harmony with the English organist Horton
> Corbett. . Otherwise entirely self taught in composition and orchestration. .
> fed large doses of Bach, which I absorbed and asked for more. Conductor
> at KHJ and KNX in the early thirties. . entered the non-sacred realm of
> pictures in 1932 and started cartoon composing in 1934 with Harmon-
> Ising Co. *[sic]* Joined in 1937 . . . have so far been able to hide from them
> the fact that I'm not much of a composer. Personal: dislike bridge, slacks
> and mannish dress on women, all chromatic and diatonic scales, whether
> written by Beethoven or Bradley. Also, crowds and most people (and
> especially biographers). Favorite composers: Brahms, Stravinsky, Hin-
> demith, Bartok. This will be boring to most everyone, so cut it as short
> as you wish. Signed: Scott[5]

Though Bradley told Dahl that his first experience in animation occurred in 1934, very early cue sheets (in the ASCAP cue sheet files) place

FIGURE 9 Scott Bradley at Harman-Ising in the late 1930s.
Courtesy of the Academy of Motion Picture Arts and Sciences.

Bradley at Ub Iwerks's animation studio, beginning in late 1931, for more than a year, linking his name to thirteen cartoons.[6] Carl Stalling also worked for Iwerks on and off from 1930 until 1936. Bradley claimed, at the end of his life, that "I never met Carl Stalling. Which is odd, isn't it, because we were in the business about the same time."[7] The assertion is odder still if their time at the same studio overlapped. No mention of Iwerks ever appeared in any of Bradley's numerous biographical blurbs or articles; perhaps because he never ran the music department for Iwerks, Bradley may have omitted this part of his history, feeling it was not as significant as his work for Harman and Ising or his pursuits as an orchestral composer. But his description of his career given in a 1937 interview—"I was sort of 'spewed' out of radio into pictures some seven years ago when I took up composing and arranging in some of the major picture studios"[8]—puts the beginning of his film music career at 1930, around the time he might have worked for Iwerks.

In 1934, the same year as the premiere of "Thanatopsis," Hugh Harman and Rudy Ising began producing a new cartoon series for MGM, having left the cartoon division they helped establish at Warner Bros. after a financial dispute with the producer Leon Schlesinger.[9] Bradley began work for Harman-Ising (see figure 9) on the inaugural short of the Happy Harmonies series, *The Discontented Canary* (Ising, 1934). He recalled: "From that time on, we [Bradley, Harman, and Ising] continued working together. They didn't work like I did in regards to music. In fact, music in those days was more like just sound effects, with a few chords here and there. I showed them what could be done and they liked the idea."[10] Three years later, Harman and Ising worked out a new contract with MGM and moved to the MGM lot, taking Bradley with them. Bradley explained, "They liked what I was writing. They left the writing to me, although we were working on a shoestring. Finally . . . we moved out to MGM. Rudy and Hugh specified to Mr. Quimby that they would continue at MGM only on the condition that they bring their own composer. I conducted the orchestra myself."[11]

Bradley remained on the MGM lot for the next two decades, scoring practically all of MGM's theatrical cartoons, as well as writing music for several feature films and numerous shorts produced for the U.S. military during World War II. In 1954 MGM terminated Bradley's weekly contract and retained him solely as a freelance composer, paying him just under $1,000 per reel. Three years later, the cartoon division finally shut its doors and he retired.

IDEOLOGIES: AESTHETIC ASPIRATIONS

Scott Bradley took great pride in composing music for animated films, expressing high hopes for the future of cartoon music and of animation in general. Few established or renowned composers of concert music paid attention to cartoon music; yet Bradley, as the sole composer for one of the major Hollywood animation studios, believed he could bring about change in his small corner of the industry.[12] He took a rather highfalutin' view of his music; Carl Stalling, in contrast, regarded his work for Disney and Warner Bros. strictly *as* work and showed little interest in calling it art.[13] Bradley apparently never lost hope that the animated cartoon would eventually become a more universally respected art form, leading to a similar cultural upgrade for its music. He felt that if he treated the music seriously, he could make the cartoons more enjoyable and give the viewer a greater appreciation for their artistry. He told an interviewer early in his tenure at MGM, "I set about to work out musical scores that would add significance to the picture, that would be musically sound and would be entertaining. How well we have succeeded is for the public to say."[14] Unfortunately, success in these efforts required that he overcome two widely accepted beliefs: that cartoons could only be funny, never serious, and that film music should be experienced and not "heard."

Bradley often took the opportunity to predict what the future of cartoon music would be or, more accurately, *should* be. He declared in 1937 that "his ideal for cartoons is the complete discarding of dialogue and the use of the orchestra as a means by which the desired sound effects are arrived at."[15] Over the next dozen years, Bradley continued to put forward his idealized concept of the cartoon in which the story and music would have equal narrative significance—an animated form of Wagner's *Gesamtkunstwerk,* or complete artwork. His first known description of this ideal form appeared in a 1941 essay, "Cartoon Music of the Future" (reprinted in appendix 2). Its requirements included

- the exclusive use of music in the symphonic poem style, "written to a definite program and recorded before a foot of animation is in production"
- original music written only for the specific story at hand, permanently called "fantasies" instead of "cartoons"
- the use of free tempi in recording sessions as opposed to reliance on a click track
- the development of "a new type of orchestral tone color"
- a complete absence of dialogue, so as not to obscure the music[16]

In *Film Music Notes* three years later, Bradley expressed the hope that future animation would "be adapted to *pre-composed* music. We have only to imagine a Debussy composing 'The Afternoon of a Faun' as the basis of such a picture, to visualize the importance of music in cartoons."[17]

Optimistic as he seemed, Bradley knew he faced an uphill battle. In the traditional methods for producing animated cartoons, the underscoring music was created only after the story, if not most of the animation, was completed. (Exceptions to this rule included Disney's Silly Symphonies and the Fleischers' Song Car-Tunes, which were prescored with a song around which the directors crafted the animation.) And Bradley was likely alone in his desire to record his scores without relying on a click track (which provides a beat for the musicians and conductor to follow) or other synchronizing device used by the film industry that enabled the sound editor to record the music in sections and then seamlessly assemble the entire score, along with added sound effects and any dialogue, into a complete soundtrack.

Bradley had more leeway in pursuing his goal of writing original music with "a new type of orchestral tone color." As his own music became more experimental and adventurous, Bradley began to see cartoons as a site for more unorthodox approaches to orchestration. He also seemed less intent on changing the entire animation industry—just his corner of it: "If I have anything to say about it, cartoon music of 1946 will be progressively modern . . . orchestration in enlarged chamber music style . . . with a total elimination of the Spring Song sort of cliche. . . . Cartoons are 'made to order' for modern music and may well prove to be an important proving ground for this kind of scoring, thus becoming a leader instead of the red-headed step-child of motion picture music."[18] In a 1948 *Sight and Sound* article on cartoon music in which he was liberally quoted, he continued to express his hopes that others would follow his lead: "Only cartoons give the picture composer a chance to hear a composition of 6 to 7 minutes' length almost without interruption. . . . I wish that our contemporary masters would take interest in cartoon work. For men like Copland, Bernstein, Britten, Walton, Kodaly, Shostakovich or Prokofieff it would be a very fruitful experience. Their contributions would certainly advance the cartoon as a genre."[19] The interest of such a "master" would justify and validate Bradley's own years of toil. Perhaps the contributions of a big-name composer would raise the public's consciousness of cartoon music even if his own attempts failed. Although he achieved few of his stated goals in his cartoon scores of the 1940s and 1950s, he could still derive considerable satisfaction from writing music for the stories he received that was as evocative and interesting as possible.

In his attempts to legitimize cartoon music, Bradley made himself known as an innovative film composer in the Hollywood film community. He took lessons with Mario Castelnuovo-Tedesco (probably in orchestration and counterpoint, techniques for which the Jewish émigré from Italy was well known), who worked on staff at MGM in the 1940s and taught a host of other aspiring composers, including Nelson Riddle, André Previn, Jerry Goldsmith, and John Williams.[20] According to the bassoonist Anthony Christlieb, a fifty-year veteran of Hollywood film orchestras, Bradley was also an avid concertgoer. He liked to attend concerts of "music of every sort. He was a regular member of the audience at the Monday Evening Concerts, which was unusual for film composers except David Raksin and Hugo Friedhofer."[21] The Monday concerts, known also as the "Evenings on the Roof" series, featured the music of contemporary composers; they thus provided a perfect forum for someone like Bradley, who was keen on staying informed of all the latest musical innovations.

Bradley also began writing cartoon-inspired suites for concertgoing audiences. Several of these works, including a suite on his music for the Happy Harmonies short *Dance of the Weed* (Ising, 1941), were based directly on scores he wrote for MGM. Bradley's *Cartoonia* suite (1938) seems to have been inspired by the prevalent themes and motifs he encountered as a cartoon composer rather than by a specific cartoon. This piece received a fair amount of public attention, particularly in Southern California,[22] and was performed on numerous occasions by major orchestras in San Francisco, Houston, and Los Angeles. No less eminent a musician than the original conductor for Stravinsky's *The Rite of Spring* and Ravel's *Daphnis and Chloé,* Pierre Monteux, conducted the premiere; another sixty performances took place throughout Southern California, "as part of the Los Angeles High School Music Education Program."[23] But as the years went by, Bradley's concert output dried up almost entirely as he focused on his work at MGM.

PRACTICALITIES: BRADLEY AND THE MGM STYLE

Perhaps the best way to understand how Bradley's approach to cartoons differed from that of other composers is to compare his creative and practical expectations with Stalling's, already discussed. Such a comparison by no means implies that one man was more creative, demanding, or innovative than the other. Their prominence in their field and the lasting impression their music has left make their work equally worthy of detailed discussion.

The most significant distinction between Stalling and Bradley arises from the remarkably different methods of storytelling employed at MGM and at Warner Bros. The MGM cartoons used less dialogue than those at Warner Bros., a practice begun with the Happy Harmonies. Harman and Ising focused primarily on the pretty fantasy worlds they constructed for each cartoon and allowed the narrative to unfold through the visuals; they therefore paid less attention to dialogue. When the Tom and Jerry series emerged as a box-office favorite for MGM in the early 1940s, the studio's other series shifted to emphasize the same style—fight, chase, conflict—that had succeeded for Bill Hanna and Joe Barbera, while still retaining the dialogue-free settings inspired by slapstick and vaudeville comedy. In contrast, the cartoons of the Warner Bros. directors delighted in humorous and witty dialogue for practically every recurring character (except the Road Runner and Hippity-Hopper, the giant "mouse"). Carl Stalling's music thus worked as part of the Warner Bros. cartoons' traditional mise-en-scène structure of dialogue, images, sound effects, and music, while Bradley's music enjoyed a more privileged position, generally sharing the stage with only the animation and sound effects.

The division of sonic space into dialogue, sound effects, and music (in descending order of importance) is a structure endemic to Hollywood filmmaking. No composer could escape the influence that sound effects had on the cartoon score. In fact, in describing the "cartoon music of the future," Bradley does not call for the elimination of sound effects. Perhaps he realized that they were ubiquitous not just because of popular convention but because they were integral to the cartoon soundtrack. Bradley seems to have incorporated as many sound effects as possible into his scores and thereby controlled, at least occasionally, the balance between two of the three elements of the soundtrack. Such musically based sound effects frequently made unnecessary the common device of a separate nonmusical sound effect to double or supplement the action in question.

Like most other cartoon composers, Bradley initially (from 1934 until the early 1940s) had no say in a cartoon's plot development unless the cartoon dealt with a musical subject or featured a musical performance as a key story element. Bradley had little input into the cartoon's narrative, nor into its timing, pacing, or other aspects that related to the music. Ingolf Dahl captured Bradley's predicament: "The cartoon, being a very extrovert and direct form of entertainment, needs the reassuring directness of symmetrically constructed music. But how to supply this when the direction has crystallized the form of the film entirely outside of musical considerations?"[24] Such a production process, though typical of practically all Hollywood films, put composers at a disadvantage by severely limiting their involvement with the larger project, but Bradley made the best of the situation. Once the visual narrative was complete, he would create a score that danced around the visuals, accentuating the action, adding to the mood, and enhancing the story in any way he pleased, for the directors, Harman and Ising, seldom interfered. Bradley could fill in the blanks in the narrative with the score, interweaving the music as closely as possible with the action without having to heed predetermined notions of rhythm and pacing. His efforts to match the pacing and quick changes in the action help explain why his scores are often melodically less flowing and more angular than those of others.

When Hanna and Barbera began directing, the scoring procedure changed, though they were no more likely to interfere than Harman and Ising had been. Joe Barbera's chief task in any Tom and Jerry cartoon was to determine the timing for all the gags, which he would write down on detail or "bar" sheets. This blueprint of the cartoon not only had space for notes on the action, sound effects, and any possible dialogue but also included two music staves per page for scoring the scene. Once all the other pertinent information had been notated, Bradley would receive the bar sheet and use it as his guide as he began to compose. He thus worked on each score earlier in the production process than with Harman and Ising, and from the early 1940s onward his music became more closely fused with the genesis of each cartoon.

As we have seen, Carl Stalling's style, particularly in his scores during his first decade at Warner Bros., tended to favor active scenes with active music. Stalling would underscore sequences that unfolded at a moderate pace with a chorus from a pop song, not seeking to explicitly synchronize the music to the action at hand. Bradley instead treated moments when visual action was slow or absent as opportunities for musical creativity. Recognizing when the story's pulse began to fade, Bradley would enliven the music, thereby enhancing its prominence in the soundtrack and maintaining the cartoon's momentum. These differences again relate to the studios' approaches to storywriting. While the (verbal) gag-driven nature of the Warner shorts was well served by Stalling's method of shifting constantly from one song to the next, the MGM cartoons, and especially the Tom and Jerry shorts, were a progression of reactions. Bradley carefully supported each story's ever-rising level of aggression until the cartoon's action and music simultaneously reached a violent explosion.

When scoring a chase sequence (for example, the Coyote chasing the Road Runner), Stalling normally chose a piece that reinforced the preconceived rhythm of the scene. If the chase moved quickly, then the music would keep pace, calculated so that the regular beats of the underscore emphasized the visual and aural synchronicities. Bradley refused to let the action—particularly in the Tom and Jerry cartoons, every one of which involved a chase of some sort—shackle his creativity. The action did not necessarily dictate the musical pacing or style. Beyond fulfilling their practical obligation to constantly feed the cartoon's forward movement, Bradley's scores provided (often ironic) commentary on the narrative in a wide range of musical styles.

A characteristic scene appears in *Puttin' on the Dog* (1943), in which Tom is being chased around a yard full of dogs. Here Bradley uses a highly flexible approach to underscoring. Because of the fast up-and-down scales, the viewer hears the cue as general romping or horseplay music; the choppy and repetitive pattern (eighth note–eighth rest–eighth note) conveys a palpable sense of chaos. None of the downbeats explicitly matches a footfall or any other visual action; the broken triplets, set against the constant eighth notes of the cello, fight against any synchronization of the aural and visual elements. Without a steady beat to dictate how the scene unfolds musically, each gesture of the cue can connect to the action without being enslaved to the beat. The score then switches to triplets without any rests, causing the momentum to increase and the tempo seemingly to speed up until complete anarchy is reached as the instruments hold out a climactic, trilled stinger-style chord—and all for a chase that lasts less than ten seconds.

Bradley's cartoons also featured fewer preexisting melodies than the Warner Bros. cartoons, in part because MGM owned less music than its competitors. Though the paucity of its library might appear to be a disadvantage, Bradley felt no great need to use music composed by others when he could write his own (which he thought would suit a situation in a cartoon better than a tune written possibly twenty-five years earlier). Whether Stalling's use of pop songs was simply a time-saving device or was an integral part of his compositional process matters little; Bradley had neither the same background nor the same time pressures on his work. His more generous schedule may begin to explain how Bradley found the time to craft his scores and write so much original music.[25] (For instance, in 1941 Bradley scored fifteen shorts, a third the number done by Stalling.) Bradley hardly sought to avoid using preexisting songs, but he did not make them the prevailing structural element of his scores.

Stalling also had the Warner Bros. studio orchestra at his disposal. As I pointed out in chapter 1, in the 1930s and '40s Warner Bros. retained a full orchestra of sixty to seventy players plus a chorus, and Stalling could use it freely. Though he generally used only thirty to forty instrumentalists, that number still qualified as large for a short, especially an animated short. Once again, Bradley worked at an apparent disadvantage, having usually nineteen players in any one score. Rather than considering it a handicap, however, he enjoyed the challenge of working with a smaller ensemble: "I conducted the orchestra myself. I noticed in an article about Carl Stalling that he used the big Warner orchestra, but you didn't need it. I used twenty pieces—that's all I needed. That's all anyone needed. You don't need a symphony orchestra for cartoons."[26] The standard complement of instruments for Bradley included four violins, two violas, cello, double bass, two or three trumpets, two trombones, flute and oboe (both doubling on other woodwinds), two or three clarinets, piano, and a percussionist; he would occasionally add extra personnel, which might include percussionists, a guitar, a harp, or an organ (a Novochord).

Timbrally, Bradley's scores differ from Stalling's not only because of the number of pieces used (the lack of a large string section is the most noticeable difference) but also because of how Bradley chose to employ the instruments he had. In a 1948 article titled "Cartoons and Modern Music," John Winge pointed out that Bradley "treated the wood-winds individually, the strings as a quintet and the piano as a solo instrument instead of a filler."[27] The favoritism that Bradley showed to woodwinds in his scores wasn't only because he couldn't afford to hire more strings. His admiration for Hindemith and, even more, Stravinsky seems to have strongly influenced his explicit use of woodwinds, both as solo instruments and in ensembles. Bradley did not rely on the traditional romantic (that is, string-heavy) sound of films, which Stalling favored, but he demanded a great deal from those musicians whom he used. One violinist commented, "Scott writes the most blank-blank-blank difficult fiddle music in Hollywood, he is yet going to break my fingers."[28]

One final distinction between Bradley and Stalling: Bradley worked on several feature films at MGM while scoring cartoons. He wrote much of the score of *The Courage of Lassie* (1946); portions of *The Yellow Cab Man* (1950), *Dangerous When Wet* (the sequence in which Tom and Jerry swim with Esther Williams, 1952), and *The Kissing Bandit* (1948); and a single reel for a deleted (animated) sequence in the 1955 film *Blackboard Jungle*, famous as the first film to include rock 'n' roll in its score (it opens with Bill Haley and His Comets singing "Rock around the Clock"). While Bradley seemed to enjoy live-action work, Stalling stated that he wrote music for one reel of a single film for Warner Bros., *The Horn Blows at Midnight* (1945), and that he took little pleasure in the experience.[29]

Perhaps Bradley's most impressive characteristic was his ability to create original music while working with the same basic plot line, involving "the chase." He wearily remarked in 1949, "It's fights, fights,

fights for me . . . and how I am getting tired of them. A beautiful, developed tune—alas, that's never the fate of Scott."[30] Little did he know
when he uttered this lament that he had yet another decade of composing fight music ahead of him.

HAPPY HARMONIES: MGM'S EARLY YEARS

The Happy Harmonies series that Harman and Ising created for MGM
took more than just its name from Disney's Silly Symphonies. As former Disney employees who had helped develop the Silly Symphonies in
the late 1920s, Harman and Ising were intimately familiar with the story
structure and artistic look of Disney's cartoons; and, as Leonard Maltin
points out, they wanted to "rival Disney's award-winning series, with
its appealing characters, imaginative stories, and elaborate trappings."[31]
Their overall style thus closely resembled the fantasy-based stories and
picturesque pastoral scenes that Disney favored. The MGM cartoons
also had few recurring characters in their fantasy series (with the exception of Bosko in the mid-1930s and Barney Bear beginning in the
late 1930s).

As noted above, Bradley began composing for Harman-Ising on their
first cartoon in the Happy Harmonies series, *The Discontented Canary.*
Much of the score is made up of popular songs, including "La Marseillaise," Henry Rowley Bishop and John Howard Payne's "Home! Sweet
Home!" and Septimus Winner's "Listen to the Mocking Bird." Most of
the music, however, consists of various arrangements of "The Man on
the Flying Trapeze." The cartoon begins with an arrangement for women's
voices singing "Trapeze"; its words apply to the canary of the film's title, who dreams of the world outside of his cage and longs to fly free.
Once he gains his liberty, he encounters unexpected real-world dangers,
including lightning storms, hungry cats, and rude hummingbirds who
literally *hum* "Listen to the Mocking Bird." The villainy of his feline
antagonist brings out the only originally composed music in the cartoon:
Bradley scores the cat's skulking around the meadow with a solo bassoon and low strings, which break just momentarily from the convention (and safety) of the familiar melodies that dominate the soundtrack.
Once the canary realizes that his life in captivity was far less stressful,
he returns to his cage to a joyous chorus of "Home! Sweet Home!"

One of Bradley's requirements in his "Cartoon Music of the Future"
was that cartoons contain original music written for the specific story,
and a complete absence of dialogue, so as not to obscure the score.[32] His

FIGURE 10 The flower and the weed in
Dance of the Weed (MGM; Ising,
1941).

best opportunity to write within these parameters came in the Happy Harmonies short *Dance of the Weed* (Ising, 1941), for which Bradley
prescored and recorded the music, much like a symphonic poem, before
the cartoon was animated.[33] A simple love story, the cartoon portrays a
clumsy male weed (who looks like a teenage rube, with a single tooth and
acne) and a serene young female flower, a ballerina whom the weed finds
dancing gracefully with other flowers. Rejected by all the other plants,
the weed makes for the flower, who at first shies away (see figure 10). But
when an errant gale blows the two into dangerous territory, the weed dig-
nifies himself by protecting them both from a three-headed snapdragon,
and the cartoon ends with the two happily united.

At the Film Music Forum in Los Angeles in 1944, Bradley showed
Dance of the Weed and spoke about it to the gathered audience:

> In this instance, the usual procedure was reversed, and the entire music
> score was composed and recorded before the story was written. I believe
> this is the first attempt to give the composer a break, and is, of course, the
> ideal way from our own selfish viewpoint. You will note that the music in
> the opening scenes is in the manner of French Impressionism. The ballet
> of the flowers is a waltz movement in which the themes of the little weed
> and the wild rose are combined. Later the terrible snapdragons (who
> menace w. & f.) are represented by bassoons and basses, while strings
> and woodwinds play a different theme in the high register. I hope you
> will notice that we use neither saxophones nor trumpets in the orchestra.
> However, we use three horns and two trombones.[34]

As Bradley indicates, both the weed and flower have their own themes
(see music example 4). The score progresses much like a ballet, as the
music both characterizes the lovers and compels their movements. The
weed's theme develops until he sees the flower, at which point her melody
takes over the score. After their encounter with the snapdragon, the two

EXAMPLE 4   Scott Bradley, themes for the weed and flower from *Dance of the Weed*.

themes come together briefly; the story ends with the weed's wistful melody. We cannot escape the feeling that the entire story is choreographed to the music rather than reacting to it more spontaneously, a notion furthered by our (and the weed's) first sight of the flower, dancing in a balletic fashion.

This precomposed cartoon score is unique, but the music does not justify Bradley's feelings that the typical scoring process should be reversed, mainly because it never establishes a substantial connection with the action. The simple love story, taking place among anthropomorphic plants, is not enough to support a particularly engaging drama or comedy. Still, in the complete absence of dialogue Bradley's music is free to tell the story, and thus he is able to satisfy at least one of his desires. After the cartoon's premiere, a reviewer predicted: "As Ravel was commissioned by Diaghilev to write his Daphnis and Chloe Ballet music, this music, too, may, with the new attitude on the part of orchestra directors over the country toward the native born composer, bring a call to Bradley to furnish scores of this highly interesting work for concerts apart from the picture."[35] Indeed, *Dance of the Weed* joined the *Cartoonia* suite as one of Bradley's concert pieces based on his cartoon music. Perhaps it was better suited to be a purely descriptive piece of music than a cartoon accompaniment. If *Dance* shows us anything about Bradley, however, it is that his dreams were remarkably close to those of Carl Stalling. Both men endeavored to work on cartoons in which the music took on the role of storyteller rather than lurking in the background. But while Stalling convinced Disney of music's worth and helped create the Silly Symphonies, Bradley had no such luck with the Happy Harmonies. Yet the Tom and Jerry series, which with few exceptions (most in the first five years of its existence) had no dialogue, allowed Bradley free rein in a tremendous amount of sonic space, which he usually had to share only with the sound effects.

MUSIC IN A VIOLENT WORLD

Tom and Jerry were not initially conceived as a recurrent comic team—in fact, they originally existed only as a one-shot story that first appeared in theaters in February 1940. The producer in charge of animation for MGM, Fred Quimby, gave his new directors Bill Hanna and Joe Barbera complete freedom to do whatever stories they wanted. The characters developed by Hanna and Barbera immediately showed tremendous comic potential, largely because the two combatants were in a constant uproar.

No doubt the never-ending cycle of pursuits, each collapsing into the next until they became virtually indistinguishable, aided in the establishment of Tom and Jerry as the paradigmatic chase cartoon. Once their success as a popular comic duo became apparent, Hanna and Barbera focused on Tom and Jerry cartoons until 1958. Each short used the same basic plot, which hardened into a subgenre in animation: the formulaic cartoon chase. By the time the next most famous animated chase duo— the Coyote and the Road Runner—appeared in 1949, the form was long since codified; Chuck Jones and Mike Maltese, respectively the director and primary writer of the Coyote–Road Runner series, had close to ten years of animated chases to refer to.

The problem with the Tom and Jerry series seems to lie not with the use of physical humor per se but with the degree of violence in that physicality. The extreme reactions that Hanna and Barbera used in the series go back to the days of vaudeville. E. G. Lutz observed in 1920, "In a boisterous low comedy it is always incumbent upon the victim of a blow to reel around like a top before he falls. It never fails to bring laughter."[36] While the practice of exaggerated reactions or big "takes" had been circumscribed on stage and in films by the natural physical limitations of the human body, animation had no such boundaries. Rather than simply spinning around every time he is hit, Tom reacts differently to each act of abuse, inevitably in a larger-than-life way: screaming as he flies through the air (his pain propelling him skyward), smiling like a simpleton as he collapses into pieces after being hit on the head, and so on.

As the story continues, the gags must also increase in size and intensity; Lutz notes, "To be sure, an animated cartoon needs a good many more incidents than one calamitous occurrence. It is indispensable . . . that it should have a succession of distressing mishaps, *growing in vio-*

lence. This idea of a cumulative chain of actions, increasing in force and resultant misfortune, is peculiarly adapted to animated drawings" (emphasis mine).[37] The cartoons work on the principle of mounting reactions: as the story progresses, the takes become bigger and more outrageous, until someone (or something) explodes. We will see that Bradley carefully follows this trajectory: as the gags intensify, so does the music.

Tex Avery, whose particular fondness for such chains of exaggerated gags made him the hero of and major influence on many Hollywood animators (including Hanna and Barbera), recognized the value of *big* takes: "We found out early that if you did something with a character . . . that couldn't possibly be rigged up in live action, why then you've got a guaranteed laugh. . . . If you can take a fellow and have him get hit on the head and then he cracks up like a piece of china, then you know you've got a laugh!"[38] The Tom and Jerry cartoons practically all boil down to a chase with various embellishments (add a dog, maid, or baby elephant to the mix), inversions (Jerry chasing Tom), or variations (Tom chasing another cat). Extreme physical behavior thus became the natural order of events; and in a series so clearly based on slapstick comedy, constant mischief gags punctuated and directed the narrative.

The extreme level of these takes compels us to consider whether the directors actually perceived the level of violence in these cartoons as being threatening. To many critics, the invariable return to the same story demonstrated that the directors had failed to consider the barbarity they were portraying. Thus the animation historian Michael Barrier argues, "Hanna and Barbera never addressed the aesthetic issues that the violence in their cartoons constantly raised; there's no reason to believe that they ever recognized that such issues existed."[39] Yet Bill Hanna once responded directly to such charges:

> Studio officials used to say things like, "You really do beat the shit out of that cat." But they were joking. My argument against our critics is that there are two kinds of violence. There is violence just for violence's sake, presented in a realistic form; and there is fantasy violence, done in comedy form. I agree with critics who say that imitative violence is bad. Now the psychologists and program practices people are easing up on us because they have come to realize that our type of fantasy violence is just for fun and is not imitative.[40]

We can see that Hanna *hoped* that audiences could read the cartoons as outrageous fun, while at the same time admitting that for him and Barbera, the humor came from seeing a character taken (often literally) to pieces. Tex Avery had a similar view of physical violence. Though not a

director on the Tom and Jerry series, Avery did work that profoundly affected the notion of violence and extremes in *all* Hollywood animation.
He too held that something "impossible" could not be perceived as truly
dangerous.

> We thought it was funny. I mean, a fellow could get hit in the head and
> stand there and have his whole body crack and fall in a pile and his own
> hands would get up and scoop it all up and put himself back together
> again. We found that you can get a terrific laugh out of someone just
> getting demolished—as long as you clean him up and bring him back to
> life again. It's exaggeration to the point where we hope it's funny. Because
> we hope the audience will say, "Well, it could never happen to a guy like
> that. All this shit could never fall on a guy."[41]

In the 1950s, the critic John Culshaw traced true violence in animation to the cartoons released during and especially after World War II,
pointing specifically to Tom and Jerry (obviously without foreseeing the
heights to which cartoon violence would rise in the future). A devoted
Disneyophile, Culshaw did not believe that the Disney cartoons (which
he used as a benchmark) were violent, interpreting all the violence prop-
agated by Mickey Mouse himself in the early 1930s as slapstick-style fun-
ning. The only violence that matters for Culshaw is violence done to the
body; and even though in Tom and Jerry cartoons the bodies are those
of animals, he insists on the human basis of the stories. Believing that
violence for its own sake in the Warner Bros. and MGM cartoons had
replaced the charm of the Disney cartoons (which then had to match the
violence of their competitors), Culshaw tries to demonstrate the (d)evo-
lution in our concept of what's funny. "The nature of the violence is
shown exactly," he complains, "because now it seems to have an entertainment value; tails are pulled off, legs broken, heads scalped, bodies
mangled."[42] As the quotation from Avery attests, the barbarous extreme
of a take itself became the joke; to keep that joke fresh, the directors had
to surpass the existing limits with each new cartoon.

Jerry typically engages in the most extreme physical violence possible, using it even when less brutal tactics might produce similar results.
In recognizing that the effects can exist only in the animated world, we
concede (albeit implicitly) their utter impossibility in the real world. This
observation may offer an insight into the cartoon universe: while some
directors retain a modicum of "reality" (usually regarding basic laws of
physics and thermodynamics), Hanna and Barbera—particularly under
Tex Avery's influence—do not, and they thus see nothing wrong with
constantly going to extremes. The bigger the set-up for a violent act, the

bigger the laugh. Audiences know that such violence cannot exist in reality, and they laugh *because* of its outlandishness. But how we should construe such humor remains an open question. The art critic Dave Hickey provides one interpretation, recalling how he and his childhood companions perceived the impotent violence portrayed in cartoons:

> What we did not grasp was just exactly *why* the blazing spectacle of lawn-mowered cats, exploding puppies, talking ducks, and plummeting coyotes was so important to us. Today, it's clear to me that I grew up in a generation of children whose first experience of adult responsibility involved the care of animals—dogs, cats, horses, parakeets—all of whom, we soon learned, were breathlessly vulnerable, if we didn't take care. Even if we did take care, we learned, these creatures, whom we loved, might, in a moment, decline into inarticulate suffering and die—be gone forever. And we could do nothing about it. So the spectacle of ebullient, articulate, indestructible animals—of Donald Duck venting his grievances and Tom surviving the lawn mower—provided us a way of simultaneously acknowledging and alleviating this anxiety, since all of our laughter was premised on our new and terrible knowledge that the creatures given into our care dwelt in the perpetual shadow of silent suffering and extinction.[43]

For Hickey, then, such violence was attractive not only because watching animals taking a beating and bouncing right back was fun, but because it helped him and his friends grapple with their fears and concerns about their approaching responsibilities as adults. Others may have different explanations, but this is not the place to determine why Tom and Jerry are so violent or to trace the effects of their actions on their audience; my point here is that the violence did not begin with them. We can also see now that Hanna and Barbera fully recognized the violence in their cartoons; after a while, it became a trademark of the series and eventually the studio. Its relation to the music remains uncertain, however. Clearly, Bradley's music enhances the action and, by extension, the violence. But is there something in the music that is redolent of violence? Does the music enhance or add to the violence? Or perhaps Bradley's zany sounds are there to remind Hickey, his friends, and all of us that what we are watching is, indeed, a cartoon, even as enough "realistic" sound (including music) punctuates the blows and flayings and explosions to convey a feeling of reality.

MUSIC AND VIOLENCE: TOM AND JERRY

From its inaugural episode in 1940 (*Puss Gets the Boot*), the Tom and Jerry series must have struck Bradley as his dream come true—in a sense.

It satisfied two of his demands for the perfect cartoon of the future, making this series as good as anything Bradley would ever get his hands on. First, the music would not have to rely on a single rigid tempo, but would change according to the needs of the cartoon (as the musical director saw them), a practice Bradley seemed to have perfected early on. Second, Tom and Jerry did not speak (as Bradley proclaimed, "fantasy is best portrayed without the irritating presence of speaking voices"). On the downside, the stories did revel in the kind of slapstick-based physical violence that Bradley disdained—he had hoped instead for "stories of great beauty and artistic (not arty) value. Think of 'Pelleas and Melisande.'"[44] When asked if either Hanna or Barbera ever evinced particular preferences for musical styles, Bradley replied: "Yes, to a certain extent—Joe [Barbera] especially liked contemporary music. Bill [Hanna] was the only director in the studio who knew anything about music. I had no interference from Bill. As time went on, Bill and Joe let me have the complete say about what music to write. Tom and Jerry never spoke a word."[45] While he may have complained about the monotony of chase cartoons, Bradley did not master his treatment of them until the 1940s. The chase music in the Happy Harmonies was often agitato orchestral music, without many points in the music to tie it to the action. Bradley thus developed a new style specifically to heighten the effect of the chases he scored so often.

Two Hanna and Barbera cartoons from the 1940s, *Solid Serenade* (1946) and *Puttin' on the Dog* (1944), provide an excellent overview of Bradley's techniques. The first involves a short chase sequence in the middle of the story. The cartoon begins with Tom singing to his cute kitty-cat girlfriend, having tied up the vicious bulldog that lives in the yard. Playing on a double bass, Tom serenades his girlfriend with "Is You Is or Is You Ain't My Baby?" Jerry, sleeping beneath the house, resolves to put an end to Tom's caterwauling. After he hits Tom in the face with two pies, the singing stops, and Tom chases Jerry through the house until Jerry unties the bulldog, who then begins chasing Tom. Insofar as it includes both original scoring and popular melodies, here in the form of Tom's extensive on-screen vocal performance, this cartoon typifies Bradley's experiences with the series.

In his exploration of film sound, the French film theorist and composer Michel Chion offers us a practical tool for understanding a fundamental component of Bradley's scores. Chion uses the term "rendering" to describe sounds that "convey the feelings or effects associated with the situation on screen," as opposed to those that literally reproduce what might actually be heard in the real world. Essential to an evocative and convincing soundtrack, Chion argues, is the use of diegetic sounds (that is, sounds emanating from within the world of the film) to "render" the emotions of a specific moment by fulfilling the viewer's expectation of how a physical gesture would sound and, thus, how it might feel.[46] The complexity in Bradley's music lies not just in the actual notes but also in Bradley's ability to illustrate both action and emotion, often at the same time.

If we consider the music (in addition to the sound effects) as trying to depict how something sounds *and* feels, suddenly the purpose of Bradley's most idiosyncratic moments of composition becomes clear: they are attempts at properly rendering an impact that will last for only eight frames (that is, about half a second), yet must resonate enough in the viewer's psyche to cause him or her to flinch at the thought (and sound) of a painful injury. Chion reminds us that when we see something fall in a film, the sound of impact must render "weight, violence, and pain."[47] The audible crash must make up for the fact that a falling object in a cartoon has no weight or mass at all, and thus we must in effect be aurally bludgeoned into believing in the impact we see. In the MGM shorts, in which falls at great distance occur as naturally as breathing, the music provides all three of the components Chion mentions: weight, often supplied by the register of the instruments; violence, conveyed by the complexity and speed of the melodic line; and pain, often communicated through a stinger chord, typically the musical equivalent of a cattle prod (Claudia Gorbman defines it as "a musical *sforzando* used to illustrate sudden dramatic tension").[48] We can see that each tool that Bradley used contributed to his larger task of giving the cartoons an innate sense of vitality and motion through the music. At the same time, the music contributes to and even challenges the narrative in each cartoon, and in doing so it is unlike what he perceived to be the uninspired, slavish scores of his colleagues, Carl Stalling included.

One of Bradley's characteristic approaches to relating music to image involved what he called "moving counterpoint," which he believed would allow him to move away from the conventional use of "sustained harmony"—that is, using the chord changes in a popular song to move the action along. Bradley certainly wanted to make the melodic lines themselves contrapuntally valid and interesting. He also strove to create a compelling relationship between the music and the image, in order to avoid rudimentary mickey- (or Jerry-)mousing. To be sure, mickey-mousing in its literal sense, the synchronization of sound and image, appears often in Bradley's work. Though he resisted the limitations of synchronization by trying, whenever possible, to write the music *before* he saw the visuals, we know that he was rarely able to do so. However, he could escape at least the appearance of mickey-mousing by refusing to use songs with straightforward rhythmic pulses. For example, an animated figure walking to the tempo of a standard pop song led to double accents on footfalls through both a visual and an aural representation of a character's movements to a constant beat—exactly the kind of synchronicity Bradley wanted to avoid.

Bradley also used musical gestures to register inner feelings. We can understand the characters by reading their facial reactions (again, since these cartoons have little or no dialogue, the expressions of the characters must be clear), but Bradley provides us a musical path to their thoughts. His cues give us a brief glimpse into the character's interior state, usually at moments of crisis, whether physical (about to be crushed, impaled, eaten, etc.) or mental (afraid of being crushed, impaled, eaten, etc.)—or even at a moment of empathy (do I help my archrival, who is himself about to be crushed? etc.). At several points, the chase sequence in *Solid Serenade* illustrates this technique: as Jerry slides onto a windowsill, we hear a glissando trombone line a moment before he reacts to Tom, who we understand is giving chase off-screen. We then hear a set of quick, syncopated chords before Jerry runs off, grabbing the window support on his way so that the sash hits Tom squarely on the neck (see figure 11). For Jerry's reactions—the first physical (sliding onto the sill), the second mental (his palpable terror as he runs off)—Bradley musically creates an expectation that the visual action would fulfill. The two elements of sound and vision together convey all the rapid events in the short scene. Bradley usually anticipated an impact or reaction by at least a second or two, so that the audience would *hear* the action before seeing it. In the swiftly paced fight or chase sequences, Bradley could prepare the viewer for each gag before it occurred and could also bridge the occasional momentary breaks in the animation. Chion mentions that a prime role of music in cartoons specifically is to "aid the apprehension of visual movements."[49] Looking at the extant bar sheets, we can see that each important hit or impact, whether a footfall or an anvil falling, comes directly *after,* or in the midst of, some sort of musical gesture.

A compositional technique with which Bradley experimented involved what he described as "Sharp dissonances and so-called 'shock chords,' usually associated with modern music . . . employed instead of actual sound effects in many instances."[50] In the traditional terminology of film music, these shock chords are stinger chords. Bradley was dis-

FIGURE 11 Out the window, in *Solid Serenade* (MGM; Hanna and Barbera, 1946).

missive of traditional sound effects, which he believed had become clichéd in animated cartoons: "It seemed to me that almost anybody could collect a lot of nursery jingles and fast moving tunes, throw them together along with slide whistles and various noise makers and call that a cartoon score, but that didn't satisfy me and, I felt sure, wouldn't really satisfy the public."[51] By coming up with musical analogues to supplement or even obviate certain sound effects, Bradley could manipulate an unusually large portion of the soundtrack. Absorbing as many of the sound effects as possible into the musical score enabled him to create an even closer relationship between these two soundtrack elements.

In *Solid Serenade,* Jerry jumps into the kitchen sink and drains it, exposing a pile of dishes. At the moment when the audience recognizes the danger Tom is in, Bradley hits a shock-/stinger-style chord and holds it; only a brief drum roll further builds the tension and drives us *into* the collision. Bradley lets Tom's actual impact go without a sting. Instead, immediately after the cat hits the dishes Bradley repeats the same chord in a deliberately off-beat pattern, conveying the pain of this headfirst dive rather than mickey-mousing the impact itself (see figure 12). Chion's description of "the Punch"—"the audiovisual point toward which every-

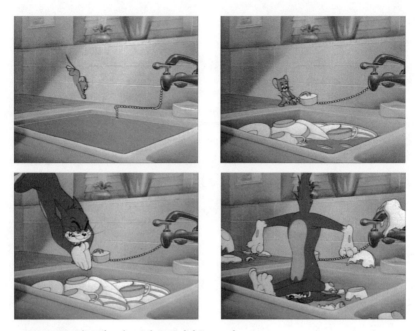

FIGURE 12 Heading for the sink in *Solid Serenade*.

thing converges and out from which all radiates"[52]—aptly applies to Tom's collision with the dishes. By scoring around this obvious point of synchronization, Bradley makes us hear an impact that occurs only as an abstract downbeat; that is, we never hear a musical sting for the actual impact, but because the chords come just before and after the hit we don't notice its absence. Bradley employed this technique to add punch to the already explicit musical effect he wrote for a scene.

In the final moments of this scene, the rhythm comes to an abrupt halt as Jerry threatens to free the bulldog, Killer. A rapid, syncopated pattern in the strings characterizes Tom's chasing Jerry across the yard. Descending a step each time it repeats, the melody moves us forward to an eventual finish line, or, as Chion would say, *vectorizes* the shot by directing it toward an inevitable goal, enabling the audience to anticipate the end of the chase before it actually happens.[53] In order to slow Tom's pace, Bradley makes a subtle shift: the upper strings play a descending three-note pattern, while the lower strings take over in a duple pattern as they continue to descend. At the same time, Bradley also foreshadows the approaching danger (the dog) with the trombones, which first hit a chord and then slide downward. This is another dou-

ble-edged gesture: the slow glissando helps render Tom's physical skid-
ding to a halt, while the final chord, played by the brass and woodwinds,
alludes to the last time we heard that timbre—when Tom's performance
of "Is You Is" ended abruptly. This sound reminds us (and Tom) of the
one bit of unfinished business that awaits him just off-screen, and as the
brass and woodwinds suddenly swell on the soundtrack we get a sense
of Killer's growing anger.

Though MGM had a far smaller musical library than Warner Bros.,
its years as the leading maker of musical films in Hollywood gave it the
rights to popular songs on which Bradley regularly drew, including "Over
the Rainbow," "We're Off to See the Wizard," "The Trolley Song," "On
the Atchison, Topeka, and Santa Fe," "All God's Chillun Got Rhythm,"
and "Manhattan Serenade." This repertoire was useful for punctuating
the story at appropriate moments with a musical gag; yet, as I mentioned
above, he disliked the practice of citing or incorporating preexisting
melodies. The possible associations that might occur to someone hearing a familiar melody were anathema to Bradley. Because he actively and
intentionally sought to invest his music with its own meaning as it related to the cartoon, he saw no reason to rely on the musical knowledge
of the audience. And since no one in the 1940s foresaw the syndication
and spread through mass media of Hollywood cartoons during the second half of the century, Bradley could not assume that anyone would see
or hear a Tom and Jerry cartoon more than once or twice. The music
had to get its point across on its first hearing.

He therefore devised a compromise: he drew on the comfort and familiarity of recognizable tunes to signal a moment of importance in the
plot: the appearance of a dramatic set piece, usually a slapstick or gag
routine. When Bradley's orchestra plays a pop tune in the big band style,
it almost always coincides with some visual comic shtick.[54] Tom and
Jerry's slapstick chases, like those in most cartoons, draw from vaudeville routines. The cartoons often shift gears seamlessly; in one moment
the story is moving forward, and in the next Tom is setting up or reacting to a gag.[55] All aspects of the story and mise-en-scène in cartoons can
potentially come to life in the diegesis; there is no formal transition into
slapstick mode, as the generic expectation of animated cartoons is that
anything can happen. By incorporating a popular melody into his score,
Bradley creates an artificial performance space in the story where the characters can act out their shtick. Rather than distracting us from the visual
narrative, the tune bubbles to the surface within the story's emotional
trajectory, thereby informing us that a dramatic shift has occurred.

Popular music never gains enough independent force in these stories to bring the action to a halt, as often happens in musical theater or opera when a song or aria appears, unless its performance occurs within the narrative itself—as happens at the beginning of *Solid Serenade*. In such cases, the number takes over the soundtrack, ending only after the song has finished or after the story can regain control of the action. Tom's song begins with him strumming on the double bass, with an off-screen (underscored) band playing along. The plucked notes of the bass solo wake up Jerry, literally moving him out of bed and onto the floor. Since the song controls the scene at this point, the action must follow the beat; thus Jerry bounces around his house in time with the percussive bass line. The only way that Jerry can stop the abuse is to stop the song, and he does so by throwing two pies in Tom's face (the first containing an iron). The break in mood is abrupt, even rude. The interruption annoys him, but strangely enough, being knocked in the face with an iron does not stop Tom from completing his song. It is the second pie, which strikes Tom just as he hits his last, high note with a final fanfare from the woodwinds, that angers him enough to chase Jerry. At this point the music shifts very noticeably from the song to the underscore. The transition exposes the story's vulnerable underbelly: the split second of silence between the end of Tom's song and the start of Bradley's original chase music displays the music's lack of direction, as the song that had once directed the scene is halted. Bradley did not (or would not) dovetail the cues, perhaps because he wanted to keep his music distinct from the songs he *had* to use. Whatever his reason, we can see how hard Bradley worked to keep the two styles separate.

Bradley incorporated popular tunes into those chase scenes that explicitly evoked comedy routines by using gag-driven choreography involving extreme physical takes. In *Solid Serenade* such a scene occurs just as Jerry unties Killer: the scoring that provided a precise counterpoint to the action segues right into the song "Running Wild," music that is far less descriptive. But it succeeds in conveying a sense of Killer's pent-up aggression, about to be released into a fit of energetic fury: just as steam comes from Killer's ears and we hear the sound of a factory whistle, Bradley calls for a big swell from the brass section that emphasizes the intensity of his anger.

Recurrent melodic themes held little interest for Bradley, who seems to have preferred writing all-new material for each cartoon. Because characters rarely appeared more than once in the Happy Harmonies, the question of writing specific themes for them did not often come up. Bradley commented on the technique in 1937: "When the studio decided to bring out our new star, 'Little Cheeser,' I concluded to surround him with character themes in much the same fashion as Humperdinck did in 'Hansel and Gretel.' . . . With the appearance of any or all of these characters, their musical themes are heard in the score. The treatment varying, of course, as the situation demands. Often all three characters are seen and their themes are then worked out contrapuntally, but the themes are always in evidence."[56] Interweaving the melodic themes enabled Bradley to remain creative while using precomposed material. By the early 1940s, characters in two cartoon series—Tom, Jerry, and Barney Bear—had their own themes, which Bradley often used when the story's direction had not yet been established, just before all hell broke loose. In the scene from *Solid Serenade* just mentioned, a quick reference to Jerry's theme represents his playfulness as he stands poised to free Killer. None of the themes lasted long, however; as the 1940s progressed, Tom's and Jerry's themes were heard less and less frequently, until Bradley finally abandoned them altogether. As for Barney, he stopped appearing in cartoons in 1949, and by then Bradley had given up themes entirely.

In *Puttin' on the Dog*, the second exemplary cartoon considered here, Bradley in effect conceals the chase music, precisely because Tom himself, a cat in a yard full of dogs, must avoid calling attention to himself. In order to follow Jerry into the dog yard, Tom dons a dog mask taken from a mannequin. Every time a dog seems to recognize that Tom is just wearing a disguise, Tom confuses or distracts the dog long enough to get away, usually employing the kind of illogical comic routine typical of cartoons and reminiscent of vaudeville. For instance, the song "That Old Feeling" begins as Tom tries to pull himself out from under a huge St. Bernard. When the dog sees his feline face, Tom does a quick turnaround so that only the dog mask—perched on his behind—is visible (see figure 13).

Bradley did not hesitate to employ tried-and-true scoring methods; specifically, he often used an instrumental line (frequently a woodwind) to represent a character's particular physical or mental gesture, the latter typically in the form of a take. In *Puttin' on the Dog*, Bradley refers to the opening motif from Wagner's *Tristan and Isolde* as Tom lifts off the dog mannequin's head—which later, seemingly alive, serves as the story's catalyst. By using a solo instrument (in this case, a clarinet), Bradley reinforces the implicit one-to-one relationship of music to motion. He successfully creates a nexus between musical and physical gestures that, though they occur simultaneously, wouldn't necessarily seem to refer to one another. Chion, in discussing the work of François De-

FIGURE 13 Tom's disguise in *Puttin' on
the Dog* (MGM; Hanna
and Barbera, 1944).

lalande and Bernadette Céleste, refers to a visual-musical link as being
formed by a process of "isomorphism, that is, by 'a similarity of movement between the sound and the movement it represents.' "[57] As long
as the musical line created an aural mirror to the action (by no means
a task easily accomplished), Bradley could write what he pleased. The
isomorphic melody became the standard musical gesture for cartoons,
with idiosyncratic bassoon or trombone melodies eventually coming to
signify movement.

In addition to using these traditional scoring methods (or perhaps to
make up for them), Bradley often juxtaposed a popular song with a modernist compositional technique. One particular sequence in *Puttin' on the
Dog* clearly illustrates how he attempted to reconcile the world of contemporary (modernist) music with animation. Bradley described the problem
and his solution:

> A little mouse was running around with the mask of a dog over his head—
> you saw only the little fellow's feet carrying this big head, and it looked
> very grotesque and funny, but I was stuck for a new way of describing the
> action musically, and for a whole day I worried about a two-measure phrase.
> Everything I tried seemed weak and common. Finally, I tried the twelve-
> tone scale, and *there it was!* This scene was repeated five times within the
> next fifty seconds, and I had only to use my scale—played by the piccolo,
> oboe and bassoon in unison. I hope Dr. Schoenberg will forgive me for
> using *his system* to produce funny music, but even the boys in the orchestra
> laughed when we were recording it.[58]

The twelve-tone scale used in this scene creates a new sound for chase
music, a chase in which something is askew (see music example 5). Bradley
employs a compositional process that is typically highly ordered and or-
ganized to convey a sense of confusion and bewilderment. The disem-
bodied head making its own way across the yard is, by itself, an unset-

FIGURE 14 The dog's head gets around in *Puttin' on the Dog*.

EXAMPLE 5 Twelve-tone scale in *Puttin' on the Dog*.

tling image (see figure 14). Bradley repeats the scale immediately—moving it from the piccolo to the bassoon—for the *real* dog that is following in the head's wake, since this dog also knows that something is amiss. Bradley denies both the head and the audience the comfort and familiarity of a melody with an obvious periodicity that fits into a single key. Because it lacks a tonal center, we don't know where the phrase begins or ends; it is an apt musical metaphor for a head that, by all accounts, should be lifeless without its supporting body, yet still walks on its own. Bradley doesn't make a fuss over using such an avant-garde scale, a reference that most of his audience wouldn't appreciate in any case; for him, it is just another way to make a cue sound unique as well as effective. Of course, when Tom playfully tugs and pulls on the bulldog's head in the mistaken belief that he has seized hold of Jerry in the mannequin head, he moves us into another comic routine and Bradley therefore brings back the same tune he had used earlier, "That Old Feeling."

The amount of violent action in these cartoons further justified Bradley's stylistic choices, as John Winge observed: "For years Bradley has been using [the Twelve-Tone System] too, as probably the only composer in his field. 'The Twelve-Tone System,' he says, 'provides the "out-of-this-world" progressions so necessary to under-write the fantastic and incredible situations which present-day cartoons contain.' . . . He has noticed, of course, that post-war cartoons are displaying a particularly great amount of violent action, super-speed, and cruel, sadistic punishment, which virtually demand the cacophonous harshness of modern composing."[59]

A shock chord similar to that used in *Solid Serenade* appears in *Puttin' on the Dog*: after Tom hits himself on the head (trying to get Jerry), the inevitable lump on his noggin grows slowly. Bradley builds a chord, note by note, entirely of fourths, effectively mickey-mousing the bump's upward growth. When the bulldog finds Tom, it has lifted the dog mask off Tom's head. The chord plays again, but with alterations (the new chord includes several tritones) to show that Tom's disguise has failed. It now indicates the dog's slowly growing awareness of and anger at Tom's (literal) duplicity. By building the chord one note at a time, Bradley stretches a traditional stinger chord out to follow the visual path of Tom's bump as it grows, and the bright trumpets convey not only Tom's pain but also his inability to hide something so obvious from the dog.

Bradley clearly delighted in appropriating modernist techniques in his scores, if only to challenge himself. When an interviewer once asked how he dealt with scoring a troublesome character in an upcoming picture, Bradley answered, "Oh, I just wadded up some whole tone stuff and threw it at him."[60] If we consider Bradley's experiments in modern music in light of his predilection for using the music to maintain the viewer's interest through a cartoon's slower moments, they take on a new significance: they provided him with novel techniques to create music that could maintain the cartoon's pace, and they also sharpened his skills as a composer as he tried to keep up with the recent developments in the field. His use of such unusual musical strokes brings us back to Bradley's self-proclaimed mission to raise the status of cartoon music in the public eye. Since, as film historian Caryl Flinn points out, "modernism remained by and large a European phenomenon,"[61] employing music that would evoke thoughts of western Europe (with its implicit association with highbrow culture) might add a bit of class to cartoons. This explanation accounts quite well for Bradley's use of a twelve-tone scale: although Schoenberg had pioneered it in the 1920s, no serial system turned up in the music of Hollywood feature films until the 1950s. Thus Bradley's practice in the early 1940s marks him as a very forward-thinking composer.[62]

Of course, the question of whether Bradley ever met or (even better) studied with Schoenberg should be addressed. Because he moved to Los Angeles in late 1933, Schoenberg certainly had the opportunity to meet Bradley, yet there appears to be no evidence that such an encounter occurred. By the late 1930s, Schoenberg's reputation as a teacher for film composers had grown immensely, and he eventually worked with, among others, Franz Waxman, David Raksin, Alfred Newman, and Hugo Friedhofer. Bradley's interest in Schoenberg's music, which he mentions in numerous articles and interviews, suggests that he might have sought out the composer hoping to find a mentor (Schoenberg was not quite two decades Bradley's senior), or at least to satisfy his curiosity.[63] It is impossible to say whether Bradley's use of such techniques was noticed by anyone other than his musicians and attendees of various film music seminars at which he spoke. But even an experienced musician would have difficulty discerning a twelve-tone scale speeding by in a three-second burst from the soundtrack; a typical audience member would be highly unlikely to notice anything unusual in the score. Bradley's aesthetic ambitions notwithstanding, some critics did not find all of his music pleasing. Michael Barrier sees little difference between Bradley's scores and the music he emulated or cited: "Separate his music from the cartoons and for some long stretches it could be confused with a particularly cold and disagreeable contemporary classical score."[64]

Does a general failure to notice or appreciate Bradley's experiments or Stalling's references to pop melodies necessarily detract from the general potency of the scores? Once again, I would say no, even more forcefully with regard to Bradley than Stalling. The latter sought to make puns within the narrative by referring to unlikely musical sources, using songs that the audience could occasionally recognize and appreciate on their own. But Bradley's sole motivation was to make his job and music more interesting; thus he sought not an intersection between the score and story but rather ways for them to support and complement each other. Not all contemporary techniques appealed to Bradley. In 1967 he observed: "My own opinion of music [of 1949] in general followed the progress (or lack of it) of contemporary thought. That is, to a certain degree. But they 'lost' me when such things as Partitas for concrete mixer, and Allemandes for piano and *silence,* e.g. John Cage's '3:45'—give or take a few seconds—were accepted as music."[65] Bradley obviously had personal limitations as a composer; with his compositional field mapped out, he could use the sonic space of the cartoon to squash and stretch, but not break, his self-imposed boundaries.

Bradley did not often disagree with the directors over his musical explorations and experiments for the Tom and Jerry cartoons. In fact, neither Hanna, Barbera, nor Bradley ever mentioned having problems working out scores. Bradley's relationship with Tex Avery was another story, however. It is worth considering briefly, not only because Bradley scored dozens of cartoons for Avery but also because the latter's fame as a director reached its height at MGM. As Barrier notes,

> Bradley and Avery—one of the least cynical of directors—did not get along. "Tex Avery didn't like my music," Bradley said. "We disagreed a lot on what kind of music was appropriate for his cartoons. His ideas on music were so bad that I had to put a stop to it. [In every picture he wanted 'Home Sweet Home' and all that corny music.]" . . . Exactly what happened, or what it meant, is not clear; but Bradley's music was never as obtrusive in Avery's cartoons as it was in many of the Tom and Jerry cartoons.[66]

Indeed, the adjective "obtrusive" neatly sums up the conflict between the two men: Bradley clearly wanted to use the same scoring style he had provided for the Tom and Jerry shorts, yet Avery's narratives consisted largely of sequences of blackout or spot gags—jokes that quickly came and went, held in place by only the thinnest of story lines. His musical taste leaned toward shorter cues that could properly highlight each gag, accentuating one punch line before moving on to the next. No doubt Avery's five years working with Carl Stalling at Warner Bros. fostered this musical preference, as Stalling's quick-cue practice seemed perfectly matched to Avery's gag-upon-gag approach. The director's supposed request for music like "Home! Sweet Home!" lends credence to the suspicion that he had become used to Stalling's style of using popular tunes to coordinate the gag with the score.

Bradley's claim to have "put a stop" to Avery's musical ideas suggests that he wrote what he pleased for Avery's cartoons. Indeed, in 1948 he boasted, "In a recent cartoon, *Out-foxed*, I wrote a short four-voiced fugue on '3 [British] Grenadiers' with the little tune 'Jonny's Got a Nickel' serving merrily as the counter subject. Cartoons usually do without fugue, but here it fits the action. Musically spoken, you can get away with almost anything in pictures if the score only captures the 'feeling' of the sequence."[67] When we look at Avery's MGM cartoons, we can see that Bradley had to compromise in order to keep him happy: the composer did occasionally briefly cite familiar melodies ("Dixie," "Be My Love," "Sweet and Lovely"), but the music in the later Avery cartoons comes almost entirely from Bradley's own hand, carefully constructed so as not to rouse the director's ire. Bradley clearly enjoyed the thought of getting away with slipping a fugue into one of Avery's cartoons. Yet he was well aware that he could get away with doing what he pleased only so long as the music fit well into the sequence. And even music that fits is not necessarily discernible: given the amount of dialogue in many of Avery's cartoons, the music has little chance to be heard except when it punctuates visual gags with brief cues or quick stings.[68]

Avery's distaste for Bradley's music not only frustrated the composer, it also gave him little reason to expand his musical vocabulary on the director's behalf. This lack of understanding between the two men seems particularly tragic because of the nature of Avery's cartoons. They exude decadence: Avery always used the most exaggerated and outrageous solution he could devise, even when a gag might normally call for a simple reaction. The media critic Norman Klein refers to Avery's cartoons as a place where "utter impossibility is defied again and again."[69] Such fantastic takes might have given Bradley numerous opportunities for experimentation. Indeed, both Avery and Bradley saw each cartoon as a chance to break the industry's conventions for stories and music, established by less adventurous animation studios; but while their ideas for change seemed compatible, their personalities were not. If only they had possessed similar ideas about music's role in cartoons, Avery might have had more complementary music scores for his shorts, and Bradley might have believed he had found a challenge finally worthy of his abilities.

THE FUTURE OF CARTOON MUSIC

In 1943, Bradley spoke of his fondness for shock chords: "The success of these experiments leads me to believe that when the hoped-for millennium arrives, music will be fully as important as the picture—in fact, one will be entirely dependent on the other. It is obvious that these animated fantasies will require a very progressive type of composer, attuned to contemporary thought in music."[70] Scores by such "progressive" composers, including Gail Kubik, Dennis Farnon, and others, began to appear in mainstream cartoons in the early 1950s, particularly those of UPA. Unfortunately, the heyday of cartoons produced in the commercial Hollywood studio system had already begun to draw to a close.[71]

When the MGM cartoon division closed its doors in 1957, Scott Bradley stopped working on cartoons and continued composing on his own. He died at the age of eighty-five in Chatsworth, California, on 27 April 1977.[72] Within ten years of his retirement, Bradley had noticed the obvious decline in the production of animated cartoons: every major studio had shut down its animation department, and the only cartoons regularly being produced used library or stock music cues written expressly for repeated use. The reality was exactly the opposite of Bradley's hopes and predictions. He mourned, "Concerning cartoon music in the 1960's,

I can only ask, *what* music? The t.v. cartoons of today are 95% dialogue, and the music is rarely heard at all, unless sound effects may be called music."[73] At the turn of the millennium, little has changed, although a few composers for television cartoons, such as Alf Clausen (*The Simpsons*) and the late Richard Stone (*Animaniacs*), have begun to take Bradley's techniques more seriously, appropriating his ideas for their own use. Bradley's scores, in stark contrast to those of his colleague at Warner Bros., could be at times intentionally crafty and abstruse and at other times remarkably simple. The true complexity in Scott Bradley's music arose from his care in placing his cues against the rest of the cartoon soundscape, avoiding the need to resort to "Jerry-mousing" while treating his music as seriously as any composer could.

3

Jungle Jive

ANIMATION, JAZZ MUSIC, AND SWING CULTURE

Boogie Woogie is the native musical expression. There is jumpin'
jive, as the locals and native animals cut loose in accepted "real
gone" fashion.

Review of Walter Lantz's *Jungle Jive,*
Motion Picture Herald, 13 October 1951

By the early 1920s, a new style of music had worked its way north from
New Orleans and begun to infiltrate numerous forms of popular culture
and entertainment, including fiction, art, and classical music. Within only
a few years, jazz permeated the collective musical culture of America,
from recordings and live performances to films focusing on the nature
of jazz itself. Cartoons got caught up in the craze as well, and they became an especially potent site for spreading the sound of jazz nation-
wide. Within two years of the Hollywood sound revolution, cartoons
began appearing with such titles as *The Jazz Fool* (Disney; Disney, 1929),
Jungle Rhythm (Disney; Disney, 1929), *Jazz Mad* (Terrytoons, 1931),
Jungle Jazz (Van Beuren; Bailey and Foster, 1930), and *Congo Jazz* (Warner Bros.; Harman and Ising, 1930), each with a different stylistic approach to the sound of jazz. The review that appears as this chapter's
epigraph shows how entrepreneurs marketing cartoons attempted to cash
in on the "swinging" qualities of a short to interest potential buyers.

Jazz would have a featured role in hundreds of Hollywood cartoons,
inspiring stories and enlivening performances in shorts from every studio.
As the public's reception of new trends in the music changed, Hollywood's
approach to the music and the imagery associated with jazz evolved over
time. Cartoons produced in the beginning of the sound era afford us a
valuable means of understanding how the general public may have viewed

jazz and its practitioners. Likewise, shorts from the 1940s and 1950s show these same perceptions changing as jazz continued to develop.

These cartoons take great pains to portray the music and those who played it, yet they cannot move beyond the level of base generalizations, for "even those cartoons ostensibly celebrating jazz by featuring it on the soundtrack" resort to the use of stereotypical images and racial conceits. Barry Keith Grant further notes the power of cartoons: "in their reliance on exaggeration and simplification in both imagery and narrative, cartoons speak a clear, simple language, like the large capital letters on children's blocks."[1] Such stereotypical depictions may not have been intentionally malicious, but we must at least consider that possibility in interpreting such virulent expressions of racism. My main interest here, however, is the way in which the music is used to construct the story or contribute to the cartoon as a whole. Because jazz has such resonant societal meanings and associations, we cannot separate the music from the culture it has come to represent. As jazz and African American cultural forms in general have been simultaneously condemned and co-opted in America through the years, we should not be surprised that the figures caricatured in the cartoons discussed in this chapter are just that—caricatures composed of nothing but stereotypical attributes. Rather than credit the achievements of these musicians, the cartoons reduce even the most brilliant, creative artists to mere racist punch lines. Thus, while my goal is to examine the different workings of jazz in cartoon scores, the issue of race and representation—and the deplorably racist effect of the imagery—will always be present in some way as well.

Although we cannot ignore the visual representations of jazz musicians in these cartoons, we must pay attention to the music, which functions simultaneously as the inspiration for the narrative and as the explicit source of the rhythm and pacing of each short.[2] As we will see, over time jazz played an increasingly important role in the medium, until it came to touch practically every Hollywood cartoon score. To understand why film composers found jazz's characteristic sound particularly useful, we should begin by examining common attitudes toward jazz as a musical genre in the 1920s.

EARLY IMPRESSIONS OF JAZZ AS FILM MUSIC

Descriptions of the innovative sound of jazz in early film music manuals provide a unique insight into general perceptions of jazz at the beginning of the century. Edith Lang and George West's 1920 handbook on accompanying declares jazz's unusual rhythmic characteristics ideal for marking special effects:

> Jazz Band—The only way to imitate a jazz band is to hear one of these unique organizations. There is no way of describing it. Each and every player must hear these peculiar effects for himself and then imitate them according to his impression thereof. The general idea is to have one hand play the tune, while the other hand "jazzes" or syncopates around it, the pedals performing the drum and bass parts. The ability to lift your audience's feet off the floor in sympathetic rhythm is the truest test; that you will distress the ears of really musical people goes without saying, but you will not distress their sense of rhythm. This rhythm on your part must be perfectly maintained, no matter what stunts you may perform with hand and feet.[3]

The impression left by this characterization is that although the music's power defies description, properly executed jazz will fulfill the accompanist's needs. Rather than offer instruction in jazz, the authors tell the reader simply to listen to someone who can play it—difficult advice to follow at a time when jazz had yet to reach all corners of the nation. Similar guidance appeared in the *Moving Picture World*, a periodical important to the early film industry. Its "Music for the Picture" column regularly featured music and its performance in the theater. In the "Questions Answered—Suggestions Offered" section, the following query appeared in 1918: "Q. In playing 'blues' how do you get the real 'nigger' effects? A. There is no way to explain the peculiar darky rhythm acquired by Southern players that make 'blues' effective. It is a thing born in the player and not made. Would advise that you hear the real thing."[4] We see here both the mythologizing that surrounded the performance of jazz from very early on and a clear desire on the part of accompanists to incorporate this novel sound into their scores.

Elsewhere, Lang and West prescribe specific uses for jazz: "One important factor in these pictorial farces is the matter of speed. 'Pep' is the key-note to the situation, with the current 'jazz' tunes as a medium. When special effects are to be introduced, or certain moods or emotions are to be 'italicized' and burlesqued, this may be done at any point of the composition played, the piece instantly to be resumed."[5] The authors once more establish a connection between the sound of jazz and those moments in the story when the music must convey a particular message. The budding accompanist might take away the idea that jazz possesses an ineffable quality that will spice up a score without altering it much aesthetically.

Early accounts of live jazz performances usually focus on their rhythm, that element of jazz's sound that white audiences found inexplicably novel. Yet those accounts cannot explain why so many people found the music so compelling, nor why listeners could not keep from moving along to the music. The presumed African heritage of black jazz musicians figured prominently in these critical assessments, where blunt references to the "primitive" and "native" elements of the music were widespread. A critic in a major New York newspaper intending to draw readers to a 1917 variety show at a local theater described "jass" as "an attempt to reproduce the marvelous syncopation of the African jungle. Prof. William Morrison Patterson, Ph.D., . . . says: 'The music of contemporary savages taunts us with a lost art of rhythm. Modern sophistication has inhibited many native instincts, and the mere fact that our conventional dignity usually forbids us to sway our bodies or to tap our feet when we hear effective music has deprived us of unsuspected pleasures.'"[6]

Phrases such as "syncopation of the African jungle" and "music of contemporary savages" allude to the notion that the supposed primitive origins of jazz or ragtime explain the music's perceived freedom. Many cartoons relied on this implicit connection when they set jazz performances in the forest primeval. But more important to the critic and the putative expert he quotes is what jazz says about "us" and "our bodies." Instead of condemning the "savages," Patterson betrays a deep sense of envy: blacks, more carefree and uninhibited, enjoy the ineffable pleasures of their "native instincts," while "modern" civilized society "has deprived us of [such] unsuspected pleasures." Primitivism was a theme running through much early writing on jazz, for it seemed to explain both the essential attributes of the music and what made it so desirable. The mass consumption of black music and culture in the 1920s and '30s by whites heading to Harlem and other black cultural centers was a direct result of such a belief in jazz's innate qualities.

EARLY JAZZ AND EARLY CARTOONS

The animated sequence in *King of Jazz* (1930, dir. John Murray Anderson), a film that features the orchestra leader Paul Whiteman, is one of the earliest appearances of jazz in animated form.[7] Several scholars have argued that Whiteman uses this film, and in particular the cartoon sequence, to insinuate that he himself was responsible for the "creation" of jazz. According to Krin Gabbard, "the cartoon ultimately portrays Whiteman as bringing jazz to Africa"; Michael Rogin sees it instead as portraying jazz as "the trophy the white hunter brings back from Africa."[8] My own interpretation is closer to Gabbard's: the film's underlying goal is to establish *how* and *why* Whiteman deserves the title "King of Jazz," and how could that better be accomplished than by implying that he introduced the music to the very people most strongly associated with it?

While the question of how someone as mainstream and pop-oriented as Whiteman could claim to be the King of Jazz is fascinating (Russell Sanjek called Whiteman a "press agent–anointed king"),[9] I am more interested here in how the music and imagery used in the opening cartoon support this claim. Like the remainder of the film, which relies mostly on mainstream pop tunes, the animated sequence presents jazz as Whiteman's group preached it to their audiences: band arrangements of current Tin Pan Alley hits and jazz melodies.[10] Songs used or referred to in the cartoon's score include "Music Hath Charms" (Tin Pan Alley), "The Campbells Are Coming" (Scottish folk tune), and a snatch of *Rhapsody in Blue*, George Gershwin's jazz-infused work, which is featured in a later segment of the film.[11] In a quick gag, probably not lost on the audience in 1930, an elephant sprays a monkey with water, angering the tree-dwelling primate into throwing a coconut that hits Whiteman on the head, effectively "crowning" him as king (see figure 15). The tune to "The Aba Daba Honeymoon," another Tin Pan Alley song whose chorus begins "Aba daba daba daba daba daba daba said the chimpey to the monk," can be heard during the monkey's very brief appearance.

"Music Hath Charms," first performed in the film during the opening credits (sung by Bing Crosby, then one of Whiteman's Rhythm Boys), receives the most attention in the cartoon's narrative. The animated Whiteman plays the song for an attacking lion who, instead of mauling the bandleader, gets caught up in the jazzy rhythm and changes from savage beast to swinging cat.[12] The instruments heard during this scene, including violin, rhythm guitar, and bass, typify the swinging sound produced by Whiteman's orchestra and others popular in the early 1930s. As jazz, Whiteman's music did not come close to the hot sound then being produced by such leaders as Duke Ellington or Louis Armstrong. For most white listeners, however, Whiteman's music was fresh and even slightly dangerous in its appropriation of black musical styles. Whiteman succeeded because his audience perceived him as "taming" jazz's "savage impulses"; that is, he used just enough of the innovative sounds of the hot jazz bands to excite his listeners safely.[13]

Walter Lantz, who directed the animated sequence in *King of Jazz*,

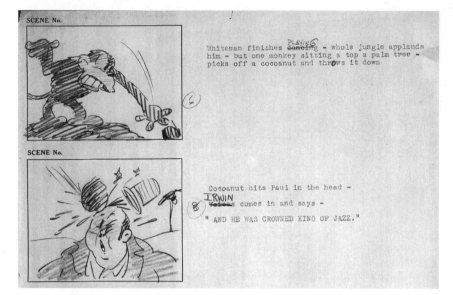

FIGURE 15   Paul Whiteman crowned king in production sketches for *King of Jazz*
(Lantz, 1930). Courtesy of the Institute of the American Musical.

recalled that contrary to usual practice, the score was recorded before
the animation was created.[14] During the scoring session he wished to set
up a system to help Whiteman synchronize the music to the animation,
but the musician saw no need for any aid. Whiteman said, according to
Lantz, "'Let me tell ya, sonny, I can keep a rhythm on anything. . . . So
you tell me how long the picture's going to be—three minutes, four minutes, whatever—and I'll give you the rhythm you want.' 'I said we wanted
four minutes,' Lantz continues, 'and I'll be darned if he didn't beat this
thing out. It came to four minutes at 2/12 [two beats per second, or one
beat every twelve frames].' "[15] The music works well for the short sequence. Because Lantz had the music recorded in advance, he could
animate the sequence so that the movements of Whiteman's animated
counterpart and of the animals he encounters in the jungle would be underscored. But the sequence's musical argument (if any) is that the music heard in the jungle usually consists of folk tunes and Tin Pan Alley
songs, in neither case music produced by Africans.

Despite its setting in "darkest Africa" (as the film's host, Charles
Irwin, describes it), Africans have a remarkably small role in the sequence. Natives appear on screen for less than ten seconds, as they dance
to the beat of the music, casting tall shadows on the wall behind them

SCENE No.

Panorama shot of cannibals dancing.

FIGURE 16   Cannibals/natives dancing in production sketches for *King of Jazz*.
Courtesy of the Institute of the American Musical.

(see figure 16). At the end of the musical phrase, however, the figures
strike a frightening pose, jumping on tiptoe, sticking out their tongues,
and bulging out their eyes. Barry Keith Grant notes that we also see
dancing "a black rabbit—'a jungle bunny'—enjoying the music."[16] The
bunny is actually Oswald the Rabbit, a character owned by Universal
(producer of *King of Jazz*) that Lantz had begun animating the previous
year, and therefore a logical candidate for a quick cameo in a major feature film.[17] Like Disney's Mickey Mouse and Warner Bros.' Bosko, Oswald had an appearance and mannerisms modeled on blackface performers from vaudeville and elsewhere. He remained a caricature, for
details rendering the true complexity of African life would have complicated his representation and thus undercut the fiction.[18]

Like Whiteman's use of jazz, Lantz's depiction of Oswald was helping to create new forms of mainstream white entertainment relying on
(white-constructed) codes meant to represent black culture. As is true today, such racial stereotypes and clichés were common then in many forms
of entertainment.[19] In his history of black images in cartoons, Henry
Sampson describes the narrative trends in animated shorts' use of black
characters: cartoons that take place on the stereotypical antebellum plantation or in the jungle and cartoons that depict vaudeville or minstrel
shows all date back to the era before synchronized sound.[20] White audiences began seeing jazz as nearly synonymous with black culture by
the 1930s, and its influence extends to many of the cartoons that Sampson
examines.

Stereotypes figured not only in the stories and design format of the
cartoons but also in their scores. Particular songs that originated in minstrel shows or vaudeville routines came to signify black culture. Although

such famous songs as "Zip Coon" and "Jim Crow" seldom appeared, others that were almost as well known took their place in sound cartoon scores.[21] The song "Sweet Georgia Brown" by Ben Bernie, Maceo Pinkard, and Kenneth Casey is an unusual example, as it frequently denotes moments in the Warner Bros. cartoons when race and gender intersect. This song was used only twice prior to Carl Stalling's arrival at the studio. Its repeated appearance thereafter is thus attributable not just to its presence in the Warner catalogue (the studio had acquired its original publisher, Jerome Remick) but also to Stalling's predilection for using song titles to guide his scores—in this case, the title refers specifically to an African American woman. Such songs may have functioned well as recognizable melodic cues for individual black characters; at the same time, the rhythms and textures of jazz provided the sound that most often signaled to white viewers the stereotyped black community and its culture.[22] Perhaps the most chilling conclusion we can draw from the persistence of such songs is that cartoons are, in many ways, a natural extension of the minstrel show. Just as Mickey and his black-faced, white-gloved brethren carry on the tradition of the minstrel figure, so their singing and dancing give new life to the same old tunes. Where but in cartoons can we today hear the plantation songs of Stephen Foster and other songs popularized on the minstrel stage? Minstrelsy never really died—it simply changed media.

JAZZ AND THE URBAN SCENE: THE FLEISCHER STUDIO

The Fleischer brothers took an unusual approach to jazz in the late 1920s and the 1930s, in that they treated it not as background but as a musical genre deserving of recognition. Instead of just using jazz idioms to color the musical score, their cartoons featured well-known songs by prominent recording artists. Fleischer was a well-known studio in the 1920s, perhaps most famous for pioneering the sing-along cartoon with the bouncing ball in Song Car-Tunes. An added attraction to Fleischer cartoons was that Paramount Pictures, their distributor and parent company, allowed the Fleischers to use its newsreel recording facilities, where they were permitted to film famous performers scheduled to appear in Paramount shorts and films.[23] Thus, a wide variety of musicians and others, including Ethel Merman, Rudy Vallee, the Mills Brothers, Cab Calloway, and Louis Armstrong, began appearing in Fleischer cartoons.[24] This arrangement benefited both the studios and the stars. Once the Fleischers chose a song from the featured artist to use in a cartoon, the writers constructed a story that made the performance of the song the centerpiece of the short. That the song's title usually was borrowed for the cartoon's title was just one way in which such cartoons helped publicize a performer's work.

The Fleischers also responded to local influences of the Manhattan music scene in their choice of performers: they combined themes from their own lives as middle-class, secular Jews in New York with their notions (cultural, musical, etc.) of African Americans, funneling all these raw materials into a popular representational form—cartoons.[25] Their earlier success with the Song Car-Tunes was owed to their use of Tin Pan Alley tunes and nineteenth-century popular songs, styles familiar in the city on vaudeville and other stages. The proximity of the Fleischer studio to premier music venues, particularly the uptown clubs in Harlem that featured artists such as Duke Ellington, Fletcher Henderson, and Cab Calloway, clearly shaped their creation of cartoons in the nascent jazz era. The aura of danger and excitement that surrounded jazz, especially during the Harlem Renaissance, likely added to the attraction. Nathan Irvin Huggins describes it: "How convenient! It was merely a taxi trip to the exotic for most white New Yorkers. In cabarets decorated with tropical and jungle motifs—some of them replicas of southern plantations—they heard jazz, that almost forbidden music. It was not merely that jazz was exotic, but that it was instinctive and abandoned, yet laughingly light and immediate—melody skipping atop inexorable driving rhythm. . . . In the darkness and closeness, the music, infectious and unrelenting, drove on."[26] Lou Fleischer, the brother in charge of music for the studio, remembered going to the Cotton Club to listen to Calloway so that he could choose the songs that might work well in a cartoon.[27] The performances themselves no doubt gave the writers at the studio ideas for future cartoons. They could easily have taken the numbers they had seen onstage and, if they had chosen to view them from the contrived primitivist perspective then dominant, created stories that blended the performers' music and the visual trappings of the clubs with the animators' ideas.

Amiri Baraka points out that whites eagerly engaged with the new black music that offered such a novel image of America,[28] desiring to experience the sensual overtones ascribed to "primitive" music. By visiting clubs in Harlem and even by viewing cartoons, whites could gain access to something they felt implicitly lacking in their lives: the freedom and hedonism believed to be characteristic of a simpler, more instinctual society (an idea alluded to by Professor Patterson). By couching the featured songs

FIGURE 17 Louis Armstrong and the
band playing in *I'll Be Glad When
You're Dead, You Rascal You*
(Fleischer, 1932).

within the stereotyped narratives that shaped the musicians' live acts, the
Fleischer cartoons enabled moviegoing audiences around the country to
experience an even more fantastical version of those narratives—narratives
previously enjoyed by a few nightclub patrons in New York City. Just as
they had done while attending live stage shows with blackface performers, white audiences could watch blacks in these newer performance venues and hope for what Huggins calls "the possibility of being transported
into black innocence."[29] The cartoons that simultaneously presented the
ideas of jazz and primitivism also (in a tone mixing envy and condem-
nation) emphasized the stereotyped notion that blacks live their lives with
careless freedom.

    Louis Armstrong and his band make their sole appearance in a Flei-
scher cartoon in *I'll Be Glad When You're Dead, You Rascal You* (Fleischer, 1932). Like most of the cartoons in this series,[30] the film opens
with a sequence of live footage following the title cards; it features Armstrong and his band performing *before* moving on to the animated story,
thereby both giving the audience the opportunity to see the actual musicians and providing Armstrong with valuable publicity (see figure 17).
But rather than performing the title song right away, Armstrong and his
men play another piece ("Shine") that segues neatly into the background
music for the animated sequence.[31] The audience must watch what
amounts to half the cartoon before Armstrong begins the title song; it is
a clever strategy on the part of the studio to keep viewers' attention on
the characters, and a technique that has parallels in the Warner Bros. style
of story construction.

    The story centers on Betty Boop and her companions, Bimbo and
Ko-Ko, as they explore the depths of the African jungle. They inevitably
become involved in a chase with some natives, which culminates in the
performance of the title song. As Bimbo and Ko-Ko try to give the slip to

their pursuer, a repetitive "ONE-two-three-four" drum beat—a musical stereotype often associated with Native American drumming patterns— starts playing in the background. This short rhythmic cue transitions almost immediately into the title song, for which the drums have set up the tempo. As the beat ostensibly comes from "native" drums and is heard as if being played off-screen, the music establishes, before any lyrics are heard, the supposedly native origin of the song, which then springs fullformed from the primordial rhythm. During the chase, the native pursuing Bimbo and Ko-Ko literally loses his head, which, detached from his body, flies after them in the sky. As the introduction to the song ends and its opening verse begins, the head dissolves into Armstrong's own live-action head in profile, singing the title song (see figure 18). This transformation focuses on another facet of the primitivist caricature, implying that Armstrong is still a denizen of the jungle himself. The skies even darken forebodingly as the native/Armstrong initially runs up behind Ko-Ko and Bimbo, who clearly fear Armstrong, his song, and (implicitly) jazz and the black community that created it.

Apparently the animators believed that placing the story within the jungle and "native-izing" Armstrong did not create an obvious enough connection between the setting and the music. The final minutes of the film are underscored with Armstrong's version of "Chinatown, My Chinatown." While a group of natives dances around a captured Betty, the animators visually transform a drummer (through the same dissolve effect used with Armstrong's head) into Armstrong's own percussionist Tubby Hall (see figure 19). "Chinatown, My Chinatown" is an interesting choice for the final cue, as its reference to an Oriental opium den evokes a different type of exoticism than that portrayed in the cartoon's action. Thus, an American interpretation of African life is mediated through a song about the presence of Far Eastern decadence in the United States.[32]

By placing Betty into a perilous setting in the jungle juxtaposed to Armstrong's savage image, the animators created a very compelling and successful story. This plot was so successful, in fact, that in the three Betty Boop cartoons starring Cab Calloway, Betty likewise finds herself in what the animation historian Paul Wells describes as a "dark, mysterious underworld, characterized by transgressive behaviour and taboo imagery. Even in its crudest forms, representations of black-ness or black-oriented contexts, operate as signifiers of danger and cultural threat."[33] Betty represents the quintessential flapper: a young, newly liberated, and highly sexualized woman. Her entrance into such a den of urban iniquity

FIGURE 18   A native becomes Armstrong in *I'll Be Glad When You're Dead.*

makes her vulnerable to the visceral temptations of jazz that I have already mentioned. Betty's presence also exposes her to black men, who, stereotypically, want to make off with and possess white women, a characteristic of "bucks," as Donald Bogle defines them in his history of blacks in film: "Bucks are always big, baadddd niggers, oversexed and savage, violent and frenzied as they lust for white flesh."[34] In the jazz cartoons with black musicians, Betty almost always ends up being chased by the animated representatives of jazz—Cab Calloway in *Minnie the Moocher* (Fleischer, 1932) and *The Old Man of the Mountain* (Fleischer, 1933), Don Redman and a bunch of other literal "spooks" in *I Heard* (1933), and natives in *I'll Be Glad,* a trope that perpetuates cultural myths about rapacious black males. To be sure, Betty is pursued by men in many of her cartoons; but the issue of race complicates the chase by making her a forbidden object of desire.

By locating Betty aurally in a jazz world, the cartoons also place her in the ideological world of black music. The dark jungles represent jazz's supposed primeval origins, while the caves that appear in all three Calloway cartoons work as metaphors for the urban source of jazz, Harlem nightclubs.[35] The portrayal of these exotic locales in cartoons provided

FIGURE 19 A jungle drummer becomes Tubby Hall in *I'll Be Glad When You're Dead.*

white audiences with a safe outing to a strange and unusual world, much like a visit to the Harlem clubs. As Huggins remarks of the clubs, "It was a cheap trip. No safari! Daylight and a taxi ride rediscovered New York City, no tropic jungle. There had been thrill without danger. For these black savages were civilized—not head-hunters or cannibals—they would not run amok."[36] Several other features of these cartoons made them attractive for white viewers. Not only were audiences transported to faraway lands, but the humorous and fantastical sight gags that characterized the Fleischer style also removed the aura of danger from Africa and even made it somewhat laughable, especially because they painted a dehumanizing image of African natives. Such portrayals could naturally be extended to the urban American black, who could become less (or more) fearsome to white audiences through such caricatures. Their experience of the forbidden music of Armstrong or Calloway as a soundtrack to the journey created an additional level of excitement.

This cartoon appeared in theaters just before Armstrong began to be criticized by other jazz musicians and the black population in general. With his wide grin, affable nature, and questionable repertoire, including his ongoing use of the song "When It's Sleepy Time Down South," Armstrong was accused of striking the pose of a "tom"[37]—a stereotypically friendly, nonthreatening male black—in order to please white audiences and ensure his popularity in the entertainment world. The cartoon also came at the very beginning of Armstrong's film career (according to Gabbard, only one feature film, unfortunately lost, predates *I'll Be Glad When You're Dead*).[38] Armstrong's early films show how others portrayed him in what many saw as a less than honorable fashion. The Fleischers were no different, as the cartoon's creators applied to his image as a black performer almost every conceivable stereotype of primitive Africans. Armstrong, of all the jazz personalities featured in Fleischer cartoons, probably received the most extremely stereotyped treatment in his single appearance. The dissolve between Armstrong's live-action head and that of his animated counterpart made the animators' visual statement about the constitution of his "inner" nature absolutely clear.

Even Armstrong's voice lent itself to the stereotype of the savage persona. In vaudeville, as Huggins points out, the dialect associated with minstrelsy characters "was coarse, ignorant, and stood at the opposite pole from the soft tones and grace of what was considered cultivated speech."[39] Of course, Armstrong's raspy and ebullient singing was a signature element of his act, yet in the context of this cartoon, his style of making music suddenly takes on primitive characteristics—especially given his frequent exclamations that often bordered on the unintelligible. Later cartoons that caricatured Armstrong fetishize the same idiosyncratic elements of his performing style; his voice is usually the most obvious, most easily imitated (albeit poorly), and therefore most often satirized aspect of his public image.

Many of these features highlighting Armstrong's "savage" qualities first appeared in *A Rhapsody in Black and Blue* (1932), a one-reel Paramount musical short that was directed by Aubrey Scotto. The film opens in a rundown home where a black man sits listening to his Louis Armstrong records and playing a makeshift drum kit while his wife admonishes him to clean the house. When she knocks him out cold with a mop, the bubbles in the soap bucket, combined with the jazz music in the background, lead to his wild fantasy in which he is the king of Jazzmania. The scene is (apparently) set in a throne room where, dressed in a military outfit, the "king" is entertained by Armstrong and his band, all dressed in leopard skins and similar costumes, while (unseen) bubble machines churn away and fill the foreground (see figure 20). Armstrong sings "I'll Be Glad When You're Dead, You Rascal You," followed by "Shine"; then the man awakens from his reverie.

A Rhapsody in Black and Blue clearly had a powerful influence on the Fleischer animators. In *I'll Be Glad When You're Dead,* they used the same songs featured in *Rhapsody* and held on to the idea of primitivism. Though the live-action short never leaves the soundstage, the Fleischers took advantage of the immense freedom of their medium by setting the story in the jungle itself. They even retain some of the camera work from *Rhapsody.* Only two musicians get close-ups in *Rhapsody,* Armstrong and his drummer, Tubby Hall; likewise, both Armstrong and Hall receive

FIGURE 20 Bubbles and animal skins
in *A Rhapsody in Black and Blue*
(Paramount; Scotto, 1932).

special emphasis in *I'll Be Glad When You're Dead,* as both have their
visages transposed with those of jungle natives.

Another take on primitivism and jazz is offered by the Warner Bros.
short *The Isle of Pingo-Pongo* (Avery, 1938). Set on a remote island, the
cartoon consists mostly of travelogue-type narration and blackout gags,
many of which involve Egghead, the character that eventually became
Elmer Fudd.[40] About halfway through the cartoon we meet the inhabitants of Pingo-Pongo, almost every one of them tall and black, having
excessively large feet and lips and a striking facial resemblance to the island's wild animals. The omnipresent tour guide chimes in: "As we near
the village, we hear the primitive beat of jungle tom-toms. We come upon
a group of native musicians, beating out the savage rhythm that is as
old and primitive as the jungle itself." After the establishing shot of four
musicians—four black natives squatting in front of four drums and beating the familiar "ONE-two-three-four" rhythm—the quartet suddenly
jumps up and does a western-style performance of "She'll Be Comin'
'Round the Mountain," complete with yodeled responses to each line of
the second verse. The unexpected (perhaps absurd) use of an American
popular tune creates the humor here, especially since "She'll Be Comin'"
is *not* as "old and primitive as the jungle itself." We have clearly been set
up to expect something in a far less familiar vein. The black natives singing
in a western harmony style adds a further sense of irony to the gag.

The narrator's line about the "primitive savage rhythm" leads the audience to connect jazz and the jungle, a connection driven home in a later
scene that portrays a "native celebration." Several male-female couples
dance a short minuet, perfectly synchronized and with arms upraised, to
imply refined, proper style. This presents yet another of Avery's comic
juxtapositions of contemporary cultural conventions with the mores of
the jungle dweller. Suddenly a short, squat native (clearly meant to be

FIGURE 21 *The Isle of Pingo-Pongo*
(Warner Bros.; Avery, 1938).

Fats Waller, as can be inferred both from his size and from his singing style) announces the next song, a rendition of "Sweet Georgia Brown" with Waller and four natives (in black tie) representing the Mills Brothers singing around a period radio microphone (see figure 21). The dancers respond, predictably, with movements that are much less refined and more stylized.[41] The startling performance by Waller and the Mills Brothers is the showstopping musical cue of the short: the brothers perform all their characteristic tricks of imitating instruments with their hands, while Waller scats his way through a chorus of the song. The number ends with a final chorus played by a native orchestra on modern jazz instruments. The cartoon's penultimate cue further confuses the musical construction of the story: when the narrator tells us it is time to bid farewell to Pingo-Pongo, the melody of "Aloha Oe," typically associated with Pacific islands (particularly Hawaii) slows down the momentum from the previous song. This conflation of white-constructed primitive attributes indicates that another stereotype is at work here: *all* peoples categorized as "primitive" look and act the same.[42]

In both films examined here, the music of African Americans, portrayed as "contemporary savages," quickly changes from stereotypical jungle melodies (beating drums) to a much more modern and swinging sound, though one still understood to be primitive in origin. The Fleischer and Warner Bros. cartoons were not alone in fostering images of the emergence of jazz from the savage hinterland; all the major studios reproduced and circulated this prevalent stereotype of jazz's origins.[43] Juxtaposing African American jazz musicians and a primitivist performance of uncivilized music, urban Americans and uneducated savages, creates a fictive identification that serves only to stereotype. Given such manipulation, we have to ask ourselves whether we are hearing the mu-

sic and the social history embedded within it, or simply what we want
to hear. All the studios helped perpetuate such myths; for some, jazz represented a total lack of civilization, while others moved the jazz sound
into rural and urban settings as well.

JAZZ AND POPULAR SONG:
THE WARNER BROS. CARTOONS

The Warner Bros. approach to jazz was very different from that of the
Fleischers. While the Warner directors and animators did *not* have direct access to famous performers, they had the next best thing—their
songs. The Warner cartoons could use contemporary jazz or big band
hits, taken from the studio's extensive holdings of popular sheet music,
and then—relying on celebrity impersonators to imitate the voices of
famous singers—have them apparently performed on screen by the biggest
names in the business. This was the method used in *The Isle of Pingo-
Pongo*.[44]

Warner Bros. already had a strong identification with the musical film:
the studio produced *The Jazz Singer* (1927) and a line of musicals that
included *Gold Diggers of 1933, Gold Diggers of 1935*, and *42nd Street*
(1933). Most of the early cartoons produced by Warner Bros. had a narrative framework similar to that of the musicals; in particular, the story
line tended to shift into song every so often before returning to "reality." But in cartoons, of course, the notion of reality is far more flexible
and is not disrupted by the introduction of music; that characters should
burst into song is just as logical and rational as anything else that happens in an animated environment. The film historian Hank Sartin does
point out one important distinction between live-action and animated
musicals: *all* characters in a cartoon can take part in any musical number. "Everyone in the cartoon is a potential performer," he observes, "and
singing and dancing are an integrated part of normal experience."[45] Because such a close relationship existed between the score and the story,
the actual music, not just its cultural implications, helped create meaning in the cartoons.

Clean Pastures (Freleng, 1937) is a morality tale that takes us back to
the heyday of the Harlem clubs, offering us an example of how (cartoon)
musicals shift between the main story and a musical interlude or number. The short derives from a very successful all-black Warner Bros. musical film, *The Green Pastures* (1936), itself an adaptation of one of the
most popular plays of the early twentieth century (written by Marc Con-

nelly, it premiered in 1930).[46] The main title begins in an unusual manner, which immediately establishes the cartoon's theme of redemption. An all-male (and clearly understood to be all-black) chorus sings the a cappella phrase "Save me, sister, from temptation" over the opening credits—a song taken from yet another Warner Bros. musical film, Al Jolson's *The Singing Kid,* released only a year before *Clean Pastures.* Its brief appearance foreshadows the cartoon's religious theme.

The plot is simple: heaven ("Pair-O-Dice") has a shortage of residents, in contrast to hell ("Hades, Inc."), where the wanton inhabitants of Harlem head after a lifetime of dancing, drinking, and carrying on (all to the tune "Nagasaki"). The angel in charge sends his assistant, an angel who is a caricature of Stepin Fechit, down to Harlem to lure the Hades-bound to Pair-O-Dice, but to no avail (see figure 22). During Fechit's entreaties to the Harlemites, Bill "Bojangles" Robinson walks by and soft-shoes "Old Folks at Home"; he is followed by Al Jolson in blackface, who sings a chorus of "I Love to Singa," further confusing the hapless spirit. Several other musicians in Pair-O-Dice (Louis Armstrong, Fats Waller, Cab Calloway) persuade the head angel that "rhythm" will make the place more attractive (see figure 23). They descend to Earth and launch into a swinging version of "Swing for Sale."

> (chorus)
>
> [Cab Calloway and his orchestra]
>
> If your rhythm's been too dreamy [echo] and you like your trumpets screamy, [echo]
> That's when you should call to see me, ['cuz] I've got SWING FOR SALE.
> If you think a waltz is horrid, and you like your rhythm torrid,
> 'Till it makes you mop your forehead, I've got SWING FOR SALE.
>
> [Mills Brothers]
>
> Rhythm is what this country needs, for years and years, I've said it.
> When you buy from me, it's C.O.D., I sell swing but not for credit.
>
> [second phrase of chorus repeated by Armstrong, including a trumpet solo]
>
> [Cab Calloway]
>
> There's no tellin' what can happen, I can start your toes a tappin'.
> I can set your fingers snappin', I've got SWING FOR SALE.[47]

The song works perfectly as an enticement to come to Pair-O-Dice. Armstrong's impassioned solo (during which his eyes bug out and his face

FIGURE 22 Stepin Fechit in *Clean Pastures* (Warner Bros.; Freleng, 1937). The sign reads "Pair-O-Dice Needs You! Opportunity. Travel, Good Food, Water Melon, Clean Living, Music, Talkies."

FIGURE 23 Jazz greats appeal to the head angel in *Clean Pastures*.

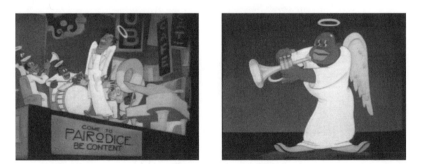

FIGURE 24 Cab Calloway and his band and Louis Armstrong in *Clean Pastures*.

turns purple), together with the vocal hand and mouth effects employed by the Mills Brothers (see figure 24), convinces the Harlem pleasure seekers to sing and dance their way to the promised land.

Clean Pastures' climax (like that of its theatrical predecessors) evokes the spirit of a revivalist camp meeting, complete with the promises of salvation available to anyone who repents of his or her sinful ways.[48] In its proposed route to salvation, *Clean Pastures* uses rhythm as a metaphor for religious faith, showing again how strongly the white population identified jazz with aspects of black culture, including religion and the unfettered expressions of emotion associated with it. Rather than offer an alternative to the swinging Harlem music, the heavenly musicians appropriate the very hottest sounds for their own purpose: to lure people to Pair-O-Dice. The joy seekers embrace a lively version of James Bland's minstrel tune "Oh! Dem Golden Slippers" on their way skyward. As hot music is combined with a traditional spiritual, both the music-loving Harlemites and the angels in heaven get what they want. Furthermore, placing the creators of "good" hot jazz in heaven suggests that certain types of black music are better than others: "hot" music made in such places as Harlem would lead to debauchery and eventually to Hades, Inc.[49] Only through the noble efforts of famous black musicians could souls be turned to a better direction. Armstrong and Calloway must have been deemed safe enough—or at least sufficiently nonthreatening to whites—to represent angels. Their success as crossover musicians, popular among both white and black consumers, no doubt helped establish them as harmless (as it would have for the other artists we have already come across, like the Mills Brothers).

Like the Hollywood musicals of the 1930s on which so many of the Warner Bros. cartoons were based, *Clean Pastures* moves from the real world (the urban city) to a surreal realm. In this case, the all-star band, singing promises of a swing-filled eternity, eventually leads the righteous away from Harlem and into heaven, beyond any bounds of earthly reality. Since neither we nor the righteous Harlemites get to see what glories await in heaven, the music *must* paint a compelling picture of the blissful times to be had. In fact, the unseen pleasures are so attractive that Satan himself comes to call at the cartoon's close (see figure 25). Using the popular images of Armstrong, Calloway, and the like enabled the writers to entice the Harlemites upward and to present an alternative to the hedonistic nightclub scene. According to Donald Bogle, paradise in *The Green Pastures* is "a perpetual Negro holiday, one everlasting weekend fish fry. Harmony and good spirits reign supreme."[50] The Warner Bros. animators use the same model for their utopia: heavenly Harlem shops and singing choirs make up their vision of paradise, without any acknowledgment of the stereotype implied in such an image.

While this imagined paradise worked for the studio, it apparently did not please the censors. In his book on censored animation, Karl Cohen

FIGURE 25 Satan comes calling in *Clean Pastures.*

cites an article from 1939 in which the Warner Bros. cartoon producer Leon Schlesinger claimed that "the phrase 'De Lawd' was cut out of the cartoon and that the censors wanted to eliminate the halo over the head of a Negro angel."[51] Michael Barrier provides more information, describing *Clean Pastures* as "one of the few cartoons to run afoul of the Production Code. The Code required rejection of any film that was a burlesque of religion, and the Code's administrator, Joseph I. Breen, condemned *Clean Pastures* as exactly that. In a letter to Leon Schlesinger, Breen cited the portions of the film set in an ersatz Heaven called Pair-O-Dice, and said, 'I am certain that such scenes would give serious offense to many people in all parts of the world.'"[52] Unfortunately, Breen's letter does not specify what in the scenes he perceived to be sacrilegious. Possibly the offense lay in their depiction of blacks not only as denizens of heaven but also as the angels who ran the place. Angels are stereotypically pure, saintly, and, most important, white—in their vestments as well as their race. The censors apparently did not like the idea of a heaven filled with people who were, according to the cartoon, gamblers, dancers, drinkers, and, above all else, jazz fans. *Clean Pastures* also resembled *The Green Pastures* in its manifest image of a black heaven; this image may have elicited some of the critiques of the cartoon. The notion of black men, women, and children—or, as Bogle calls them, "angels with dirty faces"[53]—living their (after)lives in the same heaven as white folk, portrayed in the feature film through its southern recharacterization of Bible stories, possibly appeared in *Clean Pastures* even more threatening to white viewers.

Musically, the story features several Warner Bros.–owned songs, including "Sweet Georgia Brown," "I Love to Singa," and the extended version of "Swing for Sale." The score here supplies both the foundation for the

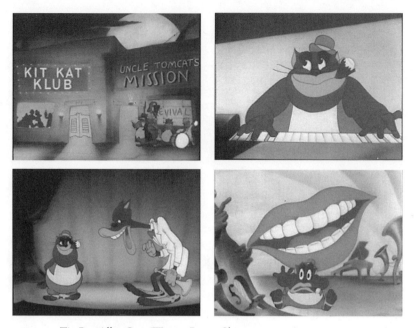

FIGURE 26 *Tin Pan Alley Cats* (Warner Bros.; Clampett, 1943).

story and the driving force behind the animation. Even in sequences in which no performers are visible, the animation still moves precisely with the music; for example, the righteous bound for Pair-O-Dice two-step their way up toward heaven in time to "Oh! Dem Golden Slippers," led by Calloway and Waller.

Clean Pastures inspired the Warner Bros. cartoon *Tin Pan Alley Cats* (Clampett, 1943), which also conveys a highly moralistic message in suggesting that jazz is the music of disorder and decadence.[54] In this cartoon, a cat (Fats Waller caricatured once again) must choose between the musically square cats in the Salvation Army, playing "Gimme That Old Time Religion" outside a seamy nightclub, or the hot tunes produced inside. Having chosen the latter (in his words, "Well, wot's de mutta wit dat?"), Fats shows off his musical skill on the piano by blazing through the opening chords to "Nagasaki," which are taken up immediately by the whole nightclub. Finally, a scatting trumpet player literally blows Fats out of this world, landing him in a bizarre netherworld filled with fantastic creatures (see figure 26).[55] Transported into a universe seemingly created from the excesses of jazz, Fats cannot make any sense of it: voices speak to him from nowhere, and its creatures—including a two-headed dog/cat mutant chasing itself—shock him. Rejecting this wacky land, Fats returns to the world he knows; he immediately runs from the club to join the righteous in their song of salvation, apparently converted to their way of thinking. Their rendition of "Old Time Religion" has no swing or joy to it whatsoever; the exaggeratedly dry performance strengthens its function as a protective mechanism against the chaotic impulses of jazz. The message of *Tin Pan Alley Cats* seems to follow the more typical line of reasoning that too much jazz will make you lose your grip on reality (as happened to Fats). Its message makes the reversal in *Clean Pastures,* in which jazz can be the means not just to damnation but also to salvation, even more surprising.[56] Of course, we can't overlook that Fats gorges himself completely on wine, women, and song before being brought back to the straight and narrow. Though the story ends with the more conservative choice, most of the film focuses on Fats's indulgences, in essence endorsing the high life over a righteous one—and leaving the audience once more with a very mixed message.

THE 1940S: RACE, RHYTHM, AND SWING

As we have seen, cartoons of the 1930s often featured musical numbers that fit into a larger story. As the public's fascination with swing music continued to grow into the 1940s, swing culture became a pervasive part of all forms of entertainment, including cartoons. Rather than spotlighting one or even two short musical numbers, these cartoons exuded swing from beginning to end: the performance never stopped. Practically every cartoon studio in Hollywood used music of the big bands and the boogie-woogie revival in their shorts—musically, visually, or both. MGM produced several jive-influenced shorts, such as *Swing Social* (Hanna and Barbera, 1940), *Red Hot Riding Hood* (Avery, 1943), and *Zoot Cat* (Hanna and Barbera, 1944). After Paramount took over the Fleischer studio in 1942 (removing the brothers and reorganizing the studio as Famous), Popeye continued occasionally to encounter jazz and swing performers, though not celebrities such as those who had habitually appeared in the cartoons of his predecessor, Betty Boop. But Warner Bros. and Walter Lantz deserve special attention: Warner for continuing to produce animated takes on the black music scene, and Lantz for dedicating an entire series to swing music.

No cartoon at Warner Bros. combined swing and animation more effectively, or with more pervasive racist imagery, than *Coal Black and de Sebben Dwarfs* (1943). The story is a modern, urban retelling of the Snow White story, with frequent references to Disney's 1937 feature version of the tale. The animation is some of the most vibrant produced by the studio at this time, and the story moves along succinctly from gag to gag.[57] Its director, Bob Clampett, felt so strongly about the need to create "authentic" images and music for this cartoon that he took his animators to a black club on Central Avenue in downtown Los Angeles, the Club Alabam, to observe the nightlife. He even attempted (unsuccessfully) to hire only black musicians to record the score.[58] He did have luck with the voice talent, however: Vivian Dandridge of the Dandridge Sisters trio played So White, her mother Ruby played the narrator, and Leo "Zoot" Watson, a drummer who worked with Louis Armstrong, took the part of Prince Chawmin', as his name was spelled in flashing lights on his car door.[59] The furor surrounding *Coal Black,* mainly due to its extreme and (therefore) offensive stereotyping of blacks, has all but eclipsed the film itself. Practically every gag, visual or aural, alludes to a stereotypical image of African Americans. One such joke gave the zoot-suited prince teeth entirely of gold except for the front two, which are dice.

Carl Stalling provided a score that mainly highlighted two songs, "Old King Cole" and "The Five O'Clock Whistle," both of which were current pop tunes (naturally, owned by Warner Bros.).[60] Other songs in the cartoon include "Nagasaki," "Blues in the Night," and a short cue of "Dixie." But the final score is hardly a typical arrangement for the Warner Bros. orchestra: instead, an ongoing groove pervades the entire cartoon. Usually cartoons rely on the delivery of a strictly verbal punch line to break any silences in the background score. In *Coal Black,* the dialogue keeps the momentum progressing smoothly as the actors speak their parts with a keen, rhythmic sense of swing, which seconds later is absorbed back into the score. Such a break in the music occurs when So White, kidnapped by Murder, Inc., is set down in the forest, presumably having won her release by putting out for her abductors (so the lipstick that covers their faces suggests). As the men place her body on the road, a quick bit of scatlike patter keeps the sense of the beat for about ten seconds as the underscoring music cuts out altogether.

All the characters in the cartoon talk in a rhythm that accentuates their jive-speak, but not everyone gets to perform musically. So White does sing a few notes when she mentions that she gets "the blues in the night"; she also sings a chorus of "The Five O'Clock Whistle" as she cooks up breakfast for her soldier boys, the dwarfs:

> Oh the five o'clock bugle, it just blew
> I'm fryin' eggs and pork chops too
> Didn't join up 'cause I'se good lookin'
> But to answer the boys when they say 'What's cookin', honey? What's
>   cookin'?'"

The dwarfs also join in with So White, as they all sing a brief chorus of "In the Army Now" (earlier in the film).

However, the performance in the film that is most important, and most closely tied to the imagery Clampett created, is given in the final scene. Having eaten the poison apple given to her by the Mean Old Queen, So White is, as the dwarfs say, "out of this world! She's stiff as wood! She's got it bad and that ain't good!" Only Prince Chawmin' and his "dynamite kiss!" can awaken her—yet he cannot. As the prince tries and fails numerous times to wake the girl, a few notes on a solo trumpet underscore each impotent peck; they progressively weaken and wobble as they slowly ascend the scale. After the prince gives up, the smallest dwarf (apparently meant to resemble Disney's Dopey) plants a kiss on So White that sends her pigtails straight into the air with little American flags on them, while the trumpet in the background doubles the joke by reaching a piercingly high note. The jazz trumpet, typically a signifier of masculinity for the black men who play it, can also serve as a sign of phallic powerlessness: musical incapacity is equated with psychological castration.[61] In this case, the prince has already been set up as less than a real man—when So White was kidnapped by Murder, Inc., the prince displayed a cowardly yellow streak that grew straight up his back. His inability to wake up So White from her sleep simply confirms his less-than-manly qualities. Only a real man (in this case, a man in uniform) has what it takes to rouse her, and thus the music reflects his rhetorical and physical power.

On a par with, if not exceeding, the insulting racial imagery of *Coal Black* is the 1941 Lantz cartoon *Scrub Me Mama with a Boogie Beat*, directed by Lantz himself and part of the Swing Symphonies series. Drawing on an entirely different set of black stereotypes, this short dwells on images of indolent blacks in Lazytown, lounging around a river landing on a hot summer day. Everybody moves slowly: two men fighting slap each other upside the head in slow motion, a listless man on the dock reacts slowly and deliberately to being stung on the nose repeatedly by a wasp, and a woman washing clothes almost stops moving altogether. A remarkably lethargic version of "Old Folks at Home (Swanee River)" underscores the sequence. As a riverboat pulls up to the dock, it releases jazz's invigorating spirit and rhythm into the town. A full band of musicians, led by a mulatto (in Bogle's rubric) female singer, injects the spirit of jazz into the locals. The singer tells the woman washing clothes that she just needs rhythm, and the woman replies, "What do you all mean 'rhythm'?" As in *Clean Pastures*, a jazz tune, in this case the title song, saves the people in the cartoon; the happy result here is not heavenly salvation but an awakening from physical stupor. The imagery becomes, if possible, even more offensive, as greater numbers of stereotypical characters (a man eating watermelon, pickaninnies, an Uncle Tom figure) appear to take part in the jamming.

During several quick shots of the musicians playing together, an unusual combination of images is presented. All four men shown are black, and three (the bass, trumpet, and piano players) exhibit the big-lipped, chimpanzee-faced design that typifies these cartoons. The clarinet player, in contrast, appears almost to have stepped out of a Harlem club, with very realistic and human-seeming face and body, as if he alone had been drawn by someone more sympathetic to the portrayal of blacks. Though this clarinetist never assumes a substantial personality in the story, his brief appearance reminds us how sharply such renderings can differ from cartoon to cartoon, and even within the same scene.

Scrub Me Mama was just one of the shorts that Lantz produced in the early 1940s in the Swing Symphonies series; not surprisingly, they emphasize swing music and swing culture, though many do not focus on music per se. More often, the stories present life as somehow unfulfilling and lacking sparkle until everybody gets rhythm—frequently bestowed on them by the boogie-woogie man, as in *Boogie Woogie Man* (Culhane, 1943), *Greatest Man in Siam* (Culhane, 1944), *Boogie Woogie Sioux* (Lovy, 1942) and *Boogie Woogie Bugle Boy of Company "B"* (Lantz, 1941). Not all the Swing Symphonies feature African American characters, however. *Pied Piper of Basin Street* (Culhane, 1945), *The Hams That Couldn't Be Cured* (Lantz, 1942), *The Sliphorn King of Polaroo* (Lundy, 1945), and several other cartoons feature musical numbers based on boogie-woogie without resorting to racist visual imagery, although other racial elements are pervasive. Jazz is brought in through standard cartoon plot devices: the pied piper's hot tunes attract rats, the three (hip) little pigs ham it up in a music teacher's shop, and so on.

Like those of the Fleischers a decade earlier, Lantz's cartoons benefited from a hometown connection. Darrell Calker, who scored Lantz's cartoons in the late 1930s and much of the 1940s, was a jazz pianist known in local clubs around Los Angeles. Lantz could thus get inspiration from local jazz and, through Calker's connections, feature in his cartoons known jazz stars—Jack Teagarden (*Pied Piper of Basin Street* and *Sliphorn King of Polaroo*), Bob Zurke (*Jungle Jive;* Culhane, 1944), and several others. But unlike the Fleischers', Lantz's cartoons did not serve as promotional shorts. The featured musicians received minor billing in the credits and were given no time on screen, live-action or animated. Only their performances make these often offensive cartoons memorable.

WHITE JAZZ

Jazz in cartoons did not belong solely to black characters. In fact, white characters appear quite frequently playing jazz; the animated sequence in *King of Jazz* demonstrates how far back these portrayals can be found. The best known, perhaps even beloved, example occurs in the Warner Bros. short *I Love to Singa* (Avery, 1936), a truncated and animated version of *The Jazz Singer* (1927) that features the opening (and closing) song from 1936's *The Singing Kid* (both Warner Bros. films starring Al Jolson). *I Love to Singa* presents the now-familiar theme of the old world clashing with the new. Professor Owl teaches strictly classical music (the sign on his housefront vehemently states "NO JAZZ"), but his youngest son, Owl Jolson, is born to be a crooner. (He literally pops out of his shell dressed in a red blazer, singing the title song.) Papa throws sonny out, but eventually the family accepts him for who he is—after he finds success singing on Jack Bunny's radio show.[62] Like that of his big-screen predecessor, the singing of Owl Jolson is relatively tame. The conflict in the cartoon between traditional and popular styles recalls that of the original film, in which the young Jakie Rabinowitz (Al Jolson) had to make a far more emotional choice between the religious faith pressed on him by his ailing father and popular fame. The similarity of the cartoon's music to that in *King of Jazz* is quite striking, as both (animated) white performers stay a safe distance from anything resembling truly hot jazz, opting instead for the safer ground of swing-infused pop songs.[63] In Whiteman's film, the songs were simply drawn from his band's typical playlist. Likewise, the director of *I Love to Singa*, Tex Avery, used the music sung by the real Jolson.

The image of hot jazz musicians, established (as we have seen) through generations of stereotyping, persisted into the late 1950s.[64] With the bebop revolution fully ingrained in the music world, and free and modal jazz just around the corner, a more modern and sanitized image of what hot jazz sounded like began to surface. The 1957 Warner Bros. cartoon *Three Little Bops,* yet another short reinterpreting the story of the three little pigs, features the trumpet work of the West Coast jazz luminary Shorty Rogers and ultra-hep narration by Stan Freberg, a star of comedy recording.[65] Suddenly there seems to be nothing anomalous about three white (or pink) characters playing jazz (see figure 27). On the contrary, the pigs set up grooves that swing everywhere they go, frustrated only by the unmelodic sounds of the Big Bad Wolf, whose unhip playing rubs the pigs and their audience the wrong way. We can see that by the time *Three Little Bops* appeared, what was once an old stereotype (only black musicians can play good jazz) had been shattered, supplanted by a new stereotype created by the musicians themselves: only tonal and melodic jazz is worthwhile.

The music the wolf plays sounds vaguely like an early form of free jazz, a style fomented in the Los Angeles jazz scene, particularly at the hands of the saxophone player Ornette Coleman. It does not gain acceptance until after the wolf has blown himself up and wound up in hell, where he can play truly hot (that is, tonal and melodic) jazz, as the pigs state the cartoon's moral,

> The big bad wolf
> He learned the rule
> Ya gotta get real hot
> To play real cool.

The wolf twice sits in with the pigs (and sneaks in a third time), only to be ostracized and kicked out of the club when his trumpet licks have nothing to do with what the pigs are playing. He is further humiliated when he tries to enter the pigs' club (the House of Bricks, "built in 1776") disguised as a 1920s hipster, complete with fur coat and playing "The Charleston" on a ukulele. His sound finally gets ultra-cool down in hell, where his trumpet suddenly takes on a muted timbre with smooth articulations. Whiteman and Jolson pleased their audience by confining themselves to playing what was, in their time, the most widely accepted (and also conventional) type of pop or jazz, shying away from the hot jazz preferred by innovative black groups. Twenty-five years later we find the definition of "conventional" shifting. The West Coast or bop style became the new norm, exemplified by the three *white* pigs. As a result, the innovative free jazz sound became the music that is too hot to touch. We cannot discount the possibility that Rogers, a known figure in the L.A. music world, might have used *Three Little Bops* to make a statement

FIGURE 27   *Three Little Bops* (Warner Bros.; Freleng, 1956). © Warner Bros., Inc.

against Coleman's experimental style of music, with which he was undoubtedly familiar.[66]

OTHER VOICES: JAZZ IN THE CARTOON SCORE

Jazz made an indelible mark on both the creation and scoring of cartoons, which portrayed jazz performances and appropriated jazz styles.
The music of race, of course, had long been woven into mainstream popular culture. Well into the 1950s, Stephen Foster's tunes and other familiar minstrelsy songs mentioned above continued their work of musically evoking a mythologized Old South. Much of the legacy of blackface
is maintained—whites are still watching from the audience and blacks
are still onstage performing—except now cartoons have replaced minstrelsy, and somehow Mickey, Oswald, and Bosko are not seen as caricatures of blacks. The black characters in the cartoons were associated
with songs, whether nineteenth-century folk or modern pop, that helped
reinforce their supposedly intrinsically primitive nature and simultaneously reaffirm whites' assumption that black culture is generally unso-

phisticated.[67] Each studio used these stereotypes, whether the references to them were oblique, direct, or somewhere in between. In whatever degree such images were used, animation's tendency to exaggerate had the power to make these caricatures especially vicious. The cartoons make no pretense of appealing to black viewers; like the minstrel shows of the not-too-distant past, the cartoons are intended to reflect the perspective of whites, drawing on white notions of how the black community functions. Long after these cartoons lost their once-prominent place in popular culture, two sets of images remain: those created of the musicians and those that became associated with the music itself.

These same images have perhaps masked the most overlooked aspect of jazz's contribution to cartoon scores in general: even when its action bore no connection to jazz or black culture in general, practically every cartoon from the late 1920s onward used components of jazz throughout its score. Jazz's broad stylistic elements, especially the approach to rhythm, became a part of the general musical vocabulary of cartoon scores, noticed only when the occasional on-screen performance by a live or animated performer might remind the viewer of their presence. The objections to the "primal" nature of African American music would not be limited to jazz, of course; we need only think back to the outcry against rock 'n' roll in the 1950s or rap in the 1980s to realize that the protests have simply found different targets as the music has evolved.

Even though feature film scores drew on jazz sounds little until the 1950s (many film music historians consider one of the first "true" jazz scores to be Otto Preminger's 1955 film *The Man with the Golden Arm*),[68] jazz had integrated itself into the public's musical psyche well before that time: just recall *The Jazz Singer* (1927). Cartoons began using jazz just as early, and yet we have only begun to understand how large a part jazz played in the creation of the cartoon sound. The viewer can watch cartoons for years and remain unaware of the variety of different cultural discourses implicit in all aspects of the production: the story, the music, the artwork. Another thread that must be made explicit is that of the African American musician. Once the various levels of meaning in one cartoon become clear, others suddenly come into focus—and we can recognize, among other revelations, how essential jazz's role in cartoons has been all along.

4

Corny Concertos and Silly Symphonies

CLASSICAL MUSIC AND CARTOONS

There is a divergence of opinion as to the use of Brahms and Chopin to accompany the antics of the *"Three Little Pigs* or *Andy Panda.*" The must-nots contend that this irreverent approach to the masters is a cheapening influence that can only end in contempt. In the other camp, the opinion is that any medium is good that will break down the feeling that the classics are sacrosanct and for the few and probably dull besides. Just who is right, time will tell.

Marie L. Hamilton, "Music and Theatrical Shorts" (1946)

If cartoons have become associated over time with any one musical genre, it is classical music. When I talk to people about cartoon music, that is inevitably what they first think of and talk about: "Cartoons are where I learned all the classics." "I love it when Elmer sings 'Kill the Wabbit!'" "I can't go to a concert without thinking of a Tom and Jerry cartoon." Apparently, countless Americans attribute their first conscious memory of the classical repertoire to cartoons. Through film, and then television, cartoons have repeatedly introduced large segments of society to this music. Among those exposed were Timothy and Kevin Burke, who write in their book on Saturday morning television: "Certainly for both of us, our first acquaintance with opera, particularly *The Barber of Seville,* came from Bugs Bunny. See, cartoons *are* educational."[1] With the increasingly limited attention given to classical music in primary and secondary schools, cartoon scores have managed to keep the classics in the public's ears, albeit in a context that gives them an entirely different set of meanings.

The general topic of classical music in cartoons is much too large to be fully treated in two chapters in a book. In this chapter, I raise a variety of issues regarding classical music's place in animated cartoons, focusing on a limited number of cartoons. I concentrate not on how the canon of classical film music was established but on how it was reduced by cartoons to an even more limited set of works, examining how cartoons made use of these pieces and their cultural baggage. In addition, I consider the culture of the concert hall and how each facet of it—the conductor, the audience, the hall itself—became a subject for parody and (occasionally) ridicule.

One note about terminology: in mentioning the "canon," I do not mean to imply that these cartoons use the music of high art. On the contrary, I believe these films subvert traditional ideas of the canon by often featuring more popular (and thus more commercial) works, both of concert music and of opera. One quality of those canonic works is their timelessness. Cartoons have helped make these works even more durable, providing audiences with new contexts to attach to the old standards. In fact, Carl Stalling earned the label "postmodernist" precisely because he was able to juxtapose a dozen pieces from a dozen eras and make them work together, a practice that by necessity leaches much of the historical significance out of a given piece.

REPERTOIRE AND THE CARTOON CANON

> You know, it is so sad. All of your knowledge of high culture
> comes from Bugs Bunny cartoons.
>> Elaine to Jerry, in "The Opera,"
>> *Seinfeld* (1992)

The exploitation of nineteenth-century music as fodder for films and cartoons is a direct consequence of the practices of silent film accompanists and composers, who used familiar, often canonic melodies in their scores. Because it was in the public domain, such music could be used in any score without any cost or copyright restrictions. As I pointed out in chapter 1, Walt Disney's reluctance to use (that is, to pay for) contemporary music compelled Stalling to fall back on older pieces: Stephen Foster, folk tunes, and classical works. Force of habit and convenience led him to draw repeatedly on the same pieces, with which he soon became strongly associated as an organist.

EXAMPLE 6 Alphons Czibulka, "Wintermärchen."

Who, then, is in the cartoon canon? At the top of the list is Wagner, with both the greatest number of overall references and the greatest number of specific pieces cited. Other favorites include Rossini, Mendelssohn, Liszt, Chopin, Franz von Suppé, Brahms, Johann Strauss, Schubert, Schumann, Tchaikovsky, and Beethoven.[2] Often just a fragment of a piece is used. Beethoven's Fifth Symphony is sometimes heard, but usually only its opening gesture, recontextualized to elicit feelings of patriotism during World War II—the symphony's main "da-da-da-daaaaah" motif was associated with the slogan "V for Victory," because it echoed the rhythm of the letter V in Morse code (dot-dot-dot-dash). Similarly, Chopin is represented in cartoons almost entirely by the opening four-note motif of his *Funeral March*.

The most famous works of a composer do not always appear in cartoons, which need short, easily digestible melodies to match the rapid-paced action that dominates their story lines. Not every piece in the canon will flourish in this environment.[3] For the same reason, many of the primary composers of the concert hall canon are underrepresented or completely absent from the cartoon canon, which thus consists of an idiosyncratic assortment of classics. Lesser-known works of well-known composers appear frequently, such as music from Wagner's early opera *Rienzi*. Composers no longer regularly heard in concert, such as Franz von Suppé and Alphons Czibulka, are favorites. The overtures to several of von Suppé's operas, including *Morning, Noon, and Night in Vienna, Light Cavalry, Beautiful Galatea,* and *The Poet and Peasant,* are often featured. Czibulka's best-known melody is "Wintermärchen" (see music example 6), familiar as the stereotypically weepy violin piece that one hears at moments of mock tragedy.[4]

The popularity of such pieces was recognized and exploited before the film era, however. Already in the late nineteenth century, Lawrence Levine notes, orchestral programmers differentiated between classical works that were popular (and thus profitable for concert promoters) and those that were aesthetically superior (symphonies and concertos by Beethoven, Schubert, and the like). Certain orchestras would thus "mount a series of 'popular concerts' for those who craved hearing Strauss's waltzes, Brahms's Hungarian Dances, Liszt's Hungarian Rhapsodies, and instrumental arrangements of Wagner's *Pilgrim's Chorus* and *Evening Star* or Verdi's arias, and . . . arrange the regular programming for those who preferred to have their culture unsullied by compromise."[5] From the start, narrative-minded film accompanists frequently used these more accessible pieces, whose lower status in the classical repertoire made them seem especially suitable for appropriation. Collections or lists of songs to be used in silent film houses, published by Sam Fox, Witmark, Belwin, and others, always included a significant number of pieces by nineteenth-century composers. These pieces shared one common characteristic: gestural immediacy. When employed in short forms such as commercials or cartoons, in which a message has only seconds to be conveyed, music must get its point across quickly. Pieces with easily identifiable motifs gave film accompanists (and later animators and cartoon composers) a simple means of connecting a tune with a visual idea, enabling them to give a sense of completion to each gesture, at once aural and visual. Not surprisingly, most classical music dismissed as too serious for use in other media (for example, the works of Mahler and Bruckner, and most pieces by Brahms and Beethoven) lacks easily excerpted melodies. Conversely, popular music that contains such melodies is used repeatedly: the very pieces cited by Levine show up over and over again in cartoons, both as underscore cues and as plot devices.[6]

By using the so-called light classics, a cartoon director could isolate and focus on particular musical gestures, one at a time. Friz Freleng once described Liszt's Second Hungarian Rhapsody, a piece that has appeared in numerous cartoons, as "one of my favorite numbers. I know it and I can manipulate it. I can make it stop, like a conductor. Or I can slow it down. That's one thing about the number: You can use a phrase, you can repeat it, and it still works!"[7] A firm grasp of the ins and outs of the work enabled Freleng to tear the music apart and reassemble it as he saw fit. Such an ability gave the director tremendous power, as he not only controlled the newly devised visual story but also shaped the musical narrative to suit his needs.

Not all gestures are created equal, however. Certain passages of the Liszt Rhapsody never appear in Freleng's cartoons—possibly because the director didn't like them, but more likely because he or his writers did not conceive of anything visually interesting to accompany those musical gestures. In contrast, those sections of the piece that did spark his or his writers' interest show up repeatedly. For instance, the same passage

EXAMPLE 7 Franz Liszt, Hungarian Rhapsody no. 2 in C-sharp minor.

from Liszt's Hungarian Rhapsody no. 2 (see music example 7), with its clusters of thirty-second-note figures followed by a long, sliding glissando, appears in both *Rhapsody in Rivets* (Warner Bros., 1941) and *Rhapsody Rabbit* (Warner Bros., 1946). The earlier cartoon depicts the building of a skyscraper (under)scored to a performance of the Liszt (see figure 28). The overarching conceit is that the foreman conducts his crew just as a conductor leads an orchestra. At one point, a bricklaying octopus puts down four bricks in a row in time with the thirty-second-note figures, and then lays a long layer of cement over the bricks, underscored by the glissando. In *Rhapsody Rabbit,* Freleng interprets the music similarly. Bugs Bunny (a concert pianist) picks up the piano keys in bunches for the first half of the passage, and then lays them all back down in a long row during the rest of the phrase (see figure 29). In both cases, Freleng takes a single gesture out of a larger piece, gives it a unique visual image for the cartoon, and then reintegrates it into a series of audiovisual gags. The independence of each gesture makes possible such a dissection of motifs.

This reliance on gesture usually prevented modernist and avant-garde music from finding any place in cartoon scores except when such sounds were being ridiculed, as in Freleng's 1955 Warner Bros. cartoon *Pizzicato Pussycat*. The plot: A mouse plays the piano beautifully. The house cat catches the mouse, sparing its life on the condition that the mouse play his mouse-sized piano inside the grand piano that the cat pantomimes playing, a deception for which the humans fall. At his Carnegie Hall debut (for which, we see on the street posters, "Leopold Stabowski"'s performance has been hastily canceled), the cat accidentally breaks the mouse's glasses. The tiny, half-blind mouse ends up playing what Will Friedwald calls "frightening Cecil Taylor-like thumps which cause press and public alike to reject the miracle cat as a fraud (the squares)."[8] Several music critics in the audience make scornful faces and

FIGURE 28 *Rhapsody in Rivets* (Warner Bros.; Freleng, 1941).

FIGURE 29 *Rhapsody Rabbit* (Warner Bros.; Freleng, 1946).

then retreat hastily from the auditorium, thereby informing the cartoon's viewers that modern music cannot and will not do at a temple of high art like Carnegie Hall. This example also shows that in practice, a cartoon score cannot successfully incorporate such pieces, as they lack the gestures that make so much late-nineteenth-century music a film composer's best friend.[9]

This point leads us back to another requirement of the repertoire: for films and cartoons, the music chosen has quite often been something recognizable or at least easily appreciated by the audience. The classical pieces promoted by various film music compendiums usually had some sort of cultural or social resonance, whether due to their original sources (e.g., Wagner's "Bridal March" in *Lohengrin,* obviously suitable for accompanying a wedding) or to an earlier cultural reassignment (e.g., Rossini's *William Tell* overture, given new life in the early 1930s as cowboy music when it was used as the theme for *The Lone Ranger* radio program).[10] The most famous gestures became independent of the pieces in which they occur. The gallop figure of Rossini's overture and the rapid scalar movement in Liszt's Rhapsody can and do make sense outside the context of the works they come from. The Rossini no longer evokes ideas of opera; its resignification by *The Lone Ranger* had led most listeners to identify it with that show or, more generally, with images of horses or chases.

In a talk given at UCLA in 1944, Chuck Jones foresaw the influence of visual media on the generations of Americans growing up with films, cartoons, and eventually television: "It is important at this time to remember that visual education has a head-start on other educational methods in that we have a sympathetic audience to start with."[11] While Jones appears to see benefits in children's being more appreciative of or "sympathetic" to learning through a visual medium than from textbooks, his phrase "sympathetic audience" evokes the arguments made against such media by the critic Theodor Adorno, who in the 1930s and '40s objected to the commodification of music by the media, particularly the radio. Adorno decried on-air music education programs such as Walter Damrosch's *NBC Music Appreciation Hour.* The music historian Joseph Horowitz summarizes Adorno's main objections to the flattening and general distortion of symphonic music by radio transmission: "In short, far from wafting symphonic culture to an ever wider audience, the radio voice fetishized the symphony. Deriding apostles of radio enlightenment, Adorno concluded that 'the isolation of the main tune, and similar features, [make] a symphony on the air [become] a piece of entertainment. Consequently, it would be absurd to maintain that it could be received by the listeners as anything but entertainment.'"[12] Adorno found the repeated use of the same few melodies in film scores just as offensive; according to Horowitz, he called this process "'plugging': the tactic of redundantly programming certain popular tunes until 'the most familiar is the most successful and is therefore played again and again and made still more familiar.'"[13] The very things about music in media that Adorno criticizes inform the entire system of film and cartoon scoring, which in turn fetishizes the already-limited symphonic repertoire that he lamented. But neither he nor Jones could have predicted how films and television would displace *all* other methods of imparting information to the masses; indeed, Jones also told his audience, "I want to make clear that I do not believe the animated cartoon will ever quite replace the old-fashioned ballet."[14] By the end of the century (he died in 2002), Jones no doubt realized that cartoons, including many that he directed, have inadvertently become for many children the earliest and sometimes almost exclusive venue for regular exposure to classical music.

Most often, classical music is introduced into a cartoon by setting the story in a performance space, either formal (Carnegie Hall, the Hollywood Bowl, a multitude of unidentified concert halls) or informal (a barn, a barbershop, a bookstore). Such cartoons had a great deal in common: from depicting the conductors to showing the behavior of the different audiences, they all follow a rigorous rubric in portraying how the culture of the concert hall supposedly works. Chuck Jones's *Long-Haired Hare* (Warner Bros., 1949) ably exemplifies the form. This cartoon satirizes all aspects of concert performances, culminates in Bugs Bunny's takeover of a Hollywood Bowl concert, and brings issues of high and low art into play, particularly the struggle of classical music versus contemporary "popular" music.

LONG-HAIRED HARE AND THE CULTURE
OF THE CONCERT HALL

Bugs Bunny begins *Long-Haired Hare,* like so many of his other adventures, singing and minding his own business.[15] In this case, he sings "A Rainy Night in Rio" without a care in the world, accompanying himself on the banjo in the woods of the Hollywood Hills. The music carries—the camera pans slowly across the terrain while Bugs's voice fades, without disappearing altogether—to the bungalow of a large, blond opera singer, one Giovanni Jones, rehearsing Figaro's aria "Largo al Factotum" from Rossini's *The Barber of Seville* in his living room. We can still hear Bugs's voice off in the distance when Jones suddenly shifts from the aria to Bugs's song ("What do they do in Mississippi when skies are drippy?"), though still singing in an operatic style. Realizing he has involuntarily switched genres, the singer finds Bugs, smashes his banjo to bits, and then resumes the rehearsal. But another of Bugs's melodies (this time "My Gal") not only derails Jones from his aria but even compels him to dance around the room, singing "one and two and three and four, she dances all day long." As before, Jones silences Bugs and his instrument, now a full-sized double harp (see figure 30). Not one to give up easily, Bugs tries one more time, playing "When Yuba Plays the Rhumba on the Tuba" as a tuba solo. Jones abuses Bugs a third time (tying the rabbit by his long ears to a tree branch); this brings from Bugs the dreaded rejoinder, "Of course you realize *this* means WAR!"

FIGURE 30 Bugs versus Giovanni Jones, round 1, in *Long-Haired Hare* (Warner Bros.; Jones, 1949).

Within two minutes, Jones establishes a key issue at stake in this cartoon and many others like it: the struggle between popular music, which was growing ever more popular, and classical music, clinging to its elevated position in the cultural hierarchy.[16] The first time Giovanni Jones silences Bugs, the rabbit simply replies, "Music hater! Oh, well." Though Bugs claims that the singer hates music, Jones in fact acts as if he alone is protecting the world of good music from the ignorant masses, which Bugs obviously represents. *Long-Haired Hare* immediately stages the high/low split, which Levine describes as a battle between the "aesthetic and the Philistine, the worthy and the unworthy, the pure and the tainted."[17] The film critic Philip Brophy zeros in on the heart of this conflict: "What is most interesting is how Bugs' singing generates a musicological discourse which *infects* the refined lineage of the operatic arias of the tenor. This clash is in effect a metaphor for the 'infectious' quality of simple pop/folk melodies and how they are regarded as disease by a musical establishment which takes pride in its sanitary measures."[18] Brophy's analysis is confirmed by Jones's reaction each time he unwittingly takes up one of Bugs's songs: his look of shock, then fury, shows that he cannot believe he would succumb to such music. The separation of popular and classical music must remain intact; the highbrow opera singer and his music live safely inside a modern, sanitized house, while the uneducated, uncouth woodland creature partakes of more plebeian pleasures in the wild.[19] Jones rages at Bugs not only because he has been distracted by the rabbit's music but also because he has wasted his precious voice, usually reserved for only the finest of music, on less refined stuff.

Opera narratives in cartoons almost always in some way involve the ongoing cultural wrangling between highbrow opera and more base popular music. Writing on the Hollywood film musical, Jane Feuer refers to this recurring plot motif as the "'opera *vs* swing' narrative." Such films rely, in part, on the same conceit: "When classical music comes to be used in a Hollywood musical (which by definition already contains popular music) the logic of the genre, which always uses cultural prejudices to its own benefit, dictates the war of musical styles."[20] Hank Sartin has shown that cartoons of the 1930s share numerous traits with such musical films; the Warner Bros. cartoons have an additional layer in common, since practically all the songs featured in those early shorts came from famous film musicals.[21] Given such a foundation laid for each cartoon before the animation had even begun, classical music presented these shorts with a target that was not only obvious but logical.

Because animation (like all forms of film) is not an elite form of media, the entire cartoon spectacle is firmly grounded in *popular* culture. From its low position on the ladder of cultural hierarchy, film viewed any and all forms of high culture as potential targets for humor. And cartoons always went further than live-action films, simply because the medium allowed it. While the Hollywood musical's "opera vs. swing" plot archetype poked fun at the traditions associated with classical music, cartoons took violent swings at them, taking each aspect of the concert hall as the spur for a possible gag.

Cartoons differ in the degree to which they juxtapose popular and classical music. Both *Rhapsody Rabbit* and *The Cat Concerto* (MGM; Hanna and Barbera, 1946), cartoons that feature performances of the Second Hungarian Rhapsody by Liszt, refer only momentarily to boogie-woogie or jazz, respectively, before returning to the "proper" music for the setting. Donald Duck's continual interruptions of Mickey and his group in *The Band Concert* (Disney; Jackson, 1935) resemble more the back-and-forth melee of *Long-Haired Hare*. In this case, Donald plays

"Turkey in the Straw" on one instrument, the flute, rather than switch-ing from song to song. This fixation with a single tune, performed in a particularly carefree manner, infuriates Mickey to no end. Nearly all these cartoons end by somehow returning to the original work. A great deal of humor comes from the effort and contortions required to play the final chords, even if the singer, the instruments, or the auditorium has been damaged or destroyed. A triumph over the fugitive influence of more con-temporary sounds remains the ultimate goal.

In *Long-Haired Hare,* only three outward characteristics—his instru-ment, his home in the "country," and his song—were needed to construct Bugs as an anti-aesthete. Playing the banjo places Bugs at a great ideo-logical distance from a classically trained opera singer accompanied by piano; it not only shows Bugs to be a truly rustic (and therefore uncul-tured) musician but also sets him in direct opposition to the singer and the aesthetic values he holds dear. His backwoods location behind Jones's bungalow magnifies his image as a yokel. Bugs also sings his song from memory. The absence of sheet music points to a lack of musi-cal training per se, implying that though Bugs may sing well, his is an unskilled performance. On the other hand, the singer uses scores and what we assume to be years of training to faithfully reproduce the notes of a time-tested aria. Even as the cartoon viciously satirizes the world of clas-sical music, it also implicitly confirms several positive stereotypes about it: professional singers, while stuffy and ridiculous, are trained artists; in contrast, popular singers may have character or charm, but they lack such training and therefore do not deserve the same respect. Bugs sings American popular songs, while Jones's music comes from the western European repertoire, further separating the two ideologically. Levine has shown that the sacralization of music that occurred in the nineteenth cen-tury strengthened Americans' belief that works of "divine inspiration" came not just from the heavens but from Europe.[22] In this cartoon, Gio-vanni Jones serves as the sole representative of all European art music, thereby becoming Bugs's prime target.

INSTRUMENTALISTS AND AUDITORIUMS

The most annoying and satisfying way for Bugs to avenge himself on the opera singer is to strike back at what he holds most dear: his sacred per-formance space. Bugs enters Jones's universe to fight him on his own turf. The rabbit can take on any of the stereotypes of the music world—or all

FIGURE 31 Bobby-soxer Bugs in
Long-Haired Hare.

of them at once, for truly outrageous results—and show the audience (both at the Bowl and in the theater) how ridiculous he thinks they look. The remainder of the story thus takes place at the Hollywood Bowl during what should have been Jones's solo performance with the orchestra. Bugs hits the shell of the Bowl with a sledgehammer (while Jones sings a solo arrangement of the sextet from Donizetti's *Lucia di Lammermoor*), and the reverberations cause Jones to fall off the stage, face-first into a tuba. Bugs sprays Jones's throat with liquid alum, causing the singer's head to shrink to a tenth of its normal size while he is singing on stage. Bugs dresses as a teenage bobby-soxer looking for an autograph from her favorite singer ("Frankie [Sinatra] and Perry [Como] just aren't in it. You're my dreamboat, loverboy, ooh-hoo-hoo-hooooo!"), but in place of a pen offers a stick of dynamite, which blows up in Jones's face (see figure 31). None of these gags rely on stereotypes of the concert hall— they are simply disruptive for their own sake.

   The stories of cartoons that take place in concert halls often revel in the opulence of the sites, especially if those sites are well-known. The Hollywood Bowl is featured in *Long-Haired Hare, Hollywood Bowl* (Lantz; Perkins, 1938), and *Tom and Jerry in the Hollywood Bowl* (MGM; Hanna and Barbera, 1950); as mentioned above, the concert in *Pizzicato Pussycat* takes place in Carnegie Hall. In all these cases, the famous venues are pictured in some detail. *Tom and Jerry in the Hollywood Bowl,* for instance, faithfully depicts the art moderne structure at the bowl's entrance as well as the familiar half-dome itself (see figure 32). These cartoons often involve an entropic story line: a seemingly small interruption of the concert early in the cartoon leads to other problems, until the performance careens into an unstoppable mass of gags. The disintegration into chaos becomes that much more heinous (or hilarious)

FIGURE 32 The entrance to the
Hollywood Bowl in *Tom and Jerry
in the Hollywood Bowl* (MGM;
Hanna and Barbera, 1950).

when it takes place in a much-vaunted location, especially when the building itself is swept into the uproar.

When unusual performance sites are featured in other cartoons, the
humor arises from their incongruous pairing with serious, highbrow music. Even when the venue is unconventional, the internal audience typically treats the occasion with no less and perhaps even more reverence
than it would in a concert hall. *Rhapsody in Rivets* takes place at a construction site, yet all the male spectators applaud the foreman respect-
fully as he steps out with the blueprints, just as if he were a conductor
walking to the podium with the score under his arm. Whether those
watching are indoors or outdoors, urban or provincial, their attitude (if
nothing else about the cartoon) remains serious. The musicologist
Christopher Small calls the concert hall a "sacred space,"[23] but by using
different settings the various shorts demonstrate that the performance
rituals associated with the music, not necessarily the structure itself, can
convey a sense of holiness. Conversely, those buildings that already con-
form to what society expects of concert halls keep their status regardless
of what takes place in them.

Small points out that "one can observe similar patterns of behavior
in other grand ceremonial buildings. . . . All have their initiates and their
outsiders, and from their behavior as they move around the building it
is generally not too difficult to tell who are insiders and who outsiders,
who are privy to its rituals and who are not."[24] In *The Rabbit of Seville*
(Warner Bros.; Jones, 1949), Elmer Fudd's unfamiliarity with concert hall
rituals reveals his lack of cultural savvy. He wanders into an amphithe-
ater while pursuing Bugs, and when the curtain rises with Elmer onstage,
he stands rooted in complete bewilderment. True, almost anyone would
lose composure who suddenly and unexpectedly found him- or herself

FIGURE 33 The musicians in *Baton
Bunny* (Warner Bros.; Jones
and Levitow, 1959).

facing thousands of people. Bugs the performer naturally adapts to the
situation immediately, and he rushes out dressed as a barber—specifically,
the barber of Seville. Elmer's ignorance of operatic conventions works
against him, turning him into a perfect foil for Bugs, who clearly knows
at least something about opera. His knowledge of classical music enables
Bugs to parody it at will.

The orchestral musicians Jones depicts in *Long-Haired Hare,* as well
as in *The Rabbit of Seville* and *Baton Bunny* (1959), have little or no
personality; their instruments become their identity. Indeed, we often see
only the instruments (see figure 33) played by faceless automatons. Small
remarks on a general tendency by those who frequent concert halls to
refer to players by their instruments rather than by name, "as if the instruments were playing themselves."[25] Jones avoids the task of charac-
terizing each individual musician by showing just a portion or even none
of their bodies. In practical terms, showing only certain parts of the players reduces the amount of work spent on portions of a cartoon viewed
as relatively unimportant: the fewer human bodies shown, the less work
for the animators, in-betweeners (who fill in the action between the animators' key drawings), and cel painters.

The orchestra itself offers an enormous variety of possible gags, and
many cartoons by other directors therefore reflect just the opposite approach. These shorts show all the musicians onstage, typically allowing
each a brief solo performance in which to demonstrate musical skill (or
lack thereof). Each instrument's idiosyncrasies can provoke a new throwaway gag, based in its shape, size, or sound; how it is played, held,
fingered, or blown; and any possible similarities that might be emphasized between the appearance of the instrument and that of its player
(tall players on double basses, overweight men on tubas, etc.). Many of

the orchestra-driven cartoons from Lantz, Columbia, and Terry, as well as Warner Bros. and MGM, consist almost entirely of such characterizations matched with the music.[26]

LEOPOLD! THE MYTHIC CONDUCTOR FIGURE

The second half of *Long-Haired Hare* involves both the Hollywood Bowl and its orchestra, but in the extended scene that ends the film the focus is much narrower: the conductor. Giovanni Jones, intent on making it through at least one aria uninterrupted, has a look of determination on his face as the orchestra launches into a furious overture (from von Suppé's *Morning, Noon, and Night in Vienna*). Bugs suddenly appears at the stage door in the orchestra pit, sporting white tie, tails, and a white wig. As he begins to walk slowly to the podium, two of the musicians, at once surprised and horrified, begin whispering "Leopold!" "Leopold!" The rest of the orchestra catches on, and the music dies away instrument by instrument until the silence is absolute. The conductor looks at Bugs and stammers, "Le-Le-Leopold!" before retiring from the podium, stepping down *backward* so as not to turn his back on the maestro. Bugs doesn't bother to give him a hard time; instead, he assumes (and subverts) the conductor's position to further humiliate Jones, now from a lofty vantage point within classical music's hierarchy. (After all, the conductor runs the show, and at the end of the performance bows and receives accolades on behalf of the entire orchestra.) Bugs takes the baton, snaps it in two, and forces Jones into an improvised vocalization that has the singer spanning his entire range and exercising all of his technical skills (see figure 34). Bugs then has Jones hold a painfully long high A. The protracted tone actually brings the Hollywood Bowl crashing down on Jones, as Bugs receives thunderous applause. The cartoon ends with Bugs picking up his banjo and playing a four-note tagline, "Good evening, friends," once more showing that he and his popular music cannot be kept down.

From the moment Bugs appears in the orchestra pit here (and in *Baton Bunny*), he assumes every stereotype ever attributed to a conductor, not just Leopold Stokowski—majestic, fearful, arrogant, and tyrannical. He personifies exactly what the audience expected from a famous conductor of the time.[27] By wearing white tie and tails, Bugs acknowledges one of the most widely recognized symbols of the concert hall: the adherence to a strict code of attire and conduct that preserves the sanctity of the experience. The cartoon's audience would probably have not

FIGURE 34 Bugs takes charge as Stokowski in *Long-Haired Hare*.

blinked if Bugs had led the concert in his usual state of dishabille, yet he explicitly chooses instead to adopt the culturally accepted practice. He dons evening attire because he wants to identify himself as a performer— one of the several reasons, according to Small, why musicians have retained the use of evening wear at all. His pose as the concert's leader, the conductor, further mandates his traditional attire. Michael Barrier notes that by dressing as the conductor, Bugs can take control of the performance rather than simply disrupting it, as before.[28] Bugs also cannot help surrendering part of his will to the power and history his clothing represents. While he cannot, or will not, perform as a "normal" conductor (his goal on the podium, after all, is to torment Jones), he also cannot be himself—his costume, which is in effect a uniform, prohibits it. "People in uniform are behaving not as themselves," Small points out, "but as representatives of the organization whose uniform it is."[29] Bugs the conductor thus becomes a contradictory mixture. Naturally, his inherent wackiness and mischief overshadow his desire to conduct, yet he still leads the concert to a successful conclusion that literally brings down the house.

As Lawrence Levine remarks, many people believe that only a "highly trained professional" has the ability and insight to properly interpret and execute "the intentions of the creators of the divine art."[30] Bugs is clearly ensconced in the world of popular music as the cartoon opens. His embrace of classical music would be that much funnier and more ironic if he took it to the greatest possible extreme, becoming the embodiment of what he has been trying to subvert all along. By assuming Stokowski's persona, Bugs can confidently carry the performance on personality alone; his conducting of Jones relies much more on attitude than on any notion of skill. Because (at least in this cartoon) Bugs is only pretending to be a professional, he eventually leads the performance into chaos. In *Baton Bunny*, Bugs is portrayed as a *real* conductor, and thus the comic confusion there occurs despite his efforts to the contrary.

Why pick on Leopold Stokowski? As one of the most famous American conductors of the twentieth century, his very visible place in the media, particularly in films, made him a target for the Warner Bros. cartoons long before *Fantasia* (Disney, 1940) explicitly associated him with animation. For instance, *She Was an Acrobat's Daughter* (Warner Bros.; Freleng, 1937), which takes place in a contemporary movie palace, features a goofy, thick-accented organist and conductor named "Stickoutski." Stokowski makes a canine cameo as the conductor Bowowski in Warner Bros.' *Hollywood Canine Canteen* (McKimson, 1946; see figure 35). Other Warner Bros. cartoons featuring cameos of him include *Porky at the Crocadero* (Tashlin, 1938), in which Porky briefly imagines himself as the great conductor; *Hollywood Steps Out* (Avery, 1941), a cartoon set at the famous Hollywood nightclub Ciro's, where Stokowski leads a conga with his signature locks in a hairnet (see figure 35); and *Stage Door Cartoon* (Freleng, 1944), a typical Elmer-chasing-Bugs plot that ends with Elmer being thrown out of a vaudeville theater while Bugs, dressed as Stokowski, looks on from the conductor's podium. *Fantasia* only reconfirmed the image of Stokowski as the quintessential longhair, particularly as he does not say anything during the entire two-hour pic-

FIGURE 35 Depictions of Leopold Stokowski in *Hollywood Canine Canteen* (Warner Bros.; McKimson, 1946) and *Hollywood Steps Out* (Warner Bros.; Avery, 1941).

ture. His silence allows his gestures and posturing to speak for him. Perhaps Adorno was thinking of such images of Stokowski when he described a conductor as "an imago, the imago of power, visibly embodied in his prominent figure and striking gestures. . . . Impressed by his medicine-man gestures, the listener thinks it takes just such an attitude to make the players give their artistic best—a best that will be taken for something like the setting of a physical record."[31] Many of Adorno's thoughts on the role of the conductor seem pertinent here, especially because neither Adorno nor the creators of *Long-Haired Hare* seem to have viewed conductors, or many other components of the modern concert hall, in a positive light.[32] Chuck Jones takes these images of Stokowski to heart, making them the essence of Bugs's performance as "Leopold." Once Bugs's masquerade begins, the mystification of the classical performance becomes much more explicit.

Bugs sends two related messages to Jones when he breaks the conductor's baton: he will not be constricted by a conventional conductor's tool, and the music that he gets out of the singer will be what *he* wants. In breaking the baton, Bugs symbolically calls Jones out, in essence threatening retaliation for the earlier abuses he endured from Jones. In addition, using his hands to conduct after casting off the baton is only one of Stokowski's idiosyncrasies that Bugs appropriates. This portrayal does not mock Stokowski: in fact, it attributes superhuman qualities to his conducting. In the final extended gag, Bugs's gloved hand waves unceasingly, forcing Jones to carry a continuous high note. The sound becomes so painful that Bugs abandons the stage to send away for earmuffs, leaving behind the glove that continues to float in midair and demand more from the singer. The gag lampoons the public's notion that Stokowski's hands were instruments unto themselves; fascination with them arose in the early 1930s, not long after he had all but given up the use of a baton.[33]

Bugs, not Jones, shows that the music is really not as important as the performance, an approach to conducting that Adorno referred to as "histrionics at the podium."[34] Through his actions as conductor, and specifically his hand motions, Bugs can "play" Jones, eliciting an improvised and yet virtuoso performance from the singer. We don't know what piece Jones would have sung had Bugs not interrupted the concert, but it doesn't matter. Jones's training enables him somehow to decode Bugs's gestures sufficiently well to follow along. Bugs's power further extends to the audience, as Barrier points out: "When the concertgoers respond with applause, Bugs conducts *them*, too, instantly silencing their applause with a gesture."[35] Chuck Jones thus presents us another stereotype: a conductor whose ability to command his surroundings is so great that he can control the orchestra *and* the audience equally well.

Such control, according to Adorno, can actually interfere with the performance: "The conductor's figure comes to be the one that acts directly on the audience; at the same time his own music-making too is necessarily estranged from the audience, since he himself is not playing. He thus becomes an actor who plays a musician, and precisely that conflicts with a proper performance."[36] Adorno clearly is attacking the charlatanism of conductors; he also brings to the surface the marked distance between the musicians and members of the audience. As a conduit between the two groups, Bugs the conductor wields a tremendous amount of power. In leading the performance, Bugs becomes a locus of power and creativity, the path through which the sensibilities of his world—anarchy and wackiness—invade the staid realm of the concert.[37]

Bugs can assume control of the performance in part because he has no regard for the understood course of events in a concert hall and does not adhere to any conventional program. Cartoon characters, who lack a commitment to what the music critic Simon Frith calls a "script or a routinized social situation,"[38] are not bound to preset roles in the concert hall. Viewers are fully aware of this freedom: the sight of a cartoon character in such a setting creates an immediate incongruity. Such incongruity involving real characters often gives rise to a sense of embarrassment; with cartoon characters, we instead wait for the fugitive element implicit in every animated individual to erupt and somehow derail the performance.

An extreme form of the conductor's contribution to the performance is portrayed in *Magical Maestro* (MGM; Avery, 1952), another cartoon

FIGURE 36   Magic runs amok in *Magical Maestro* (MGM; Avery, 1952).

built around "Largo al Factotum." A lowly magician seeks to join in the
performance of a famous opera singer (Poochini). Rejected by the singer,
the magician replaces the true conductor by stealing his tails, his bouf-
fant, Stokowski-styled hair, and his red nose with three waves of a magic
wand, and proceeds to wreak havoc on Poochini's performance. Recall
that in *Long-Haired Hare*, as Bugs unintentionally compels Giovanni
Jones to sing popular music, the singer is able to maintain some of his
composure as a performer by not breaking character. Similarly, musical
continuity is maintained in *Rhapsody Rabbit:* when a boogie-woogie interlude interrupts the Hungarian Rhapsody, Bugs quickly squelches it.
The magician/conductor in *Magical Maestro*, however, deliberately dis-
rupts Poochini's performance, relying on the wand/baton he wields as
the site of his power. Instead of letting the music pass through him to the
audience, this conductor takes the upper hand and repeatedly forces the
musician to perform against his will. Every time the magician points his
wand/baton at Poochini, he asserts his power dramatically: the rabbits
that assist the magician appear magically at the singer's side; the singer,
his costume, and his song are completely and instantaneously transformed; and so on (see figure 36).[39]

As in *Long-Haired Hare,* the antics of the magician/conductor in *Magical Maestro* make visible a class struggle, played out in the songs that appear throughout the cartoon. An entire musical revue and magic show passes before the audience as they watch the singer bounce from classical to blues to classical to country and back again to classical. Some of the songs are "A Tiskit, a Tasket" (performed by the singer in a little boy's sailor suit, complete with red balloon), "Mama yo quiero" (in the voice, outfit, and headdress of Carmen Miranda), and "My Darlin' Clementine" (in the western attire of a square-dance caller, complete with chaps), and there are several ethnic interludes (Chinese, Pacific Islander) as well. In both cartoons, the superiority of classical music to popular music is constantly challenged; but in *Magical Maestro,* the attack on classical music is mounted *inside* the concert hall, where it should reign supreme. Of course, the powers of a magician are required to succeed in such an enterprise. Popular music had already made its first inroads into high-art strongholds (the 1938 and 1939 Carnegie Hall revues of gospel, jazz, and blues in the series "From Spirituals to Swing" come to mind), and its appearances in such venues were growing more regular—a state of affairs commented on by the cartoon. We unfortunately don't see how the audience reacts to the various songs (with the exception of one man, who seems to hate Poochini no matter what he is singing).

The conductor may lead the performance, but the action in *Magical Maestro* suggests he is not immune to the slapstick behavior occurring elsewhere in the hall. His position as leader and occasional disciplinarian makes him all the more ripe for ridicule. Several cartoons use this theme, including *The Mad Maestro* (MGM; Harman, 1939), *Tom and Jerry in the Hollywood Bowl,* and *Baton Bunny*—as well as parts of *Pigs in a Polka* (Warner Bros.; Freleng, 1943), *A Corny Concerto* (Warner Bros.; Clampett, 1943), and *Carmen Get It!* (MGM; Deitch, 1962). In each of these shorts, the conductor's stand is the point from which chaos and entropy flow. Yet all of them combined could not overcome the order and majesty attributed to the conductor and his control over music in *Fantasia.*

DISNEY AND *FANTASIA*

Disney released *Fantasia* in 1940, at the full flowering of what the composer and critic Virgil Thomson called the "music appreciation racket."[40] *Fantasia,* which is probably the most ambitious attempt in the history of film (animated or otherwise) to integrate classical music into the medium, provides a decidedly positive view of both the culture of the concert hall and the people who make its music. *Fantasia*'s reception is important because of its position, even to this day, as the preeminent animated film about music and classical music culture. It also shows us how one studio used animation to glorify classical music, instead of seeking to tear it down.

Joseph Horowitz observes that a favorite topic for American and English cinema in the early and mid–twentieth century was "suave or tempestuous embodiments of charismatic longhairs";[41] such films idolized composers, pianists, violinists, opera singers, the concert hall life, and even the music itself, in a sometimes not-too-oblique attempt at cinematic music appreciation. Animation made it possible to create illustrated stories for each piece of music. *Fantasia*'s technological achievements—particularly Fantasound, a multichannel recording process and broadcasting system that predated surround sound by a decade[42]—also won the Disney studio new prestige, as it brought the classics into the world of more mainstream entertainment with impressive success.

At the same time, this fixation on classical music's place in society alienated many viewers and was one of the factors that led to the film's near failure in its initial release.[43] Those responsible for that emphasis, as well as for choosing the pieces used in the film, were clearly Walt Disney and Leopold Stokowski (Robin Allan calls them "two showmen with equally powerful egos").[44] Disney knew the risks in making classical music the film's focus, but he proceeded with the project because, as Barrier notes, *Fantasia*'s "highbrow associations . . . might bring him even greater prestige than *Snow White* had."[45]

Audiences have enjoyed *Fantasia,* in time making it a classic of American animation; yet the film has never been perceived as anything more than a popular appropriation of classical music, despite its "highbrow associations" and aspirations. Because of its medium, it drew scathing censure from music and film critics alike for cheapening and popularizing the classics. Not all held a negative view, however. Harold Rawlinson acknowledged the concern, commenting, "Good music will demand a good film. Do not vulgarize a masterpiece by fitting a frivolous idea. First-class poetry requires first-class music—and we must not cheapen another man's work." Yet, he argued, Disney's explicit respect for the canon enabled him to avoid that pitfall: "Such works as a Beethoven Symphony and Moussorgsky's 'A Night on a Bare Mountain' were not cheapened by being the inspiration of Disney's work."[46]

Fantasia, which used the featured music as the seed for an audiovisual ballet, differed in two important ways from the cartoons discussed above (such as those produced by Warner Bros.), which more often took the music as a point of comic departure: the Disney name and the animated film's length (two hours). Both forced reviewers to take *Fantasia* seriously as either an assault on or a well-intentioned tribute to the canon, and most leaned toward the former position. Animated shorts clearly lacked the power and draw of a Disney feature; they were largely perceived as throwaway comic filler, which any theater across the country could show or shelve as it pleased.[47] This lack of prestige may in fact have benefited the shorts, enabling them to fly mostly under the radar of any cultural critics who might otherwise have objected to their treatment of the classics. No cartoon, spoofing the classics or not, could expect more coverage than a blurb in a film exhibitor's daily. For example:

"CAT CONCERTO": SUPERB FANTASY

M-G-M's Academy Award–winning Tom and Jerry cartoon in which Tom turns concert pianist. With a beautifully satiric rendering of Liszt's 2nd Hungarian Rhapsody, Tom and Jerry perform an assortment of didoes that are guaranteed to leave the most phlegmatic moviegoer helpless in the aisles. Beginning wonderfully straightlaced, the reel runs only a short distance before Jerry booby-traps the piano into remarkably clever situations. Film winds up to a socko finish with Tom a quivering wreck slumped shirtless over the keyboard, and the victorious Jerry proudly taking bows from the top of the piano.[48]

The anonymous commentator sums up the cartoon's thrust in one word: satire. Nothing more is said about the music, and for good reason: these cartoons are meant to entertain, and the "review" was simply intended to sell the short to prospective customers (theater owners or managers).

Unlike animated shorts, *Fantasia* was the subject of countless reviews and critical essays in magazines from *Ladies' Home Journal* to the *Etude.*[49] The writers often remarked on Disney's approach to the classics, his method of combining music and image, and even his dedication to children's entertainment. Disney and Stokowski, who felt very strongly that America's youth needed to be educated about classical music, took seriously the story told by each segment—even "The Dance of the Hours," which features dancing crocodiles and hippopotami. Disney's reverence for the canon is demonstrated by his studio's many thoughtfully developed artistic interpretations of such works. He may also have hoped that *Fantasia* would become a useful tool of those supporting music appreciation. The combination of animation (including the most famous cartoon character of the time, Mickey Mouse, in his own musical sequence) and classical music might appeal greatly to children, thereby helping music educators to shore up their position against the ever-growing interest in swing, race records, and other forms of popular music.

Disney apparently tried in *Fantasia* to protect classical music from being degraded by popular culture. His aim proved difficult to achieve, as animation, no matter how lofty its high-art aesthetic aspirations, was never seen by the public as anything but pop culture. Disney's later films present the classics with greater flexibility, if not downright satire. The film historian Harry Benshoff points out that *Make Mine Music* (1946) and *Melody Time* (1948) "turn away markedly from classical music to embrace more popular musical modes such as jazz and big band. When classical music is used, it is tempered with voice-over narration (as in Prokofiev's 'Peter and the Wolf') or burlesqued outright (hear Nelson Eddy as 'Willie the Whale')—both examples from *Make Mine Music*."[50] Not until the release of *Fantasia 2000* (2000) would the studio focus its attention as pointedly on classical music as it had done in *Fantasia*.

By the time *Fantasia 2000* arrived, notions of the canon had shifted drastically. In *Fantasia*, popular music appeared only in a short interlude involving some of the orchestra's musicians. As they retake the stage after the film's intermission and begin to tune up, a contrabass player takes up a snatch of melody from Beethoven's Pastoral Symphony and turns it into a jazzy bass line. A clarinetist plays an upbeat tune, and soon all the violins and several other instruments join in—that is, until Deems Taylor returns, at which point everyone abruptly stops (except the clarinetist, whom Taylor has to quiet by discreetly clearing his throat). In this case, the jam session is brief and accidental, perhaps the fault of some of the younger musicians who can't leave the less serious stuff outside the concert hall. Significantly, the jazz-inspired riff was on Beethoven, making it one of dozens of tunes from the time that jazzed the classics. Thus even the paltry fifty seconds of contemporary music in *Fantasia* drew its inspiration from the canon. Sixty years later, popular music had a much stronger hold in the *Fantasia* franchise: *Fantasia 2000* dedicated a segment to Gershwin's *Rhapsody in Blue,* complete with an introduction by Quincy Jones. While *Fantasia* was hosted by two stars of the classical music world (Deems Taylor and Leopold Stokowski), *Fantasia 2000* was introduced by prominent entertainers associated with Hollywood, including Steve Martin, Penn and Teller, and Bette Midler. Apparently classical music was no longer off-limits to movie, music, and other popular culture icons—or perhaps the Disney folks hoped that people would simply come to see their favorite stars and the brilliant animation, regardless of the music featured.

One area of high-art music was left untouched by both *Fantasia* films but singled out for special attention by every cartoon studio: opera, the subject of the next chapter.

5

What's Opera, Doc? and Cartoon Opera

The visual, dramatic, and musical trappings of nineteenth-century opera have become a standard reference point for animated cartoons, and thus no understanding of the battle between classic and cartoon is complete without an examination of opera. Dozens of possible cartoons might be considered, but the best-known example is *What's Opera, Doc?* (Warner Bros., 1957), Chuck Jones's interpretation of Wagner's operatic universe. Disney's *Fantasia* takes a long look at classical music, loving and serious; *What's Opera, Doc?* instead takes *on* classical music. This cartoon and others like it have helped form a new cultural concept of opera, an awareness built on comic appropriations of the form rather than on the operas themselves (see figure 37). A detailed analysis of *What's Opera, Doc?* is the central focus of this final chapter, which also briefly reviews the history of films about opera and the persistent use of Wagner's music in film and cartoon scores. We will consider the animated influences on Jones's story, as well as the short's musical, dramatic, and technical elements.

The score for *What's Opera, Doc?* uses musical conventions from late-nineteenth-century Romantic music and cites melodies from more than a half-dozen different Wagner operas. The screenplay's rapidly changing plot points embrace a complicated collection of generalizations about opera, specifically those associated with Wagner (mythology, magic, love, and fantastic, otherworldly settings). Wagner's concept of the *Gesamtkunstwerk*—the "total artwork," fusing together and giving equal weight to the poetry, the music, and the staging—is here approached from a modern (or perhaps postmodern) angle. In fact, animation offers the perfect medium for realizing Wagner's hopes for a *Gesamtkunstwerk*, since it sets no physical bounds to the animator's creativity. This cartoon not only represents a total work of art but aspires to sum up the totality of Wagner's artworks in a *single* serving. The creators preserved what

FIGURE 37 Robb Armstrong, *Jump Start*, July 2, 2001. Reprinted by permission of United Feature Syndicate, Inc.

they perceived as the most important ideas, both musical and dramatic, thereby allowing Jones to take, as he put it, "14 hours of *The Ring of the Niebelungen* and reduce it to six minutes."[1]

Despite the fact that he was producing a cartoon, Jones, along with the cartoon's writer, Michael Maltese, approached Wagner carefully. Jones once explained, "Many cartoons using classical music have failed because they don't take the music seriously enough. I always felt that Bugs and Elmer were trying to do the opera right."[2] Jones also told me, "We didn't want people to laugh at the music, we wanted them to laugh at what was interpreted by Bugs and Elmer. . . . It seemed to me that we were paying great respect to the music itself, but we're saying that if you put a bunch of clowns in front of it, it will be a lot different."[3] His sentiment may have been noble, but we will see that *What's Opera, Doc?* actually stands as a testament to what Jones *believed* he knew of Wagner and opera. Dramatically and musically, Jones established a specific set of criteria that he felt needed to be met in order to have a complete opera.[4] He constructed the cartoon out of a hodgepodge of famous tunes with familiar plot devices, taking the most familiar parts from the whole of the composer's dramatic oeuvre, and poured them into the shell of Wagner's single most famous work: the *Ring* cycle.

CHARACTERISTICS OF OPERA AND ANIMATION

Opera has always been an easy target for Hollywood cartoons—almost too easy. Its combination of music and drama, set in distant or even mythical places and featuring characters who often dressed in outlandish costumes as they sang in other languages (frequently about ultra-romantic situations), presented fertile material for satire. The cartoons simply import the dramatic situations and music and then commence with the comedic treatment, leaving intact only the barest framework of the original. The public's familiarity with operatic stereotypes ensures that audiences get the gags, which rely on generalizations about opera and opera singers. Simply placing opera into an animated medium is intrinsically humorous, because it violates cultural tradition—we laugh at the juxtaposition of high and low. As the cartoons added their (sometimes not so) gentle commentary on operatic conventions, the almost absurdly serious nature of the dramatic form became even funnier.

Such opera parodies are not purely in the domain of cartoons. In fact, probably the most successful large-scale spoof on opera in the twentieth century is the Marx Brothers' 1935 film *A Night at the Opera,* which juxtaposes action on and off the opera stage. As this and other comedies constantly parodied cultural ideals, they created, as Lawrence Levine says, "a rapport with their audiences that generated a sense of complicity in their common stand against the pretensions of the patrons of high culture."[5] Cartoon characters work with the same sense of narrative logic as the Marx Brothers; when Bugs Bunny and other characters enter the opera house they inevitably bring along the outside world, and their injections of popular culture during performances create a string of culture clashes that grow in intensity throughout the short. (We have already seen such a collision of worlds in *Long-Haired Hare,* discussed in chapter 4.) *What's Opera, Doc?* is a notable exception to this pattern, for it takes place within an understood universe of Wagnerian opera; thus the *only* music that exists for anyone—including Bugs, whom we expect to transgress the highbrow conventions of the story—is Wagner's.

Film parodies usually refer to particular operas and arias, and often feature actual opera stars playing either themselves or fictitious characters. Nearly all cartoons are less specific in their approach to opera, in part because many of the writers and directors had only a superficial knowledge of the subject.[6] The directors Bill Hanna and Joe Barbera (both at MGM), as well as Chuck Jones (Warner Bros.), have all stated in their respective autobiographies that they had little background in music and often left decisions about it to their writers or even the composers.[7] Such ignorance may well have worked to their advantage: rather than focusing on details, the cartoon director relies on familiar references and broad, sweeping generalizations to create humor based on stereotypes. Moreover, general ignorance of opera may add to its cultural authority; the musicologist Jeremy Tambling argues that "where opera is only very imprecisely known about, its myth-making powers seem further ensured in terms of promoting images of taste and the good life."[8] For Jones and others, the idea of opera probably was inextricably bound to notions of high art and the upper classes. These associations may explain why the Warner Bros. cartoons that involve opera almost always are set in the opera house, creating an image of that stage and hall as a sacred space (albeit one that must be assaulted), while the music itself does not really matter . . . so long as it's Italian.

The predominance of Italian opera (in particular, bel canto—literally, "beautiful" or "fine singing," an operatic style of the late eighteenth and early nineteenth centuries that is typified by Rossini, Donizetti, and Bellini) marks another idiosyncrasy of opera in cartoons. Tambling explains that films privileged Italian operas because of the tunefulness of their arias, duets, and choruses.[9] These same films eschewed Wagner because the vocal lines lacked such catchy tunes. Conversely, while Rossini and Donizetti have singable, memorable phrases in their bel canto arias, those composers are no match for Wagner when it comes to creating short motifs in the orchestral accompaniment, and Wagner is a favorite in cartoons as well as in films for underscore cues. David Huckvale notes that "the appeal of Wagner's nonvocal or orchestrally arranged music has always been considerable."[10]

Cartoon characters often sing in the opera's original language, if for no other reason than the inherent added humor: a cartoon animal singing opera is funny, and a cartoon animal singing in a foreign tongue is funnier still. In *One Froggy Evening* (Warner Bros.; Jones, 1955), for example, the main character, Michigan J. Frog, sings the beginning of "Largo al Factotum" in a public park for his owner, who cannot seem to convince anyone that he can sing at all. The majestic, even brassy voice that comes out of the frog's mouth is a far cry from what we expect to hear. This enormous voice becomes one of the short's fundamental comic devices. Joe Adamson, in a biography of Walter Lantz, describes a similar scene in a Woody Woodpecker cartoon, *Barber of Seville* (Lantz; Culhane, 1944): "Woody just launches straight into the 'Largo al factotum' from *The Barber of Seville*—no translation, no motivation, no explanation. He suddenly becomes a musical purist . . . and the effect is funny."[11] By using opera in its original *foreign* tongue, the cartoon also highlights the vast cultural distance between the music and the cartoon itself. A "serious" performance of an aria in a short—that is, overdubbed in Italian by a professional opera singer, as was done in *One Froggy Evening* and in Tex Avery's *Magical Maestro* (MGM, 1952)—sets up the audi-

ence for the disintegration that inevitably follows. Such respectful treatment of the original cannot go unchallenged; indeed, veneration of the
original exponentially increases the chances that the performance will
go awry. In this respect as well, *What's Opera, Doc?* defies the norms established by other cartoons, presenting a story that is funny without
sacrificing the integrity of the opera's narrative.

THE STORY: ELMER CHASES BUGS, WAGNER STYLE

Part of the unique standing that *What's Opera, Doc?* holds in the animation world is due to its being one of the few complete operatic parodies, beginning and ending in the narrative space of an operatic drama.[12]
It is also the only cartoon to deal exclusively with Wagner.[13]

Following the main title music and the appearance of the Warner Bros.
shield to the tune of "The Merry-Go-Round Broke Down," the cartoon
begins with a shot of a set of theater curtains surrounding its title (see
figure 38). Two more title cards follow with the primary credits; in this
sequence of less than thirty seconds we hear various instruments of an
orchestra tuning, including snatches of Wagnerian leitmotifs. The screen
goes blank for a moment, before a tremendous storm rages, with the shadows of an unseen pair of hands seemingly conducting nature's fury. We
then see the silhouette of an ominous figure to whom the hands belong—
a horned fiend that appears to loom over the surrounding mountains (see
figure 39).[14] The overture for *The Flying Dutchman* is played in a faith-
ful rendition by a full orchestra. (In fact, as we will see below, all of the
music in this short appears in its natural state, that is, fully orchestrated
in the Wagnerian style.) The camera pans downward to reveal the horned
creature as Elmer Fudd, wearing Viking helmet, body armor, and carrying a spear. He admonishes us to "Be vewy quiet—I'm hunting wabbits!"
(see music example 8). As he says "hunting wabbits," he turns his head
upward and his arms move to either side in the first of many parodies
on the stances struck by opera singers as they act.

As he looks over hill and dale, a different kernel of the Valkyrie leitmotif underscores each sequence of steps in a series of pseudo-balletic
gestures. Discovering "wabbit twacks," Elmer rushes over to a rabbit
hole and begins stabbing in his spear while yelling "Kill the wabbit!" to
the tune of the Valkyrie leitmotif (see figure 40). Bugs sticks out his head
from a nearby hole, repeating in disbelief "Kill the wabbit?" Elmer continues his assault on the first hole, yelling "Yo-ho-to-ho!" until Bugs walks
up and asks him, "Oh, mighty warrior of great fighting stock, / might I

Be ve-wy qui - et   I'm hunt-ing wa-bbits

EXAMPLE 8 Melody for "Be vewy quiet—I'm hunting wabbits!"

FIGURE 38 Title card of *What's Opera, Doc?* (Warner Bros.; Jones, 1957).

FIGURE 39 Elmer, the mighty hunter, in *What's Opera, Doc?*

enquire to ask / what's up, doc?" After Elmer reiterates, "I'm going to kill that wabbit," Bugs answers: "Oh, mighty warrior 'twill be quite a task / how will you do it, might I enquire to ask?" Elmer shows off his magical hardware, singing, "I will do it with my spear and magic helmet." "Spear and magic helmet?" Bugs replies. Elmer demonstrates the helmet's power by destroying the tree Bugs is standing under with a bolt of lightning, sending Bugs running for the hills, with a "Bye!" reminiscent of Martha Raye.

Elmer runs after Bugs (with music from *Rienzi* underscoring the chase)

FIGURE 40 Elmer in a rage in *What's Opera, Doc?*

until he spies a "new" character on the scene. Bugs, dressed in a pink top and sporting blond braids, eye shadow, and false lashes, reappears at the top of a hill lounging on the back of an enormous white horse. The horse begins to gallop down the hill, and we see that Elmer, stricken with love, cannot take his eyes away from Bugs. When the horse reaches him, Elmer sings: "Oh Bwunhilda, you're so lovely" (see music example 9). They then dance a brief ballet together (to the Venusberg music), culminating in Bugs running up a hill topped by a neoclassical, Greek-inspired structure with white columns, where he lies on a large couch and begins to sing (to the tune of the "Pilgrims' Chorus") the love duet "Return My Love" (see figure 41):

> *Elmer:* Return my love, a longing burns deep inside me.
> *Bugs:* Return my love, I want you always beside me.
> *Elmer:* Love like ours must be.
> *Bugs:* Made for you and for me.
> *Duet:* Return, won't you return my love; oh, my love is yours.

The song ends with a magnificent crescendo, just as Bugs's wig falls off and Elmer realizes he has been fooled. Bugs rushes off (losing the rest of his costume along the way) as slowly building timpani indicate Elmer's rising anger. As the skies go purple and red, he bellows out, "I'll kill the wabbit! Arise storms! Lightning! Earthquakes! Hurricanes! SMOG! Strike lightning! Strike the wabbit!" With these final words (accompanied once more by the *Dutchman* overture) bolts of lightning level the distant mountains. As Elmer runs over to see the results, we find Bugs lying motionless, his hand poised dramatically over his head, a beam of sunlight breaking through the clouds to illuminate him. Overhead, a flower, whose stem was broken in the melee, slowly drops watery tears

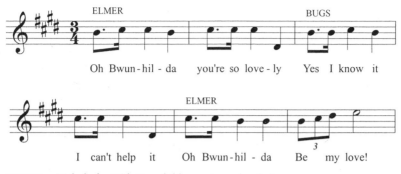

Oh Bwun-hil-da   you're so love-ly   Yes I know it

I can't help it   Oh Bwun-hil-da   Be my love!

EXAMPLE 9 Melody for "Oh Bwunhilda, you're so lovely."

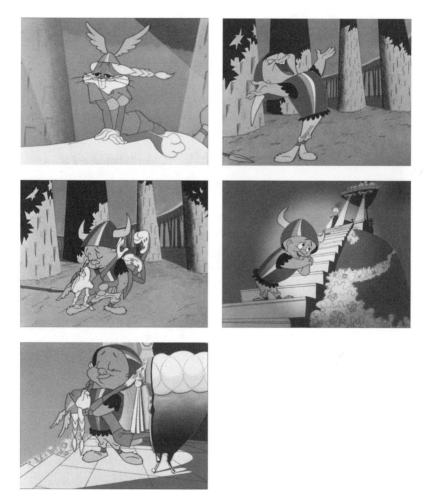

FIGURE 41 Love duet and ballet in *What's Opera, Doc?*

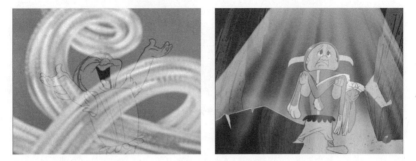

FIGURE 42 Elmer mad and then sad in *What's Opera, Doc?*

on the seemingly fallen hero. Stricken, Elmer exclaims, "What have I done? I've killed the wabbit! Poor little bunny, poor little wabbit . . ." He begins carrying Bugs off into the distance as the instrumental strains of the "Pilgrims' Chorus" are once more heard (see figure 42). Just as all seems lost, Bugs holds up his head, turns to face the audience, and proclaims, "Well, what did you *expect* in an opera? A *happy* ending?"

WAGNER'S PRESENCE IN FILM AND CARTOON MUSIC

Anyone seeking to create a thorough satire of opera for an American audience needed to look no further than Richard Wagner, who already during his lifetime was an icon of the opera world. *What's Opera, Doc?* cites a half-dozen operas, but much of the action centers on an extended excerpt from *Tannhäuser*, refashioned into the love duet and ballet interlude between Bugs and Elmer. Reverence for Wagner's music in general reached almost cultlike proportions in the United States in the late nineteenth century, and in his history of Wagner's American reception Joseph Horowitz shows that *Tannhäuser* enjoyed a particular distinction: its finale is the first piece of Wagner's music known to have been performed in the United States, in November 1852, and when it opened at the Bowery Theatre in New York on 4 April 1859 it became the first of his operas to receive a complete staging in the country.[15] Overtures are often excerpted from operas for concert performances, because they are relatively short, are tuneful, and require no vocalists or even instrumental soloists. More than a century after his music premiered in the United States, Wagner still ranked among the top six composers whose work is performed by American symphony orchestras (after Beethoven, Brahms, Tchaikowsky, Mozart, and Johann Strauss), and the *Tannhäuser* overture remained his most frequently heard piece.[16]

According to Horowitz, Wagner entered American popular culture through two routes: band music and film scores, both forms of entertainment that provided the sounds of Wagner to listeners without any "high-cultural uplift."[17] At the end of the nineteenth century, military-style bands were found throughout the nation, in small and large communities alike. Their conductors all looked to the preeminent bandleader in the country, John Philip Sousa, for repertoire suggestions; what Sousa played, the country played.[18] Wagner topped Sousa's list of favorite composers, and his band drew on numerous arrangements of Wagner's works. The band performances took Wagner's music out of its original context; and when excerpted for use in film scores, Horowitz shows, its excision from its place within the *Gesamtkunstwerk* was even more radical.[19] Selections from Wagner operas appear frequently in manuals for accompanists of silent film, with each piece meant to convey a different mood or emotion through music. For example, Wagner's name is listed in Erno Rapée's *Encyclopedia* under all sorts of descriptive headings, from neutral andantes to wedding music.[20] Both band and film music exposed listeners to a wide variety of composers and musical genres in settings that carried none of the specific cultural associations of the concert hall.

Wagner's music appears in cartoons from the beginning of the sound era onward.[21] Consider the scores of Carl Stalling, whose approach to classical music and general style were widely emulated in all the studios (see chapter 1). A significant portion of the classical music in his scores was Wagner's, especially in the Warner Bros. cartoons. During Stalling's twenty-plus years at Warner Bros., Wagner cues appear in 120 different cartoons. The specific selections break down as follows:

Lohengrin ("Bridal Chorus")	22 cartoons
Rienzi overture	21 cartoons
Tannhäuser overture	16 cartoons
Twilight of the Gods	16 cartoons
The Valkyrie	15 cartoons
The Flying Dutchman	10 cartoons
The Rhinegold	8 cartoons
Parsifal	4 cartoons
Siegfried	4 cartoons
The Mastersingers of Nuremberg	2 cartoons[22]

Not only was Wagner often used in cartoons, but his instrumental music was clearly preferred. Though drawn from his operas, it is primarily symphonic rather than vocal in nature. This bias displayed by Stalling reflects not only the general preference mentioned above but his own background. As a musical director in theaters Stalling was responsible for *all* music played during each show, which could go on for three hours or more; some days the shows ran back to back for almost half a day. Wagner had a formidable presence in Stalling's musical library in a variety of forms, notably excerpts arranged for organ and similar extracts orchestrated for a typical theater orchestra of winds, brass, a few strings, and keyboard. Stalling's experiences with this music in his early film days likely predisposed him to use the same pieces for dramatic purposes in later years.[23]

Because of his background as a film accompanist, Stalling reflexively took advantage of the cultural significance of the music he used to tell the story. In *Captain Hareblower* (Warner Bros.; Freleng, 1954), for instance, the Dutchman motif from *The Flying Dutchman* was meant to create a notion of danger on the high seas, not just through the illustrative nature of the music itself but also through its evocation of Wagner's opera. Just as J. C. Breil used "The Ride of the Valkyries" to accompany the "heroic" ride of the Ku Klux Klan in D. W. Griffith's *The Birth of a Nation* (1915), so Stalling quotes Wagner, knowing well the audience's familiarity with such music and using it to his advantage.

Warner Bros. was not the only cartoon studio to focus on Wagner. Fifteen years before *What's Opera, Doc?*, the Disney studio devised an animated scene based on *The Valkyrie* to be used in *Fantasia*. (Disney had originally planned to update *Fantasia* following its original release by replacing sections of the film with new musical sequences.) According to the film historian Robin Allan, more than a hundred sketches created in 1941 for an animated sequence on "The Ride of the Valkyries" show "the descent of the Valkyries from the clouds and their conducting of slain warriors to Valhalla." Walt Disney planned to address the music seriously; in a story conference he warned, "You'll get embarrassing animation if you get Brunnhilde up there mugging, or one of those things." The director of the sequence, Sam Armstrong, had intended to base the sequence on the imagery of traditional Norse mythology rather than the purely Germanic Wagnerian version.[24] Within a year, however, the United States was fully embroiled in World War II, and the presence in film of Wagner's music took on an entirely new, politicized meaning.

THE PREHISTORY OF *WHAT'S OPERA, DOC?*:
CARTOONS AND WORLD WAR II

During World War II, several Hollywood animation studios (Warner Bros., Disney, MGM, Lantz) produced cartoons for the U.S. government to use in the war effort as training films; every studio took issues surrounding the war as fodder to inspire new stories, often used to entertain the soldiers overseas.[25] As noted in chapter 1, German and Japanese characters were frequently humiliated in cartoons from all the studios.[26] Numerous cartoons from this period did more than refer to the enemy: they were specifically intended to depict the Axis powers not just as the enemies of good but also as disagreeable, shifty, bumbling, and ridiculous in every possible way.

For the Nazis, Stalling provided several themes; the most commonly used song was "Ach du lieber Augustin." Often Stalling transformed the chorus, with its "oom-pah-pah" feel, into a kind of ridiculous waltz, whose sound rendered the Nazis less menacing by making them look (and sound) foolish.[27] Stalling also used Wagner's music, as well as selections from Johann Strauss, to represent Nazis. What seems to me an obvious choice—Beethoven's Fifth Symphony—for the Nazis is not used, possibly because the main four-note motif had been appropriated as a musical signature for the Allied efforts.[28]

One of the Warner Bros. wartime cartoons that deals specifically with the Nazis and Germany, *Herr Meets Hare* (Freleng, 1945), is a significant precursor to *What's Opera, Doc?* and a source for much of its visual imagery, in particular the ballet sequence featuring Bugs in drag. The film begins as Bugs has made one of his inevitable "wrong turn[s] at Albuquerque"; this time it lands him in Germany's Black Forest, where he meets none other than Hermann Göring, taking a break from the war by going hunting (in lederhosen, in case we forgot he is German). Bugs disguises himself as Hitler, but when Göring realizes the subterfuge, Bugs runs off, only to reenter the scene wearing a wig (yellow hair with long braids down the back), sporting a Viking-style helmet, and riding a white steed (unmistakably a Clydesdale) that almost prances in, accompanied by the main melody of the "Pilgrims' Chorus" from *Tannhäuser.* Seeing Bugs/Brünnhilde, Göring zips off screen and rushes back dressed in a long brown loincloth and his own Viking helmet (whose horns grow in size, becoming quite erect, as the Nazi eyes his companion lecherously; see figure 43).[29] The two then dance—not to Wagner but to two Viennese waltzes by Johann Strauss: "Vienna Life" and "You and You," the latter from *Die Fledermaus.*

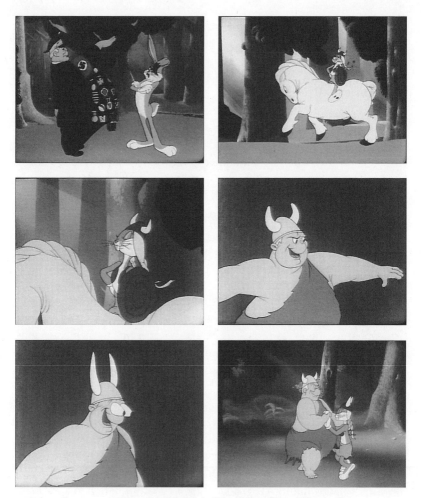

FIGURE 43 Bugs meets Hermann Göring in *Herr Meets Hare* (Warner Bros.; Freleng, 1945).

Bugs's entry onto the scene, as he rides a large white horse while dressed as Brünnhilde, shows up fundamentally unchanged in *What's Opera, Doc?:* the music and much of the staging stay the same. When Bugs and Göring dance together, however, their waltz is almost slapstick, unlike the refined ballet performed by Bugs and Elmer in *What's Opera, Doc?* A dance between Bugs and an admirer appears in both films, but with radically different motivations. Göring, lost in the moment, simply follows Bugs's lead; Elmer and Bugs, in the midst of an artistic performance, enact some of the cultural expectations for such a presentation. Jones did not formally acknowledge the influence of *Herr Meets Hare* on his Wagnerian exploration, although similarities between the two can be at least partially attributed to Michael Maltese's role as writer for both shorts. Perhaps it was in part to distance himself from Freleng's earlier short as well as to inject his own sensibility into the story that Jones created a parody of the opera world itself in his cartoon, focusing only on the performers and the performance and forgoing any references to the composer, conductor, musicians (except for the tuning at the beginning), or audience. Production notes from *What's Opera, Doc?* reveal that several gags that might have more clearly differentiated the two stories were not used. For instance, after Bugs flees from his first encounter with Elmer, the story sketches indicate that Bugs was to steal Elmer's magic helmet and conjure a small storm with it, only to have Elmer sneak up and quickly repossess it. Immediately after this interaction, Bugs would dress as Brünnhilde and toy with Elmer for a while before beginning the love duet.[30]

Though *What's Opera, Doc?* appeared more than a decade after the end of World War II, it is possible that the cartoon contained implicit criticism of Germany in addition to its undisguised satire on opera and high-art music. Through its association with Hitler and Nazi Germany, Wagner's music had become something to fear, something to hate—Leni Riefenstahl's use of *The Mastersingers* in *Triumph of the Will* (1935) was simply one of the more explicit instances of a connection made between Wagner and Hitler in film.[31] In *Herr Meets Hare,* the director clearly intended *all* of the German references as a comment against Hitler, the Nazis, and Germany as a whole, and Stalling clearly viewed Wagner as the suitable musical backdrop for such criticism. The war did not change the music that Stalling and other composers for animation used; rather, it complicated the associations produced when such pieces were heard, adding a political and emotional charge at a time when practically everything in the media referred to the war in one way or another. The comedic elements inherent in what Jones retained from Freleng's cartoon (Bugs in drag and the dance sequence) do little to evoke World War II; Jones's cartoon instead takes on Wagner (as well as opera) directly, with any more general mockery of German culture remaining secondary.

PRODUCTION ISSUES: VISUAL APPEARANCES

Certainly the most obvious sign that Jones viewed *What's Opera, Doc?* as something special is the amount of extra time and attention that went into the cartoon's production. Michael Barrier mentions several of the unusual elements of the film: "Jones said, 'it was one of the few times that we actually corrected a storyboard before I did all the [character] layouts.' [Maurice] Noble made extensive inspirational sketches because, as Jones said, 'a lot of the story had to be told in graphics . . . the imagination of the environment was important.'"[32] Corrections were made on the storyboard because Jones and Michael Maltese, the writer, wanted the story to be completely worked out before animation began, while Noble's inspirational sketches gave the animators a tangible model on which to base their work. Noble's role as layout artist was therefore essential to the film's overall look, as he visually constructed the mythic world for Elmer's and Bugs's interactions. Leonard Maltin calls Noble's designs "bold and forceful, with vibrant colors and shadows." Noble told Maltin, "They thought I was bats when I put that bright red on Elmer with those purple skies. I had the Ink and Paint Department come in and say, 'You *really mean* you want that magenta red on that?'"[33] When production was finished, these details added up to a cartoon unique in its appearance and in its artistic approach. The work was enormously time-consuming, and it forced members of Jones's production unit to give less time than was typical to a Road Runner cartoon, the formulaic series they created and maintained.[34] The director and several of his unit recalled forging their time cards so that they appeared to be giving equal attention to the Road Runner short, when in reality the Wagner was occupying almost all their time.[35]

Barrier also notes that the entire soundtrack for *What's Opera, Doc?* was recorded before animation began. Recording the singing parts in advance is a necessary step in any cartoon, because the animators must synchronize the mouth movements of each character to the final vocal tracks. Jones's concept for *What's Opera, Doc?* took this requirement a step further: all the music had to be in its final form for the animation to proceed so that at all times the characters could move in a choreographed fashion.[36]

THE MUSIC

What's Opera, Doc? divides easily into two narratives at work simultaneously—the visual, discussed above, and the musical. Table 3 presents the musical skeleton of the short, and shows that it breaks down into three categories:

Table 3. MUSIC IN *WHAT'S OPERA, DOC?*

Title	Composer	How Used	Time (min.sec)
1. Merrily We Roll Along	Charlie Tobias, Murray Mencher, Eddie Cantor	Underscoring	0.13
2. The Flying Dutchman	Richard Wagner; arr. Milton J. Franklyn	Underscoring	0.49
3. Mighty Hunter	Milton J. Franklyn	On-screen vocal	0.11
4. Ride of the Valkyries	Richard Wagner; arr. Milton J. Franklyn	On-screen vocal	0.28
5. Siegfried	Richard Wagner; arr. Milton J. Franklyn	Underscoring	0.47
6. The Flying Dutchman	Richard Wagner; arr. Milton J. Franklyn	Underscoring	0.15
7. Rienzi	Richard Wagner; arr. Milton J. Franklyn	Underscoring	0.09
8. Tannhäuser	Richard Wagner; arr. Milton J. Franklyn	On-screen vocal	1.27
9. Return My Love	Richard Wagner, Michael Maltese	On-screen vocal	0.54
10. Ride of the Valkyries	Richard Wagner; arr. Milton J. Franklyn	On-screen vocal	0.20
11. The Flying Dutchman	Richard Wagner; arr. Milton J. Franklyn	Underscoring	0.24
12. Tannhäuser	Richard Wagner; arr. Milton J. Franklyn	On-screen vocal	0.41

A. Purely orchestral forms of Wagner's music used to underscore or mickey-mouse action on screen

B. Melodies of Wagner's transformed into some type of vocal melody

C. Original music—written to emulate Wagner's sound—to underscore or mickey-mouse the action on screen

The production emulates not only the sound but the form of opera, specifically in its stylized movements. Bugs and Elmer's dance to the Venusberg music adds another dimension to the cartoon, which already included singing, instrumental music, and dramatic acting before the addition of ballet (which in Wagner's operas plays a substantial role only in the Venusberg sequence in *Tannhäuser*). Ever vigilant about realism in portrayals of such performances, Jones researched the scene thoroughly: "When we were making the film, Titania Riabachinska and David Lichine of the Ballet Russe de Monte Carlo were working on the Warner Bros. lot, and we went to the studio where they were rehearsing to sketch them before creating the *What's Opera, Doc?* scene."[37] Rather than precisely copying the movements of the ballet dancers by rotoscoping them—that is, tracing a live-action film of the dance, projected one frame at a time, to reproduce it more naturalistically in the animation[38]—Jones and his animators instead relied on their studies to create a more realistic duet between Bugs and Elmer. In the process, they steered clear of *Herr Meets Hare*'s farcical dance.

Similarly, Jones's fastidious attention to detail regarding how in general opera singers move and act broadened the characters' depth. While animation in general requires that attention be paid to the smallest movement, animators often do not take great pains at literalism when rendering visual representations of performance. For instance, they might not bother to make sure that the character is playing in the correct range of the piano at various moments in a performance (in *Rhapsody Rabbit* [Warner Bros.; Freleng, 1946], Bugs is not). We find in *What's Opera, Doc?* a remarkable focus on all aspects of the performer's physical toil, and these too inspire some subtle humor. Such careful planning is evident at a number of points in the opening confrontation between Bugs and Elmer. For instance, Elmer rhythmically punctuates each syllable of the exclamation "Wab-bit tracks!" by jabbing his spear into the ground. And after Bugs fearfully questions Elmer's intentions to "Kill the wabbit," he affectedly flutters his eyelids to the rhythm of the Valkyrie/"Kill the wabbit" leitmotif (being played at that moment on the flute). Finally, between the lines "Oh, mighty warrior 'twill be quite a task" and "How will you do it, might I enquire to ask?" Bugs visibly takes a dramatic, full breath as a singer might in preparation for an important line (see figure 44).[39] Jones may have believed that he was faithfully representing the outward appearance of opera singers, but in making the performance by Bugs and Elmer so highly stylized he underscored the level of artifice that exists in all opera performance. The pensive, heaving breaths taken by both characters throughout the cartoon call attention to the unnatural demands that opera singers must place on their bodies.

Bugs's and Elmer's singing raises an issue touched on earlier: the his-

FIGURE 44   Dramatic action and heavy breathing in *What's Opera, Doc?*

torical tendency of cartoons not to use melodies (as opposed to musical cues) from Wagner. If we analyze the vocal lines in *What's Opera, Doc?*, we find that each fits one of three descriptions:

A. A leitmotif from Wagner used as a sung melody. For example, Bugs's "Oh, mighty warrior of great fighting stock" (to Siegfried's leitmotif) and Elmer's "Kill the wabbit!" (to the Valkyrie leitmotif).

B. Vocal music from Wagner performed in the style of a bel canto aria. For example, Bugs and Elmer's love duet, "Return My Love" (to the "Pilgrims' Chorus," at some length).

C. A completely new melody in the style of a Wagner recitative (his least tuneful music). For example, Elmer's opening line, "Be vewy quiet, I'm hunting wabbits."

A and B have precedents, in that cartoons, as needed, constantly appropriate familiar melodic lines from all forms of music, opera included. But the third possibility is surprising: why write music in Wagner's style, which has already proven to be unpopular for use in films? Because Jones wanted to parody *all* aspects of Wagner and his art, this familiar aspect of his operas had to be incorporated. Even more important, performers and audiences alike know that singing in opera, no matter how unmelodic it may sound, is nonetheless supposed to represent something innately beautiful; "Opera singing . . . is self-consciously beautiful, and it takes itself completely seriously," as Jeremy Tambling explains.[40] In other words, the voice itself—not what is being sung—is of paramount importance for the fan of opera.

Of all the selections from Wagner's operas used in cartoons, the one least familiar to today's opera fans appears the second most often (after

Lohengrin's famous "Bridal March"): music from the overture to Wagner's highly successful third opera, *Rienzi*. Stalling used this piece for particularly intense moments; Rapée's *Encyclopedia* appropriately classifies it as "heavy" dramatic. In this music, like that of Franz von Suppé and Alphons Czibulka, we see how cartoon scores became a haven, if not a final resting place, for once-popular concert pieces that have fallen out of favor or vogue. Probably the most famous use of this piece in film outside animation occurs in the scene from *The Birth of a Nation* mentioned above; Martin Marks has documented that the *Rienzi* overture, in combination with "The Ride of the Valkyries" and Louis Hérold's overture for *Zampa* (also popular in the nineteenth century), constitutes the background to the Ku Klux Klan's final heroic ride in the film.[41]

Jones acknowledged, years before *What's Opera, Doc?* appeared, that such familiarity with music was important to help the audience in understanding when a pun (or an extended satirical situation) was being presented: "In this field of satire, one factor constitutes a limitation of sorts: the piece selected should have a certain amount of familiarity, because this adds anticipatory enjoyment for the audience."[42] In light of this comment, we can presume that Jones and Maltese, along with Stalling and Milt Franklyn (Stalling's orchestrator and the primary composer for *What's Opera, Doc?*), picked those excerpts from Wagner whose melodies they believed the audience would recognize. This principle of selection begins to explain the musical choices for the film from *The Flying Dutchman, Rienzi, Tannhäuser, The Valkyrie,* and *Siegfried.* Instead of trying to satirize any one of Wagner's operas, Jones appropriates what is most powerful or widely recognized, confident that such tunes will get the biggest audience reaction. It is unlikely Jones knew much about the true sources of the music being used; he repeatedly stated in his two autobiographical books and in interviews that he knew little of music, or Wagner, beyond his favorite (mis)quotation of Twain's on the subject, "Wagner is better than it sounds."[43] Thus, the music used in *What's Opera, Doc?* was what Jones and Maltese understood to be Wagner's most popular melodies—a misquotation viewed by David Huckvale as a "deliberate confusion" on Jones's part.[44] This is not to say he did not know how to present the music appropriately; on the contrary, as Jones recalled, the production purposely mimicked grand opera: "To keep Wagnerian opera's sense of grandeur, we used a huge eighty-piece orchestra. It would have been less majesty [sic] to do anything unfair to the music. Although when I visited Wagner's grave, I did hear a whirring sound."[45]

STORYTELLING IN *WHAT'S OPERA, DOC?*

As the critic Jaime Weinman suggests, Jones seems to take his subject matter *very* seriously.[46] But at the same time, he conflates various idiosyncrasies of Wagner's characters without any sense of wrongdoing; the characters are there to be violated. For instance, David Schroeder points out that Bugs takes on the visual appearance of a Rhinemaiden with his golden locks and helmet, while Elmer, whose first prominent vocal utterance echoes the Valkyrie leitmotif, wears the cuirass and horned helmet specifically associated with the Valkyries.[47] The musical and visual attributes that Bugs and Elmer exhibit constantly shift from gag to gag. It is this scattershot approach to hitting all the familiar stereotypes that enables the cartoon to capture so many elements of Wagner's music.

Yet even those who see *What's Opera, Doc?* with little or no knowledge of Wagner, the *Ring*, or the composer's notion of *Gesamtkunstwerk* find the cartoon funny. Because Jones and Maltese drew on the most typical, if not stereotypical, scenes in Wagner's narrative arsenal, most viewers are familiar enough with the standard plot points of operas to get the idea. There are five main episodes, each accompanied by a cue from Wagner:

1. Overture	*The Flying Dutchman*
2. The mighty warrior (Elmer/ Siegfried) on display as warrior/hunter	Valkyrie and Siegfried leitmotifs
3. Love duet between hero and heroine (Bugs/Brünnhilde)	*Tannhäuser* (Pilgrims' Chorus)
4. Magical power of the gods/ battle sequence	Valkyrie leitmotif
5. Tragic death scene	*Tannhäuser* overture

The most noticeable shift in the drama occurs when Elmer, chasing Bugs on foot across the countryside, is brought to an abrupt stop by the sight of Bugs, in drag as Brünnhilde, riding down to greet him (see figure 45). The music marks this drastic change in direction (and attire) by switching from *Rienzi* to the beginning of the *Tannhäuser* overture, replete with bold trombones to properly illustrate the majesty of Bugs's descent from on high. It makes no difference that no such scene ever takes place in Wagner's world; Bugs (or, rather, Jones) resolves the conflict with Elmer by switching to the narrative logic (or illogic) of cartoons, in which his

FIGURE 45 Bugs as Brünnhilde in *What's Opera, Doc?*

cross-dressing subterfuge, inspired by *Herr Meets Hare,* is sure to succeed. In fact, we can trace none of these episodes directly to any Wagnerian original. Jones, Maltese, and their creative colleagues instead fab-
ricate such generalized situations (dressed up in Wagnerian garb) that
most in the audience never know the difference.

The scene in the film that most perfectly combines the Warner Bros.
approach to comedy with Wagner's melodramatic style occurs early on,
when we first encounter Elmer's character. Though the ubiquitous music from *Tannhäuser* is prominent in *What's Opera, Doc?,* no melody in
this short is more memorable and arresting than the Valkyrie leitmotif,
appropriated and then fused with Elmer's hunting cry of "Kill the wabbit!" (see music example 10). Elmer makes this declaration in the briefest
of scenes, yet this phrase has lasted more indelibly than any other in the
collective memory of countless cartoon viewers. The phrase "Kill the wabbit" encapsulates almost two decades of struggle for Elmer (he began hunting Bugs in 1940), and it is grafted onto a leitmotif that perfectly exemplifies the form: short, distinct, unique, and thus easy to identify. Uniting
the epitome of Wagner with the essence of Elmer was a brilliant idea; it
is so effective, in fact, that those who see the cartoon seem unable to tear
apart the two icons—one visual, one aural. This musical gesture still sig-
nifies Wagner, but it is now Wagner as portrayed by Bugs and Elmer.

The irony of the mundane Elmer expressing his desires through music,
and especially through *Wagner's* music, makes for a truly comic moment;
the film critic Philip Brophy declares that "it is almost as if this is actually
a *serious* cartoon—which is precisely what makes it so comical."[48] Of all
the serious moments in *What's Opera, Doc?,* none is more so than this
one, and it is therefore the funniest moment as well. Part of the scene's
gravity comes from Elmer's expression of murderous lust. By the time this

Kill the wab-bit   Kill the wab-bit   Kill the wab-bit

EXAMPLE 10 Melody for "Kill the wabbit."

short appeared in 1957, the meetings between Bugs Bunny and Elmer Fudd had moved well beyond the predictable. As an adversary, Elmer did not offer much of an opponent for Bugs; he was just too gullible. In order to revitalize the feeling of conflict for *What's Opera, Doc?*, the stakes between hunter and hunted had to be higher. In earlier cartoons Elmer proclaims "I'm hunting wabbits," or "Ooooh, I'll get you for this, you, you . . . wabbit!" Here, he audibly states that he wants to *kill* Bugs.[49] Although other Warner Bros. directors had characters "die" on screen (for example, Clampett, in *Hare Ribbin'*, 1944; Freleng, in *Back Alley Oproar*, 1948), and attempted murder and involuntary manslaughter occur in almost every cartoon, *What's Opera, Doc?* marked a particularly dramatic exploration of these ideas for Jones. The safety of the operatic diegesis allows Jones to deal with death almost lightly: the comic juxtaposition between the opera and cartoon worlds predisposes the audience to ignore issues of mortality—after all, how can a cartoon character be killed? At the same time, however, Elmer's hunt and Bugs's subsequent death suggest that in Jones's mind, a death is a natural if not essential part of an operatic narrative, an inference confirmed by Bugs's parting shot as the cartoon ends.

Thus we come to the other shaping force behind this story, which allows Jones and Maltese to bring two worlds into conflict: the metanarrative of the animated cartoon, in this case the chase. Fundamental to this type of story line is expecting the unexpected, since Bugs has every right to use *any* means at his disposal to keep Elmer from catching or killing him (or both). Cartoons that fall into the chase subgenre usually consist of disparate scenes in rapid succession. *What's Opera, Doc?* contains the expected and reassuring story details that any Wagner opera should have, while still displaying the unpredictability for which the Warner Bros. cartoons had become famous. By putting the two styles together, Jones can appeal to the cartoon and opera fan at the same time. Seeing Elmer and Bugs in the same story is enough for any cartoon fan to fathom the core narrative of the cartoon: Elmer hunting Bugs. And in case some of us do not get the point immediately, Jones clearly indicates the chase subplot with the opening words/arioso: "Be vewy quiet—I'm hunting wabbits!" The subplot is more than simply just the motivation for the story itself: the ongoing conflict between Bugs and Elmer bridges the gaps between the five operatic episodes. Elmer's consuming desire to catch Bugs transcends time, place, and setting; Bugs always verbally toys with Elmer, and then mentally and physically abuses him until a critical moment when somebody gets "hurt." Knowing that all this will unfold gives the cartoon fan a sense of security; so, too, an opera devotee takes comfort in the belief that generic norms will be maintained, though they are norms of a different nature.

Indeed, the story must end in accordance with the audience expectations not just for a cartoon but also (as perceived by Jones) for an opera. Christopher Small points out that all such stories "partake of the nature of myth," and that even the conventional "happy" ending leaves us wondering, "What makes people happy?"[50] In this case, Elmer triumphs over Bugs, for Jones's notion of Wagner's universe dictates that the story involve a tragic death—even though such a death confounds the archetypal Warner Bros. chase, in which Bugs prevails. Elmer/Siegfried carries the lifeless Bugs/Brünnhilde off into the distance, perhaps to a funeral pyre. Lest we forget we are watching a cartoon, Bugs breaks character and the fourth wall to address the audience with "Well, what did you *expect* in an opera? A *happy* ending?" A death provides the audience with what they "expect" from a dramatic opera, while Bugs's trickery at the expense of death fulfills our desires that he outsmart Elmer the hunter. Everybody is happy.

When the thrust of the opera's narrative momentarily weakens in the cartoon, the protagonists' personalities as *cartoon* characters reenergize the scene. The humor comes from the collision between their established personas and the fantastic yet straitlaced world of Wagner, not from the pratfalls and explosions typical to cartoons, especially those in the vaudeville-based style of the Warner Bros. shorts. Jones apparently felt that some sign of respect toward the composer was necessary, insisting, "There are *no gags* in the film. We believed that a rabbit and a hunter working with that grand music in a fully Wagnerian environment would be funny enough in itself. But with the humor coming from personality rather than from gags, the need to play the music properly and to make the action logical became more emphatic."[51]

The claim that there are absolutely no gags in *What's Opera, Doc?* is not quite true; more accurately (and what Jones likely meant), there are few cartoon-based gags in the film. In his quest to preserve Wagner's dramatic integrity, Jones refrains from the physical or word-based humor that usually pervades his cartoons. Instead, he relies on the seeming mis-

match of high and low art forms to create comedic tension. As Michael
Barrier puts it, "Jones obviously respects *both* his principal ingredients,
Bugs Bunny and Richard Wagner. He invites his audience to sneer at neither one, but to enjoy the incongruity of Bugs Bunny in a Wagnerian setting instead."[52]

Those gags that do occur are not as explicit or gratuitous as in most
cartoons. For instance, as mentioned earlier, when a distressed Bugs
rhetorically repeats back Elmer's "Kill the wabbit!" he blinks his eyes
rapidly, exactly in sync with the Valkyrie motif on the flute; thus his gesture is both distraught and momentarily comic. And when Elmer con-
jures the forces of nature to "strike the wabbit," the final and most deadly
earthly power he calls down is "Smog!"—a curse he yells at the top of
his lungs. The topical joke about the pollution in Los Angeles (especially
in the 1950s) briefly startles the audience out of the opera's universe.[53]
In a gag that plays with Wagnerian convention, as Elmer stabs furiously
at Bugs's rabbit hole, he yells out "Yo-ho-to-ho!" rather than the familiar
"Ho-yo-to-ho!" of *The Valkyries*. In case we think that Elmer has simply switched his syllables, he ends his onslaught with a final "Yo-ho!,"
just short of a slightly more congenial "Yoo-hoo!"

When Elmer destroys the mountains around him in retaliation for
Bugs's drag deception (see figure 46), Jones puts the narrative perspective
of the short into question. As the mountains come crashing down, the audience wonders whether the action is taking place on the stage of an opera
house or in a world of animated make-believe. We can see the falling
mountains either as a stage's backdrop—perhaps even sets at Bayreuth—
crumbling, or as proof that Elmer indeed has the powers he claims to
wield in Wagner's universe. The beginning of the cartoon as described
above, a title card and credits shown while the sounds of a tuning orchestra
(including bits of leitmotifs) are heard, complicates the question of interpretation. Maurice Noble recalled, "We'd had a production designer that
wanted to have the proscenium arch right on stage all the time. I said,
well, to hell with that, you know, I wanted to have *super* grand opera.
We threw away the arch completely and immediately began writing on a
grand scale."[54] Jones also stated repeatedly that in *What's Opera, Doc?*
he took two unpredictable elements (Bugs and Elmer) and simply dropped
them into the ordered world that Wagner had created.[55] The audience un-
derstands that they are seeing an animated spoof on opera and all its stereotypes; whether they believe the story is set in the Rhineland where the
Ring takes place does not matter as long as Bugs and Elmer play out their
parts to the fullest, which they do.

FIGURE 46 The world comes crashing
down in *What's Opera, Doc?*

Perhaps one of the few stereotypes that Bugs does not take on is the prototypical woman of opera. The roles of female characters in cartoons are limited at best, and the use of opera and opera narratives did nothing to add to them, despite the ease with which images of the loud female opera singers, or the proverbial fat lady, might be spoofed. The Rossini and Donizetti arias mentioned above as frequently used in cartoons are performed by men; no such famous aria for women appears. The few women that are depicted in operatic roles are usually a hybrid form, wearing the costume associated with Wagner's Rhinemaidens but singing Italian words. Occasionally we see someone performing as Carmen, as in *Chile Con Carmen* (Lantz, 1930) and *Carmen Get It!* (MGM; Deitch, 1962). Apparently, the use of female characters simply did not occur to the directors. Jones once commented on the general absence of female stars in Hollywood cartoons, "This always comes up. . . . It's a pity. I can only beat my breast and say that I should be nailed to the wall. But I didn't [consider having any female characters]. So I don't know how to answer that except to say I'm sorry."[56]

Jones fails to mention the host of instances when male characters dress in drag, a device he uses in all three of his opera cartoons: *Long-Haired Hare, The Rabbit of Seville,* and, most extensively, *What's Opera, Doc?* He injects his characters into an unusual performance space, but he compels them to adopt only the attire appropriate to their environment and not the physical form of its usual inhabitants. For Bugs, this means assuming the costume of a Wagnerian diva, but not her stereotypical size.[57] The horse Bugs rides while posing as Brünnhilde, however, more than makes up for his (unusually—for a diva) svelte figure. Jones exaggerates Bugs's steed to the point of absurdity, enabling the bunny as Brünnhilde to make a truly grand entrance. As already noted, Jones clearly modeled

FIGURE 47 The disdainful steed in
What's Opera, Doc?

his horse on the one that appeared in a similar scene in *Herr Meets Hare,*
which itself seems to have been influenced by the centaurs in the Pastoral
Symphony section of *Fantasia,* which in turn were inspired by classical
Greek vase paintings. In his autobiography *Chuck Amuck,* Jones explains:
"Missing the great pink, busty quality of the proverbial Wagnerian diva,
we invested all the fat curves we owned in Brünnhilde's charger." He
tells the story slightly differently in *Chuck Reducks:* "Since we didn't have
a voluptuous soprano at hand, I designed a voluptuous horse as a stand-
in."[58] The horse acts as a surrogate because Jones cannot change Bugs
physically. He even gives the horse a bit of personality: at one point during
Bugs and Elmer's ballet, Bugs hides coyly behind the horse as Elmer gives
chase playfully, while the horse looks on at their capers with a clearly
perceptible sneer (see figure 47).

WRESTLING OPERA

In his discussion of storytelling and the use of myth, Christopher Small
claims that "the historical accuracy of a myth is more or less irrelevant
to its power as paradigm."[59] Rather than striving for complete historical accuracy—using a scene directly from a Wagner opera with its original
music intact—Jones and Maltese instead go for a more entertaining approach: they create a cartoon that is *culturally* accurate, satisfying the
common notions of what Wagner's operas look and sound like. Nothing
that occurs in the narrative of *What's Opera, Doc?* is drawn directly from
Wagner—all the events are parodies or stereotypes—and the cartoon likewise almost entirely avoids using its own heritage of comedy and timing
developed over twenty-five years (rooted largely in film comedies and
vaudeville routines). That is, we can imagine the better part of the action

of *What's Opera, Doc?* occurring in any Wagner opera; nothing Bugs or Elmer does goes beyond the bounds of operatic spectacle. Thus Jones adroitly likens the operatic nature of his own medium to the cartoonish tendencies of Wagner's world—perhaps his intent all along. Because of its spectacular nature (fairly reeking of high culture), opera invited its own comeuppance; what better way for Jones to simultaneously deal with the two entertainment media than by showing that opera and cartoons appeal equally to the desire for melodramatic spectacle?

For most people in the 1950s, as Joseph Horowitz notes, Wagner represented "Opera" both musically and stylistically;[60] *What's Opera, Doc?* gives those who never had the opportunity to see an opera a glimpse of what it's like even as the cartoon levels some satire at a few of the sacred icons of the spectacle. This approach may begin to explain the short's success. A film like *Fantasia* presents a novel and in some respects modern way of looking at a piece of classical music, but the Disney studio's reverence for classical music prevented the animation from having any significant effect on the music. Warner Bros. (and other studios, including Lantz, MGM, and Fleischer) allowed much more interaction between the worlds of animation and music, and as a result the story often commented explicitly on the music. *What's Opera, Doc?* is a case in point, through its lampooning of high culture. Jones represented opera through a fixed musical and visual vocabulary; as long as the overall gesture worked, the means to accomplishing it didn't matter. *What's Opera, Doc?* exists as a testament to opera's most familiar stereotypes, many of which had, by 1957, become associated with Wagner; the two were inseparable for Jones, and thus there was no need for Wagner's name ever to be seen or heard in the cartoon.

I began chapter 4 by noting that cartoons have come to provide rudimentary training in music appreciation, since many people claim to have first been exposed to classical music while watching cartoons. The same is true of opera, as recently demonstrated on *The Jeff Foxworthy Show.* In an episode titled "Wrestling Opera" (1997), the main character, played by Jeff Foxworthy, has to take his child to an opera for a school trip. In one scene his stereotypically redneck friends discuss the outing:

> *Andre:* And why are you bad-mouthing opera? I know you like the music.
> *Florus:* I do not. Take it back.
> *Andre:* You like cartoons, right?
> [Florus smiles and nods, then drops his smile.]
> *Florus:* Is this a trick question?

> Andre: Well, cartoons are full of opera music. Remember Elmer Fudd on stage
>   in a little Viking hat? (*Hums*) Da da di daaaa da, da da di daaaa da,
>   da da di daaaa da.
> Florus: Yeah . . .
> Andre: That's Wagner. That's opera.
> Bill: Yeah, but if you take Elmer and Bugs out of it, opera's really boring.[61]

The *Jump Start* comic strip at the beginning of this chapter (figure 37) offers another example of the extent to which popular notions of opera are drawn from cartoons. We don't know what opera Joe and his wife Marcy are attending, and it doesn't matter—his musical knowledge of opera derives, as he says, completely from Bugs Bunny.

In a 1946 article, Chuck Jones foresaw the possible role his cartoons might take: "The animated cartoon can match, enhance, make credible the melodic fantasy of the composer. Overlapping here a little bit, I believe that the educational system will one day demand a library for its public schools of just such painless introductions to classic and semiclassic music."[62] Many would argue that such exposure renders Beethoven, Mendelssohn, and Wagner anonymous (in cartoons, there is no time to mention the names of the composers being spoofed), chopping up their respective works and reducing them, like a stockpot of classical melodies, down to the barest essence of the now-defunct canon—the same short melodies that found their way into silent film underscores only decades earlier. Yet the music in cartoons can inspire audiences to learn more about the composers caricatured and parodied. Similarly, though *What's Opera, Doc?* and cartoons like it are often accused of undercutting and weakening classical music's rightful place in the cultural hierarchy, in reality they do as much to maintain music's elevated status as do more worshipful representations. Just as *Fantasia* firmly places Bach and Beethoven in the temple of high culture, so too *What's Opera, Doc?* reminds us that classical music is high art; every time we see these cartoons, we are reminded that the object of their parody—opera—occupies a place of honor in our culture. By focusing on music and concert hall culture as worthy subjects for deflation, these cartoons more firmly set the music and spectacle in their high place.

A Brief Conclusion

Even a quick glance at the animation industry in our own time reveals that a great deal has changed. With the demise of the animation units run by or for major Hollywood companies, the power shifted to independent animation studios that could supply the seemingly insatiable demand for children's television programming. In the 1970s and 1980s, Hanna-Barbera, Filmation, DIC, Ruby-Spears, and other studios paid little attention to (or money for) such luxuries as unique sound effects or original music. At the same time, there was an explosion of cartoons featuring rock bands, including Pebbles and Bamm-Bamm, Josie and the Pussycats, and Jabberjaw.[1] The stock music these cartoons typically used is a topic worthy of future investigation. Both the animation, which relied on the photocopying of drawings and repetition of backgrounds ad infinitum, and the music, which drew on stock cue libraries and generic mood music, diminished in originality, though these cartoons were more popular than their predecessors among consumers (a popularity due in no small part to television's national and eventually global reach).

A renaissance in cartoon production occurred in the late 1980s. Reawakened interest in the now-classic Warner Bros. cartoons led Steven Spielberg to produce *Tiny Toon Adventures*, based on Warner stars and cartoons; at the same time, networks and cable channels commissioned entirely novel series, including *Ren & Stimpy, Rugrats, Animaniacs, Batman,* and *Doug*. Many of these went out of their way to identify themselves—through their story lines, design characteristics, voice actors, and music—with the animation styles of their precursors. Warner Bros., the producers of *Tiny Toon Adventures, Animaniacs,* and *Pinky & The Brain,* among others, seemed especially interested in reviving the sound and feel of Carl Stalling's music, which had been reintroduced to the public when the first *Carl Stalling Project* CD was released in 1990. Composers like Richard Stone helped reacquaint audiences with Stalling's style of composing, raising their awareness of the complexities and subtle humor that pervade all of the Warner Bros. cartoon scores. The popularity of the *Carl Stalling Project* and Stone's revival and supplementation of the melodic arsenal established by Stalling (many new tunes came into the public domain after Stalling retired) compel us to reexamine the modern cartoon score, which has reclaimed its role as a link between popular culture of the present and years past—a role practically abandoned during the 1970s and 1980s.

Meanwhile, shows like *South Park*, which use little synchronized underscoring (that is, mickey-mousing), instead turn their musical attention to the production of showstopping musical numbers. Again, such shows have classic Hollywood cartoons to inspire them, often using the shorts from the old school as a source for parody; with astonishing regularity, 1930s cartoons are used as the point of departure in modern cartoons. In fact, the first broadcast episode of *South Park*, "Cartman Gets an Anal Probe," features what amounts to an audio sample of a chorus of Owl Jolson singing "I Love to Singa" from the 1936 cartoon of the same name: it comes out of Eric Cartman's mouth with brilliant results.[2] By making *I Love to Singa* the joke, *South Park* shows just how much modern animation relies on its predecessors. The cutesy-sounding music itself is certainly funny, but the actual gag rests on a joke made more than a half century earlier.

Music does more nowadays than tell stories or provide an emotional barometer. The employment of contemporary music written in Bradley's highly synchronized style, or of a modern reinterpretation of Liszt's Second Hungarian Rhapsody, reaffirms the continuity of music in Hollywood animation throughout the past century. Thematically, stories or gags involving music are still vital; the conflict between high and low art remains as popular a trope in cartoons now as it was when Disney made fun of highbrow concert musicians in the early 1930s. Likewise, contemporary popular music has become a fundamental element in contemporary cartoons. The scores for *The Powerpuff Girls*, for instance, are largely driven by electronic dance beats, taking the place of the jazz combos and orchestras that pervaded 1940s cartoons. Popular songs also feature as a major element in the stories of many cartoons, in particular when they are performed as part of the plot. And, of course, we can't overlook the road map for cartoon music drawn by Scott Bradley and Carl Stalling some seventy-five years ago. Not only did Stalling and Bradley work as composers in animation, but they defined its rules as they went along;

their impact has been so great that no one since has escaped their influence. Time has not lessened their impact or altered the function of cartoon music; on the contrary, it still serves as both the motivation for gags and their accompaniment. Modern cartoons have the great advantage of being able to use the better part of a century's worth of cartoon music history as a template for making their own gags that much funnier.

Carl Stalling Documents

"CARL STALLING," *EXPOSURE SHEET* 2.7 (15 APRIL 1940): N.P.

Some time ago we promised to keep his secret. Carl saw the light of the musical world in Lexington, Missouri. Right from the beginning Carl started teething on a tuning fork, and at the ripe age of fourteen, he was playing piano for the picture shows, and later teaching piano in the Conservatory. Just to give you a rough hint as to the approximate era all this was happening, Carl says he remembers playing piano furioso for "The Great Train Robbery," which makes your guess as good as ours!

From piano, he graduated to an orchestra of his own, and finally to playing an organ at the time that Talkies were coming into the world.

When Walt Disney came to the west coast, Carl accompanied him as musical director. Here he did the story and music score for the first Silly Symphony, "Skeleton Dance," and two or three others which followed. He also composed "Minnie's Yoo Hoo," which was used as the theme music for all the Mickey Mouses for the next four years.

Then, when he left Disney, came Ub Iwerks, and finally here at Schlesinger's.

As if you didn't know, Carl says, "My hobby? Horses!" Sounds like a gag—hobby horses!! He also goes in for the growing of citrus fruits.

When asked for a happy memory, Carl remembers the time when he was playing a theatre in K.C. It had high windows all around the walls, and they were always kept open to let in the air. At one time the silent "Sea Hawk" was playing, and Carl, at the organ, was throwing his all into a swell storm effect—all stops open! Just as the storm on the screen began, the gods took the situation in hand, and gave out with a real storm above the theatre! The competition was too much for Carl, and throwing up his hands in great disgust, he just sat back and let the heavens take over. But finally the storm became too terrific, and the windows were closed. Thus was saved the Maestro's career!!

"THIS MONTH'S THUMBNAIL SKETCH," *WARNER CLUB NEWS*, MARCH 1948

How long do you think it would take you to write eight million musical notes?

Carl Stalling, director of music for Warner Bros. Cartoons, says it has taken him 20 years, and concluded with, "That includes waving them at the musicians. Here, take a look at my biceps!"

"I started scoring music for cartoons in 1928," he continued, "when I joined, if you'll pardon the expression, Walt Disney. The title of the first picture was 'The Galloping Gaucho.'" Then pointing to the score of the latest Warner Bros. Cartoon, "High Diving Hare," he said, "And I'm still at it!"

Since that first cartoon, Carl has scored, composed and conducted the music for about *six hundred* animated cartoons—and that's a record of some sort!

There's another record in Carl's history, the *Tic-Tempo* record. In fact, you couldn't write about Carl without mentioning the *Tic-Tempo* because this is his baby.

It is a method of synchronizing a picture to a recorded tempo with mathematical precision, and is used today in all studios, not only for animated cartoons, but for live action as well. This should rate an Oscar of some sort.

By way of statistics and background we find that this only musical Stalling was born in Lexington, Missouri on the 10th of November, 1891. He started playing the piano (for money) at the age of fourteen, and is a graduate of the Kansas City Conservatory of Music. He studied piano under the late Boguslawski and pipe organ under Pietro Yon, honorary organist to the Vatican.

Carl gained recognition as feature pipe-organist and pianist in the theatres of Kansas City and Chicago, and one time was member of Leo Forbstein's orchestra. Leo Forbstein, as you all know, is Musical Director on the Warner Bros. main lot.

It is worth noting that four [*sic*] men who have contributed a great deal to the animated cartoon industry have come from Kansas City. They are: Carl Stalling, Friz Freleng and Walt Disney.

By way of romance we find Carl meeting, falling in love, and marrying Gladys Baldwin, who was teaching violin at the Conservatory. This was a musical natural and they have been living in perfect harmony for thirty years; that is, if you discount the discord which occasionally creeps in at the pari-mutuel window, which has just closed in Carl's face—too late to place his wife's winning wager.

Somewhere in the foothills, near Upland, California, there is a citrus ranch and a rambling redwood house. Here it is that Carl and Gladys relax over the weekend. (Santa Anita is midway between Hollywood and Carl's orange grove.)

This year Carl is celebrating his forty-third year in the show business; twenty of them being with animated cartoons, the last twelve of which have been with Warner Bros. Cartoon Studio.

Monotonous? Listen to what Carl said to that:

"There's no business like show business, and I get just as much of a kick out of hearing my latest score as I did when I heard my first one, twenty years ago!"

Scott Bradley Documents

SCOTT BRADLEY, "CARTOON MUSIC OF THE FUTURE,"
PACIFIC COAST MUSICIAN 30.12 (21 JUNE 1941): 28

A few weeks ago we were running a group of animated cartoons in the projection room at M-G-M.

One of the most interesting subjects was an old cartoon, made in 1930, and the studio audience howled with laughter; not because it was funny, but because it looked and sounded so dated and "corny"! And this vintage product was only ten years old! So great has been the technical and musical progress in animated cartoons since those first clumsy efforts that it may well have been pre-war.

Yet we may look back ten years hence and laugh at our present efforts as we now laugh at the 1930 model Disney and Harman-Ising cartoons. The musical accompaniment for these 1930 films was terrifying; a seven-piece orchestra blaring out jazz as fast and loud as the sound track would take it and four drummers trying desperately to get the sound effects in the proper place. (We never dubbed in the effects in those days.) Today we use orchestras of as many as 35 players for single-reel cartoons, using music especially composed for well-written scenarios, and played by symphony musicians.

As one of the minor prophets of this era of animated cartoons, I should like to hazard a guess as to the part music will play in cartoons of the future; for music has finally become equal in importance to color and story.

First, music will be composed in the symphonic-poem manner, i.e., written to a definite program and recorded before a foot of animation is in production. What a happy day that will be for the composer who, at the present time, hears his music cut and mutilated to suit the action or story.

Second, it will attract the foremost composers, especially those capable of writing humorous music—the most difficult of all, as the very limited repertoire will attest. A Shostakovitch, or a Kodaly, capable of writing such clever humor as "Hary Janos," or Prokofieff with his "Peter and the Wolf," would find a fertile field for their amazing talents. And their collaborators will be writers of the highest type, capable of adapting their talents to the music. Furthermore, it will—or should be—original music which will have the advantage of being associated strictly with the story, instead of having been written and associated with subjects not practical to its medium.

Third, they will not be called "Cartoons" at all but, rather, "Fantasies," in which slap-stick and impossible physical gags will be replaced by stories of great beauty and artistic (not arty) value. Think of "Pelleas and Melisande," with the mystical beauty of Debussy's music, animated by artists of great talent, and mise en scene by Dali! American Indian legends and the great wealth of Old World folk-lore would provide endless subject matter both to authors and composers.

Fourth, the present rigid methods of recording, wherein we must follow a "click track" in order to co-ordinate the music with the animation, will be abandoned in favor of free and flexible tempi governed by the emotional quality of the music. There will be unlimited variation in composition, giving the composer complete freedom of expression, and giving the music cutter a chronic headache trying to "break down" the sound track!

Fifth, there will—or should be—no dialogue at all, for fantasy is best portrayed without the irritating presence of speaking voices. Furthermore, it will have the added advantage of being equally understood in Athens or Zanzibar and most important to the composer, it will allow the maximum of opportunity for his music to be heard without the necessity of dubbing under the voices. What a Utopia for the long-suffering Composer, when he actually hears his "brain child" as he hears it in the mixing booth! (Off-stage voice: "What an optimist you are, Scott.")

Finally, for composers, it will require a new type of orchestral tone color, since sound effects will be contained in the orchestration, and the possibilities will be boundless. I have been experimenting in this field for several years but it is still in its infancy. The composer will finally come into his own and receive equal screen credit with the author and producer. The orchestra will, of course, be of symphonic size and quality and the premiere will be reviewed by a music critic instead of a gossip columnist. In brief, fellow composers, Forward March! The world is your oyster, the sky is the limit, and the once lowly and despised slapstick cartoon will be your liberator.

BRADLEY'S NOTE TO INGOLF DAHL, "NOTES ON CARTOON MUSIC," *FILM MUSIC NOTES* 8.5 (MAY–JUNE 1949): 3–13

This note, appended to Bradley's copy of Dahl's article, is now among the Scott Bradley Collection at the American Heritage Center, University of Wyoming. It refers specifically to the autobiographical "memo" reprinted in chapter 2.

PREFACE 1967

Prof. Ingolf Dahl's article accurately reflects my views, and the status of Cartoon music, as of 1949. Naturally, my own opinion of music in general followed the progress (or lack of it) of contemporary thought. That is, to a certain degree.

But they "lost" me when such things as Partitas for concrete mixer, and Allemandes for piano and *silence,* e.g. John Cage's "3:45"—give or take a few seconds—were accepted as music.

However, this does not indicate that I am a reactionary *in toto.* My dislike for women's slacks, etc. has changed 180 degrees. For the current mini-skirt craze, I quickly cry: "Vive la legs"!!

Concerning Cartoon music in the 1960's, I can only ask, *what* music? The t.v. cartoons of today are 95% dialogue, and music is rarely heard at all, unless sound effects may be called music.

Finally, for the avant-garde music student who may be weary of the squeaks and groans, I offer a soothing panacea: Go to your piano, and play the Chopin Mazurka in A-minor, opus 68. And welcome back to the world of beauty and order.

Scott Bradley

NOTES

INTRODUCTION

1. Kristin Thompson, "Implications of the Cel Animation Technique," in *The Cinematic Apparatus*, edited by Teresa de Lauretis and Stephen Heath (New York: St. Martin's Press, 1980), 110–11.

2. Thompson, "Implications of the Cel Animation Technique," 110.

3. For a recent evaluation of the state of film music, see Robynn J. Stilwell, "Music in Films: A Critical Review of Literature, 1980–1996," *Journal of Film Music* 1.1 (Summer 2002): 19–61.

4. George Tootell, *How to Play the Cinema Organ: A Practical Book by a Practical Player* (London: W. Paxton, n.d.), 84.

5. Edith Lang and George West, *Musical Accompaniment of Moving Pictures* (Boston: Boston Music Company, 1920; reprint, New York: Arno Press, 1970), 35–37.

6. Erno Rapée, *Encyclopedia of Music for Pictures* (New York: Belwin, 1925; reprint, New York: Arno Press, 1970); this work was originally published under the title *Erno Rapee's Encyclopædia of Music for Pictures*.

7. "Jazz and 'Aesop's Film Fables' Good Mixers," *Motion Picture News*, 2 June 1923, 2651. Michael Barrier refers to this short article in *Hollywood Cartoons: American Animation in Its Golden Age* (New York: Oxford University Press, 1999), 51.

8. *Sam Fox Incidental Music for News Reels, Cartoons, Pictorial Reviews, Scenics, Travelogues, etc.*, 4 vols. (Cleveland: Sam Fox Publishing, 1931); *Classified Catalogue of Sam Fox Publishing Co. Motion Picture Music* (Cleveland: Sam Fox Publishing, 1929); *Sam Fox Loose Leaf Collection of Ring-Hager Novelties for Orchestra*, vol. 1 (Cleveland: Sam Fox Publishing, 1926); *PianOrgan Film Books of Incidental Music, Extracted from the World Famous "Berg" and "Cinema" Incidental Series*, 7 vols. (New York: Baldwin, n.d.).

9. Kurt London, *Film Music* (London: Faber and Faber, 1936; reprint, New York: Arno Press, 1970), 149–53.

10. Stephen Handzo, "Appendix: A Narrative Glossary of Film Sound Technology," in *Film Sound: Theory and Practice*, edited by Elisabeth Weis and John Belton (New York: Columbia University Press, 1985), 409.

11. Raksin did receive significant attention for his feature film scores, particularly *Laura*.

12. Roy M. Prendergast, *Film Music: A Neglected Art* (New York: W. W. Norton, 1977); Jon Newsom, "'A Sound Idea': Music for Animated Films,"

Quarterly Journal of the Library of Congress 37.3–4 (Summer–Fall 1980): 279–309.

13. Douglas Kahn, *Noise, Water, Meat: A History of Sound in the Arts* (Cambridge, Mass.: MIT Press, 1999), 148–51; Scott Curtis, "The Sound of the Early Warner Bros. Cartoons," in *Sound Theory, Sound Practice*, edited by Rick Altman (New York: Routledge, 1992), 191–203.

14. Michael Barrier, Milton Gray, and Bill Spicer, "An Interview with Carl Stalling" (1971), in *The Cartoon Music Book*, edited by Daniel Goldmark and Yuval Taylor (Chicago: A Cappella Books, 2002), 49.

CHAPTER 1. CARL STALLING AND POPULAR MUSIC
IN THE WARNER BROS. CARTOONS

1. *The Carl Stalling Project* was on the *Billboard* "Top Pop Albums" chart for two weeks, peaking at number 188 (Joel Whitburn, *Joel Whitburn's Top Pop Albums, 1955–1996* [Menomonee Falls, Wis.: Record Research, 1996], 738).

2. Joe Adamson, "Chuck Jones Interviewed," in *The American Animated Cartoon*, edited by Gerald and Danny Peary (New York: E. P. Dutton, 1980), 135.

3. Mike Barrier, Milton Gray, and Bill Spicer, "An Interview with Carl Stalling" (1971), in *The Cartoon Music Book*, edited by Daniel Goldmark and Yuval Taylor (Chicago: A Cappella Books, 2002), 56. Stalling would have been around twelve years old when he saw *The Great Train Robbery;* he was born on 10 November 1891 in Lexington, Mo.

4. See appendix 1 for biographical material on Stalling.

5. Advertisements in the *Kansas City Star,* 26 February 1922; 3 June 1923; 17 June 1923; 14 December 1926; 17 December 1926.

6. Stalling makes clear that he did not score *Steamboat Willie,* and Wilfred Jackson (who was involved with the recording session for *Steamboat Willie*) agrees (Barrier, Gray, and Spicer, "An Interview with Carl Stalling," 38). Disney was, in fact, on his way to New York to record the soundtrack for *Steamboat Willie* when he stopped in Kansas City to leave the other two Mickey films with Stalling (Michael Barrier, *Hollywood Cartoons: American Animation in Its Golden Age* [New York: Oxford University Press, 1999], 52–53).

7. Barrier, *Hollywood Cartoons,* 65.

8. Barrier, Gray, and Spicer, "An Interview with Carl Stalling," 49. Stalling provided arrangements for more than forty shorts from 1931 to 1933.

9. Stalling was musical director for the cartoons throughout this period, although he did not score every short produced. His arranger, Milt Franklyn, received cowriting or codirection credits with Stalling beginning in the 1940s, and eventually took over when Stalling retired. Eugene Poddany, who went on to work with Chuck Jones at MGM in the 1960s, wrote three scores in 1951 when, in Stalling's words, "I bumped my head and a clot as big as my hand formed between my skull and my brain. I was ill for four or five weeks" (Barrier, Gray, and Spicer, "An Interview with Carl Stalling," 50).

10. Edith Lang and George West, *Musical Accompaniment of Moving Pictures* (Boston: Boston Music Company, 1920; reprint, New York: Arno Press,

1970), 36. Stalling's copy of this book can be found in the Carl W. Stalling Papers, American Heritage Center, University of Wyoming; while it is not inscribed with a date, the abundance of materials in the collection from Stalling's days as an accompanist suggests that this book, too, dates to those years.

11. Tim Anderson, "Reforming 'Jackass Music': The Problematic Aesthetics of Early American Film Music Accompaniment," *Cinema Journal* 37.1 (Fall 1997): 12. See also Erno Rapée, *Motion Picture Moods for Pianists and Organists* (New York: Schirmer, 1924; reprint, New York: Arno Press, 1974).

12. Lang and West, *Musical Accompaniment of Moving Pictures,* 36.

13. Jeff Smith, *The Sounds of Commerce: Marketing Popular Film Music* (New York: Columbia University Press, 1998), 29–30.

14. Lang and West, *Musical Accompaniment of Moving Pictures,* 37.

15. Anderson, "Reforming 'Jackass Music,'" 12.

16. Charles Merrell Berg, *An Investigation of the Motives for and Realization of Music to Accompany the American Silent Film, 1896–1927* (New York: Arno Press, 1976), 244, 199.

17. Anderson, "Reforming 'Jackass Music,'" 14. The use of popular music to comment on or somehow become involved with the film's story (diegesis) has become a standard element in the construction of modern soundtracks. See Jeff Smith, "Popular Songs and Comic Allusion in Contemporary Cinema," in *Soundtrack Available,* edited by Pamela Robertson Wojcik and Arthur Knight (Durham, N.C.: Duke University Press, 2001), 407–30.

18. Barrier, Gray, and Spicer, "An Interview with Carl Stalling," 26.

19. Barrier, *Hollywood Cartoons,* 155–65; Steve Schneider, *That's All Folks! The Art of Warner Bros. Animation* (New York: Henry Holt, 1988), 34–39; Hank Sartin, "From Vaudeville to Hollywood, from Silence to Sound: Warner Bros. Cartoons of the Early Sound Era," in *Reading the Rabbit: Explorations in Warner Bros. Animation,* edited by Kevin S. Sandler (New Brunswick, N.J.: Rutgers University Press, 1998), 69.

20. Tom Gunning, "Crazy Machines in the Garden of Forking Paths: Mischief Gags and the Origins of American Film Comedy," in *Classical Hollywood Comedy,* edited by Kristine Brunovska Karnick and Henry Jenkins (New York: Routledge, 1995), 96.

21. Russell Sanjek, *Pennies from Heaven: The American Popular Music Business in the Twentieth Century* (New York: Da Capo Press, 1996), 55. While other Hollywood studios had an interest in hiring songwriters to create new music for their musical films, Warner Bros., according to Sanjek, was "unique in the rush by movie companies to purchase music houses[,] . . . look[ing] to the day when it might be freed of onerous and increasingly exorbitant synchronization fees" (i.e., fees paid for the use of music). Warner Bros. purchased Witmark in January 1929, and in May purchased a half interest in Remick, which also included parts of DeSylva, Brown & Henderson; Harms; and several others (Smith, *The Sounds of Commerce,* 30).

22. Contract quoted in Barrier, *Hollywood Cartoons,* 160.

23. Smith, *The Sounds of Commerce,* 30–31.

24. For more on Warner Bros. and the Vitaphone short subjects, see Roy

Liebman, *Vitaphone Films: A Catalogue of the Features and Shorts* (Jefferson, N.C.: McFarland, 2003).

25. Friz Freleng with David Weber, *Animation: The Art of Friz Freleng* (Newport Beach, Calif.: Donovan Publishing, 1994), 77.

26. Michael Barrier and Milton Gray, "Bob Clampett: An Interview," *Funnyworld*, no. 12 (Summer 1970): 13.

27. Avery, quoted in Barrier, *Hollywood Cartoons*, 341.

28. Chuck Jones, interview by author, tape recording, 14 September 1994.

29. Rudy Ising recalled that the soundtracks for the original Merrie Melodies were to have been performed by "name bands," but only the first few shorts credit Abe Lyman's Brunswick Record Orchestra. Later performances were presumably done by the Warner Bros. studio orchestra, which had already been recording the Looney Tunes scores (Schneider, *That's All Folks!*, 35–39). Like Disney's Silly Symphonies, the Merrie Melodies did not use recurring characters; instead, each episode featured novel plots and personalities.

30. Barrier, *Hollywood Cartoons*, 324. In 1937 the veteran animator and new director Isadore "Friz" Freleng also briefly left Warner Bros., trying unsuccessfully to breathe life into MGM's animated adaptation of the popular newspaper comic *The Captain and the Kids*. He returned the following year.

31. Bob Clampett developed Tweety; but after he left Warner's in 1946, Freleng put his spin on the supposedly innocent little canary, pairing him with Sylvester for years to come.

32. Barrier, *Hollywood Cartoons*, 471.

33. Freleng, *Animation*, 102. Freleng was discussing the importance of music to the Warner Bros. cartoons, lamenting how limited the early shorts were by the rule that each cartoon include a song. I believe his judgment to be too harsh; Marsales's scores may not be as creative as Stalling's or as contrapuntally involved as Scott Bradley's, but they are very good by the standard of what composers at other studios—including Joe de Nat (Columbia), Philip Scheib (Terrytoons), and James Dietrich (Lantz)—were producing in the early 1930s. Moreover, the comparison between these earlier scores and those of Stalling and Bradley is unfair, because the former did not have the luxury of exposure sheets to help them guide their composing and aid them in creating synchronous music (my thanks to Mike Barrier for this observation).

34. Barrier, Gray, and Spicer, "An Interview with Carl Stalling," 42.

35. Freleng, *Animation*, 148. When writing out the piano score, he would make notes to his orchestrator, Milt Franklyn, indicating instructions for specific moments, such as "trombones here," "mysterioso effect here," and so on. Franklyn would then take the score and orchestrate it, returning it to Stalling scored for orchestra and (presumably) ready to record.

36. Barrier, Gray, and Spicer, "An Interview with Carl Stalling," 49.

37. Leon Schlesinger, contract, 1 September 1940, USC Warner Bros. Archives, School of Cinema-Television, University of Southern California.

38. Perhaps one of the most interesting documents in the Stalling Papers is a mimeographed alphabetical list of song titles (several pages long), divided up by publisher: Harms, Witmark, Remick, and Advanced. Judging from the well-thumbed condition of the pages, we might assume that this list served as Stalling's

guide to or reminder of the songs he had easy access to through Warner Bros.'
publishing concerns.

39. Adamson, "Chuck Jones Interviewed," 135. Jones told the same anec-
dote in an earlier interview: "If it was a lady in a red dress, he'd *always* play 'The
Lady in Red,' or if a bee, he'd *always* play 'My Funny Little Bumblebee,' which
was written in 1906 [emphasis mine]. Sometimes it worked and sometimes it
didn't—that 'Funny Little Bumblebee' thing was so obscure no one could make
the connection. You had to be a hundred and eight years old to even know there
was such a song" (Greg Ford and Richard Thompson, "Chuck Jones," *Film Comment* 11.1 [January–February 1975]: 23). The bumblebee song (properly titled)
is "Be My Little Baby Bumble Bee" (1912), which provided the title music for
the cartoon *The Bee-Deviled Bruin* (Jones, 1949). I emphasize Jones's use of the
word "always" to underscore his explicit disapproval of—if not outright disdain
for—Stalling's technique, though in fact the composer used "Be My Little Baby
Bumble Bee" only *once* during his tenure at Warner Bros. Jones's taunt about
"Fingal's Cave" is similarly inaccurate; Mendelssohn's melody shows up a dozen
times, but never for a cave scene (in a cartoon directed by Jones or anyone else).
Moreover, "Bumble Bee" was hardly obscure: it was a tremendous hit in the Flo-
renz Ziegfeld–produced show *A Winsome Widow,* and was recorded that same
year to great acclaim by the hugely popular duo of Ada Jones and Billy Murray.
See Gerald Bordman, *American Musical Theatre: A Chronicle,* 2nd ed. (New York:
Oxford University Press, 1992), 276; Joel Whitburn, *Pop Memories, 1890–1954:
The History of American Popular Music* (Menomonee Falls, Wis.: Record Re-
search, 1986), 239.

40. Freleng, *Animation,* 105. The color gray was hardly a safe choice, as
Stalling could have used "The Old Gray Mare."

41. Ford and Thompson, "Chuck Jones," 23.

42. Smith, "Popular Songs," 416, 417.

43. The song comes from a patriotic wartime musical, *Banjo Eyes* (opened
25 December 1941), starring Eddie Cantor; the song was introduced by James
Farrell and chorus (information from the *Playbill* of the original production).

44. Smith, "Popular Songs," 418.

45. Steve Neale and Frank Krutnik, *Popular Film and Television Comedy*
(London and New York: Routledge, 1990), 108.

46. Anderson, "Reforming 'Jackass Music,'" 17.

47. Will Friedwald, quoted in Greg Ford, brochure notes for Carl Stalling,
The Carl Stalling Project: Music from Warner Bros. Cartoons, 1936–1958
(Warner Bros. Records 26027, 1990), n.p.

48. Smith, "Popular Songs," 418.

49. Chuck Jones, "What's Up, Down Under? Chuck Jones Talks at *The
Illusion of Life* Conference," in *The Illusion of Life: Essays on Animation,* edited by Alan Cholodenko (Sydney: Power Publications, 1991), 39.

50. John Robert Tebbel, "Looney Tunester," *Film Comment* 28.5 (September–
October 1992): 66.

51. Barrier, Gray, and Spicer, "An Interview with Carl Stalling," 53.

52. Irwin Chusid, brochure notes for Raymond Scott, *Reckless Nights and
Turkish Twilights: The Music of Raymond Scott,* the Raymond Scott Quintette

(Sony 53028, 1992), 2. See also Chusid's essay on Scott, "Raymond Scott: Accidental Music for Animated Mayhem," in Goldmark and Taylor, eds., *The Cartoon Music Book*, 151–60.

53. Schneider, *That's All Folks!*, 54.

54. Gunning, "Crazy Machines in the Garden of Forking Paths," 93–94.

55. Henry Jenkins, *What Made Pistachio Nuts? Early Sound Comedy and the Vaudeville Aesthetic* (New York: Columbia University Press, 1992), 70–71; cited in Paul Wells, *Understanding Animation* (London: Routledge, 1998), 135.

56. Claudia Gorbman, *Unheard Melodies: Narrative Film Music* (London: BFI Publishing; Bloomington: Indiana University Press, 1987), 58.

57. Because each gag or series of gags in a cartoon is allotted only a relatively limited amount of time, every punch line must be delivered quickly and succinctly before the next joke occurs and the previous one is forgotten.

58. A few other examples of songs Stalling used that are listed in Erno Rapée's *Encyclopedia of Music for Pictures* (New York: Belwin, 1925; reprint, New York: Arno Press, 1970) include Chopin's "Marche Funèbre" for deaths or funerals, Stephen Foster's "Old Folks at Home" or Daniel Decatur Emmett's "Dixie" for the South, J. B. Lampe's "Vision of Salome" for settings in the Middle East or the Orient, and "Chinatown, My Chinatown" by Jean Schwartz and William Jerome for scenes involving Chinese characters. One could develop an entire history of film-accompanying practices from the contents of Stalling's library at the time of his death in 1972. For the discussion here, the tremendous number of popular songs, either in sheet music form or in arrangements for band or small orchestra, is by far the most significant component of the collection. Music written and published specifically for use in film scores is also present, evidenced by the multitude of volumes from series such as "A.B.C. Dramatic Set" by Ernst Luz, "Breil's Dramatic Music" by J. C. Breil, and "Moving Picture Series" by various authors. See the Stalling Papers.

59. Henry Sapoznik, *Klezmer! Jewish Music from Old World to Our World* (New York: Schirmer Books, 1999), 81.

60. Sapoznik, *Klezmer!*, 55–56. A copy of the book *Twenty-five Hebrew Songs and Dances,* arranged by Maurice Gould, compiled by Julius Fleischmann (New York: Fischer, 1912), is in the Stalling Papers, and the volume includes "Mazel Tof." The page on which the tune appears was torn out and later replaced, suggesting that this is the version used by Stalling.

61. Karl F. Cohen, *Forbidden Animation: Censored Cartoons and Blacklisted Animators in America* (Jefferson, N.C.: McFarland, 1997), 72.

62. Several other cartoons deal with the Japanese during the war—notably, *The Ducktators* (McCabe, 1942), *Tokio Jokio* (McCabe, 1943), and *Bugs Bunny Nips the Nips* (Freleng, 1944)—but Stalling was not musically venturesome in their scores. Among the Japan-oriented songs he used in them are "Kimygayo" and "From Nippon Bridge." For more on the musical representation of Japanese characters in American films during World War II, see Anthony Sheppard, "An Exotic Enemy: Anti-Japanese Musical Propaganda in World War II Hollywood," *Journal of the American Musicological Society* 54.2 (Summer 2001): 303–57.

63. See chapter 5 for more on Stalling's musical characterizations of Nazis, especially in Freleng's *Herr Meets Hare*.

64. Six of the ten published works Stalling uses in *Porky's Moving Day* are by Zamecnik, whose work other composers for cartoons also drew on; both Frank Marsales and Bernard Brown (who worked in 1935 between the tenures of Marsales and Stalling) used him often. *Buddy's Pony Express* (Hardaway, 1935), scored by Brown, consists almost entirely of Zamecnik cues, including one of Stalling's favorites for horse chases: listed as "In the Stirrups" on the cue sheets, it is titled "Western Scene" in volume 4 of *Sam Fox Moving Picture Music* (Cleveland: Sam Fox Publishing Company, 1924), 5.

65. For Disney and Iwerks, Stalling typically had no more than a dozen musicians to work with, although the wind players played two or more instruments. At Warner's, between thirty and sixty players were available to him at any one time. In these early days, he was no doubt getting used to his new job and his sudden jump in output. Eight of the ten cartoons Iwerks produced in 1935 were scored by Stalling, but in 1937, the year after he arrived at Warner Bros., he scored three dozen cartoons (Leonard Maltin, *Of Mice and Magic: A History of American Animated Cartoons*, rev. ed. [New York: New American Library, 1987], 407, 422).

66. Much of this material can be found in the Stalling Collection.

67. Chuck Jones, *Chuck Reducks: Drawing from the Fun Side of Life* (New York: Warner Books, 1996), 158.

68. While he is not formally named in this cartoon, the cat in *Mouse Warming* is identical in appearance and personality to Claude Cat, who appears in several other Jones cartoons.

69. Chuck Jones, *Chuck Amuck: The Life and Times of an Animated Cartoonist* (New York: Avon Books, 1990), 224–25.

70. The most obvious exception to Stalling's aversion to musical repetition is his use of the theme from Mendelssohn's "Fingal's Cave" overture as a walking melody for the mynah bird in the half-dozen Inki cartoons.

71. Freleng had his share of pantomimic stories, but he relied much less on facial expressions than did Jones. Particularly in his musical cartoons, in which the score dominates the soundtrack almost entirely (*Rhapsody in Rivets*, 1941; *Pigs in a Polka*, 1943; *Rhapsody Rabbit*, 1946), the visual humor created with the characters' bodies is histrionic rather than subtle.

72. Barrier, *Hollywood Cartoons*, 490.

73. Practically the same confrontation between Bugs and Sam occurs in the first Yosemite Sam cartoon, *Hare Trigger* (1945); but there (in a scene set on a train) rather than having dramatic music the scene is completely silent, so that the sound of their spurs can be heard as they walk toward each other.

74. Among those viewing Stalling as a postmodernist is the composer John Zorn, probably the most vocal of all of Stalling's supporters: "On first hearing, Stalling's immense musical talents are immediately apparent, and certainly all these basic musical elements are there—but they are broken into shards: a constantly changing kaleidoscope of styles, forms, melodies, quotations, and of course the 'Mickey Mousing.' . . . Stalling developed this technique while playing piano for silent films in Kansas City, honed it to a science with Disney and elevated it to an art with Warner Bros." (Zorn, "Carl Stalling: An Appreciation," brochure notes for Stalling, *The Carl Stalling Project*, n.p.).

75. Schneider, *That's All Folks!*, 149. See also Eric O. Costello's online en-

cyclopedia on the Warner Bros. cartoons (*The Warner Bros. Cartoon Companion*, 1998, http://members.aol.com/EOCostello/ [accessed 1 June 2004]), which is dedicated to explaining all sorts of arcane information about the series. The bulk of its entries are devoted to explicating various intertextual references.

CHAPTER 2. "YOU REALLY DO BEAT THE SHIT OUT OF THAT CAT": SCOTT BRADLEY'S (VIOLENT) MUSIC FOR MGM

1. For example, the chapter on music in animated films in Roy M. Prendergast's *Film Music: A Neglected Art* (New York: W. W. Norton, 1977) looks solely at Bradley as a representative Hollywood cartoon composer. Other criticism that similarly views him in this manner includes John H. Winge, "Cartoons and Modern Music," *Sight and Sound* 17.67 (Autumn 1948): 136–37; Ingolf Dahl, "Notes on Cartoon Music," *Film Music Notes* 8.5 (May–June 1949): 3–13; and Jon Newsom, "'A Sound Idea': Music for Animated Films," *Quarterly Journal of the Library of Congress* 37.3–4 (Summer–Fall 1980): 279–309. For contemporary writing explicitly on Bradley, see R. Vernon Steele's "Scoring for Cartoons: An Interview with Scott Bradley," *Pacific Coast Musician* 26.10 (15 May 1937): 12–13, and the five articles that Bradley himself wrote throughout the 1940s and 1950s: "Cartoon Music of the Future," *Pacific Coast Musician* 30.12 (21 June 1941): 28; "'Music in Cartoons,' Excerpts from a talk given at The Music Forum October 28, 1944," *Film Music Notes* 3.4 (December 1944): n.p., reprinted in *The Cartoon Music Book,* edited by Daniel Goldmark and Yuval Taylor (Chicago: A Cappella Books, 2002), 115–20 (all citations are to the reprint); "Open Forum," *Hollywood Reporter,* 28 October 1946, 10; "Personality on the Sound Track: A Glimpse behind the Scenes and Sequences in Filmland," *Music Educators Journal* 33.3 (January 1947): 28–30; and "Evoluzione della musica nei disegni animati," in *Musica e film,* edited by S. G. Biamonte (Rome: Edizioni dell'Ateneo, 1959), 217–21.

2. Scott Bradley, interview by Michael Barrier and Milton Gray, 11 March 1977, 1. My thanks to Mike Barrier for making this interview available to me.

3. [Inset photo], *Pacific Coast Musician* 23.11 (17 March 1934): 1. The soloists for "Thanatopsis" were Myrtle Aber (Bradley's wife), Clemence Gifford, Hardesty Johnson, and Frank Pursell.

4. "Oratorio Society Gives Fine Dual Performance," *Pacific Coast Musician* 23.12 (24 March 1934): 5.

5. Dahl, "Notes on Cartoon Music," 4. I have reprinted the "telegram" exactly as it appeared in the original. Parts of Dahl's article, including this biographical statement, have been reprinted in Newsom's "A Sound Idea." The notes on the reverse of an early publicity photo of Bradley, now in the photo files of the *Los Angeles Examiner* (Los Angeles Examiner Collection, Specialized Libraries and Archival Collection, University of Southern California), fill in some more gaps in his musical biography: he was "identified with orchestras and bands in the East . . . and has directed light opera such as 'Red Mill.'"

6. These cue sheet records have been condensed and reproduced in Clifford McCarty, *Film Composers in America: A Filmography, 1911–1970,* 2nd ed. (New York: Oxford University Press, 2000), 46.

7. Bradley, interview by Barrier and Gray, 2.

8. Steele, "Scoring for Cartoons," 12.

9. Michael Barrier, *Hollywood Cartoons: American Animation in Its Golden Age* (New York: Oxford University Press, 1999), 188–89. Barrier argues that Harman and Ising most likely stopped producing cartoons for Schlesinger because he did not want to increase their budget for each short. His own 1933 contract with Warner Bros. had lowered his operating budget by almost $4,000 from its 1931 level. MGM offered to pay Harman and Ising $12,500 per cartoon—still $500 short of the minimum budgeted for each Disney cartoon in 1933 (some cost as much as $20,000).

10. Bradley, interview by Barrier and Gray, 1. Bradley also mentions that Harman and Ising "had a picture they wanted to do at Paramount Studios, and they were looking for someone to do the music. Frank Marsales was working for Rudy and Hugh, but his hand was injured. . . . I was at home and not working at the time, and they called me. I had never met them nor they met me. . . . I knew they were working with a small budget, so instead of charging them $500.00 for the job, I gave them the music for $250.00." This "picture" is most likely the 1933 version of *Alice in Wonderland*, directed by Norman McLeod, which includes a sequence animated by Harman and Ising.

11. Bradley, interview by Barrier and Gray, 1.

12. The list of "classical" composers who wrote music for animation includes Paul Hindemith, Dimitri Shostakovich, Paul Dessau, and Alfred Schnittke. None of these composers worked on Hollywood-produced cartoons, however (although Dessau, who created semi-improvised scores for several early Disney pre-sound shorts, came close).

13. Though a single interview with Stalling near the end of his life cannot offer a complete picture of his opinions on animation, it does begin to convey his attitude toward his work; see Michael Barrier, Milton Gray, and Bill Spicer, "An Interview with Carl Stalling" (1971), in *The Cartoon Music Book,* edited by Daniel Goldmark and Yuval Taylor (Chicago: A Cappella Books, 2002), 37–60.

14. Steele, "Scoring for Cartoons," 12.

15. Steele, "Scoring for Cartoons," 13.

16. Bradley, "Cartoon Music of the Future," 28.

17. Bradley, "Music in Cartoons," 119. The one-page biography included with this "talk" (probably written by Bradley himself) echoed a similar sentiment: "His ambition is to score a feature-length cartoon, using an original, pre-composed score—the exact opposite of 'Fantasia.'"

18. Nathaniel Shilkret, "Condensed from 'Some Predictions for the Future of Film Music' in *Music Publishers' Journal*—Jan., Feb. 1946," *Film Music Notes* 5.8 (April 1946): 14.

19. Winge, "Cartoons and Modern Music," 137.

20. See James Westby, "Castelnuovo-Tedesco in America: The Film Music" (Ph.D. diss., University of California, Los Angeles, 1995). Included in the Bradley collection at the University of Southern California are three short pieces—for piano only—titled "Movie Sketches," written by Castelnuovo-Tedesco and signed by him to Bradley; the piece subtitled "The Sorcerer" is inscribed "To Scott Bradley 'his apprentice sorcerer'" (Scott Bradley Collection, MGM Col-

lection, USC Cinema-Television Library, University of Southern California). Westby has told me that these pieces were composed in 1941—a date consistent with the reference to Disney's *Fantasia,* released in 1940.

21. Anthony Christlieb and Carolyn Beck, eds., *Recollections of a First Chair Bassoonist: 52 Years in the Hollywood Studio Orchestras* (Sherman Oaks, Calif.: Christlieb Products, 1996), 27. Christlieb also states:

> I did all Scott Bradley's TOM & JERRY cartoons at M-G-M from 1936 to 1941. Scott was an elegant composer of music for cartoons, one of the best anywhere. He was well schooled in his craft. It seemed that at the conclusion of any picture that was being scored, a cartoon was in the wings, waiting to be scored if a few minutes were left over on the recording sessions. . . . Ingolf Dahl once did a treatise on cartoon music ["Notes on Cartoon Music"], detailing all the difficulties involved. One such difficulty would be ways one has to contract or elongate a melodic line to fit the action. His most quoted source was Scott Bradley. Scott once confided to me that his contract to M-G-M amounted to $10,000 a year, a shocking revelation that to me only denigrated the music department and at the same time revealed that the players were not the only ones being taken advantage of.

My thanks to Neil Lerner for bringing this memoir to my attention.

22. Numerous references to performances of Bradley's works, including *Cartoonia,* appear in *Pacific Coast Musician* throughout the late 1930s.

23. Bradley, "Music in Cartoons," 119. My thanks to Mike Barrier for first pointing out to me the information about Monteux's involvement with *Cartoonia.* The autograph copy of the score is dated August 1937. Immediately following his retirement from MGM in 1958, Bradley seems to have renewed his interest in public performance: *Cartoonia* was performed by the San Fernando Valley Symphony during a concert on Friday, 22 May 1959. In addition, the program notes indicate that the piece had been performed the previous year by the Houston Symphony, under the direction of Leopold Stokowski (Bradley Collection, box 2:2).

24. Dahl, "Notes on Cartoon Music," 6.

25. Having more time did not necessarily spell great success for a composer: most of the other major studios—Disney, Lantz, Columbia—similarly produced only fifteen to twenty cartoons a year, yet their music received far less praise from contemporary critics than that of MGM (and Bradley).

26. Bradley, interview by Barrier and Gray, 1–2.

27. Winge, "Cartoons and Modern Music," 136. My thanks to Leonard Maltin for helping me to track down this article.

28. The violinist is quoted in Winge, "Cartoons and Modern Music," 137; also quoted in Leonard Maltin, *Of Mice and Magic: A History of American Animated Cartoons,* rev. ed. (New York: New American Library, 1987), 290.

29. Barrier, Gray, and Spicer, "An Interview with Carl Stalling," 54.

30. Dahl, "Notes on Cartoon Music," 6.

31. Maltin, *Of Mice and Magic,* 281.

32. Bradley, "Cartoon Music of the Future," 28.

33. In "prescoring," the cartoon's score was recorded before the animation was complete—a reversal of the normal process. *Film Music Notes* printed Bradley's comments on the ideal cartoon just two weeks after *Dance of the Weed*

first appeared in theaters (its score was recorded on 19 February 1941). It is fair to assume that he made them with this cartoon in mind. Obviously he was pleased with the process and thought all cartoons should be done the same way.

34. Bradley, "Music in Cartoons," 116.

35. "Cartoons," *Film Music Notes* 1.3 (December 1941): 6.

36. E. G. Lutz, *Animated Cartoons: How They Are Made, Their Origin and Development* (New York: C. Scribner's Sons, 1920; reprint, Bedford, Mass.: Applewood Books, 1998), 230. Lutz also points out that "an effect like this is easy to produce in animated cartoons."

37. Lutz, *Animated Cartoons*, 225–26.

38. Avery, quoted in Joe Adamson, *Tex Avery: King of Cartoons* (New York: Da Capo Press, 1975), 190.

39. Barrier, *Hollywood Cartoons*, 422.

40. Eugene Slafer, "A Conversation with Bill Hanna," in *The American Animated Cartoon*, edited by Gerald and Danny Peary (New York: E. P. Dutton, 1980), 258.

41. Avery, quoted in Adamson, *Tex Avery*, 193.

42. John Culshaw, "Violence and the Cartoon," *Fortnightly*, no. 1020 (December 1951): 834.

43. Dave Hickey, "Pontormo's Rainbow," in *Air Guitar: Essays on Art and Democracy* (Los Angeles: Art issues. Press, 1997), 48.

44. Bradley, "Cartoon Music of the Future," 28.

45. Bradley, interview by Barrier and Gray, 2.

46. Michel Chion, *Audio-Vision: Sound on Screen*, edited and translated by Claudia Gorbman (New York: Columbia University Press, 1994), 224, 109.

47. Chion, *Audio-Vision*, 112.

48. Claudia Gorbman, *Unheard Melodies: Narrative Film Music* (London: BFI Publishing; Bloomington: Indiana University Press, 1987), 88.

49. Chion, *Audio-Vision*, 122.

50. Bradley, quoted in "News Items . . . Comments," *Film Music Notes* 3.3 (December 1943): n.p.

51. Steele, "Scoring for Cartoons," 12. Bradley's willingness to make such a statement, particularly in a music and performance journal like *Pacific Coast Musician,* demonstrates his lack of concern about offending his colleagues in the cartoon music world, as he undoubtedly was referring to the cartoons produced in the 1930s by the Columbia, Lantz, Terry, and Warner Bros. studios.

52. Chion, *Audio-Vision*, 61.

53. Chion, *Audio-Vision*, 13–14.

54. In addition, Bradley usually used a band arrangement of a popular tune at the very beginning of a cartoon (following the title cards) to establish a playful or boisterous mood.

55. Henry Jenkins, *What Made Pistachio Nuts? Early Sound Comedy and the Vaudeville Aesthetic* (New York: Columbia University Press, 1992), 146.

56. Steele, "Scoring for Cartoons," 12.

57. Chion, *Audio-Vision,* 121.

58. Bradley, "Music in Cartoons," 118.

59. Winge, "Cartoons and Modern Music," 136–37.

60. Steele, "Scoring for Cartoons," 13.

61. Caryl Flinn, *Strains of Utopia: Gender, Nostalgia, and Hollywood Film Music* (Princeton: Princeton University Press, 1992), 21.

62. Earlier examples of twelve-tone scores do exist, such as Hanns Eisler's music for the title sequence of Fritz Lang's 1943 feature *Hangmen Also Die.* Eisler's project, as detailed in *Composing for the Films* (New York: Oxford University Press, 1947) and elsewhere, so appealed to Bradley that when Eisler was excoriated in the *Hollywood Reporter* in 1946 for owing his composing jobs in Hollywood to his supposed Communist leanings, Bradley defended him in a reply published on the journal's editorial page. He made special note of Eisler's music having been "(sometimes erroneously called 'ultra-modern') and as such appeal[ing] to the musical intelligentsia" ("Open Forum," *Hollywood Reporter,* 28 October 1946, 10). Bradley's own music for cartoons received very similar criticism, particularly from the directors with whom he worked.

63. Sabine M. Feisst, "Arnold Schoenberg and the Cinematic Art," *Musical Quarterly* 83.1 (Spring 1999): 99. Feisst told me that her own research on Schoenberg, which included going through all of his old address and date books, turned up no mention of Bradley's name. If any meeting between the two men occurred, it likely was unplanned and went unrecorded.

64. Barrier, *Hollywood Cartoons,* 421.

65. From a note typed and dated 1967, signed by Bradley and attached to a copy of Dahl's 1949 article, "Notes on Cartoon Music" (Scott Bradley Collection, American Heritage Center, University of Wyoming). See appendix 2 for the complete text of this note.

66. Barrier, *Hollywood Cartoons,* 421–22. The bracketed sentence is taken from the unedited version of this interview, graciously provided by Barrier.

67. Bradley, quoted in Winge, "Cartoons and Modern Music," 136.

68. Avery's degree of control over the recording levels in his cartoons is not known.

69. Norman M. Klein, *7 Minutes: The Life and Death of the American Animated Cartoon* (New York: Verso, 1993), 199.

70. Bradley, quoted in "News Items . . . Comments," n.p.

71. As the popularity of television as a form of entertainment was beginning to grow, film companies were selling their theaters in response to the Supreme Court's 1948 decision holding Paramount and others guilty of violating antitrust law. New theater owners no longer had to pay for and show the studios' cartoons. In this period, cartoons with experimental scores would likely have been even more difficult than others to sell to potential exhibitors.

72. My thanks to Mike Barrier for providing me with this date.

73. Bradley, note attached to Dahl, "Notes on Cartoon Music."

CHAPTER 3. *JUNGLE JIVE:* ANIMATION,
JAZZ MUSIC, AND SWING CULTURE

1. Barry Keith Grant, "'Jungle Nights in Harlem': Jazz, Ideology and the Animated Cartoon," *University of Hartford Studies in Literature* 21.3 (1989): 5–6, 10.

2. The literature on the representation of race in film and in animation is extensive. My discussion, which touches on several aspects of the racist elements of film, focuses on music's role in the creation of jazz's image in cartoons. For an excellent introduction to the history of African Americans in film, see Donald Bogle's *Toms, Coons, Mulattoes, Mammies and Bucks: An Interpretive History of Blacks in American Films* (New York: Continuum, 1994); Karl F. Cohen's *Forbidden Animation: Censored Cartoons and Blacklisted Animators in America* (Jefferson, N.C.: McFarland, 1997), which discusses several aspects of racist cartoons; and Henry T. Sampson's magisterial *That's Enough, Folks: Black Images in Animated Cartoons, 1900–1960* (Lanham, Md.: Scarecrow Press, 1998), which chronicles almost every appearance in a cartoon of a black character (or a stereotype of one). Barry Keith Grant's article on jazz and animation, "Jungle Nights in Harlem," was also an important guiding factor in my consideration of these issues.

3. Edith Lang and George West, *Musical Accompaniment of Moving Pictures* (Boston: Boston Music Company, 1920; reprint, New York: Arno Press, 1970), 58–59. This excerpt comes from a section titled "Special Effects, and How to Produce Them."

4. "Music for the Picture: Questions Answered—Suggestions Offered," *Moving Picture World*, 23 March 1918, 1662.

5. Lang and West, *Musical Accompaniment*, 37.

6. Walter Kingsley, "Whence Comes Jass? Facts from the Great Authority on the Subject," *New York Sun*, 5 August 1917, 3; reprinted in *Keeping Time: Readings in Jazz History*, edited by Robert Walser (New York: Oxford University Press, 1999), 6.

7. Though earlier examples of jazz in animation exist, their focus on jazz is not so explicit, and they do not demonstrate (as Whiteman does) the construction of the jazz aesthetic for white consumers.

8. Krin Gabbard, *Jammin' at the Margins: Jazz and the American Cinema* (Chicago: University of Chicago Press, 1996), 11; Michael Rogin, *Blackface, White Noise: Jewish Immigrants in the Hollywood Melting Pot* (Berkeley: University of California Press, 1996), 139. For a complete description of the scene in question, see Gabbard's introduction, 11–14.

9. Russell Sanjek, *Pennies from Heaven: The American Popular Music Business in the Twentieth Century* (New York: Da Capo Press, 1995), 30.

10. Grant, "Jungle Nights in Harlem," 7.

11. The repeated use of *Rhapsody in Blue* was by no means accidental, as the piece was written for and premiered by Whiteman's orchestra on 12 February 1924, at Aeolian Hall in New York City (Hugh C. Ernst, "The Man Who Made a Lady out of Jazz [Paul Whiteman]," in Walser, ed., *Keeping Time*, 39–40).

12. Whiteman's method of taming the beast is only one of several similarities between this segment and Walt Disney's cartoon *Jungle Rhythm* (1929), in which Mickey performs for (and on, as in *Steamboat Willie*, 1928) many of the jungle animals, having first calmed and impressed them with his vocal musical prowess. While the Disney title might imply a link to jazz, Mickey nonetheless steers clear of contemporary music and instead performs songs such as "Yankee Doodle" and "Turkey in the Straw," no doubt because of Disney's reluctance to

use current popular songs with their inevitably expensive licensing fees (as discussed in chapter 1).

13. The Aeolian Hall concert of 1924 is seen as the performance in which Whiteman supposedly "made a lady out of jazz" (Ernst, "The Man Who Made a Lady out of Jazz," 39). Whiteman in *King of Jazz* reprises his role as the musician who helps tame jazz and make it respectable. We also cannot ignore that Whiteman was a white man: his race surely helped reassure uncertain white listeners.

14. Lantz would in any case have needed at least to record Whiteman for the sequence in order to have something to animate to. It would make sense to record the entire short sequence in one session, especially since sound recording and mixing technology at the time was still (comparatively) primitive (Michael Barrier, *Hollywood Cartoons: American Animation in Its Golden Age* [New York: Oxford University Press, 1999], 174).

15. Leonard Maltin, *Of Mice and Magic: A History of American Animated Cartoons*, rev. ed. (New York: New American Library, 1987), 162.

16. Grant, "Jungle Nights in Harlem," 7.

17. Walt Disney and his colleagues were the first to animate Oswald; when Lantz took over, his character and appearance changed significantly. For more on Oswald's transition from Disney trickster to Lantz cutie-pie, see Barrier, *Hollywood Cartoons*, 48–49.

In the midst of a discussion of recurring figures in African storytelling traditions, Samuel Floyd "posit[s], as have others in casual conversation, that Br'er Rabbit later metamorphosed into Bugs Bunny, trickster hero of millions of Americans, white and black, child and adult" (Floyd, *The Power of Black Music* [New York: Oxford University Press, 1995], 29). Some of Oswald's traits no doubt influenced Bugs's personality.

18. When Hugh Harman and Rudolf Ising left Warner Bros. in 1933, they took Bosko with them. In the cartoons they produced with Bosko for MGM the somewhat indeterminate character was transformed into a black human child who, unlike his non–*Homo sapiens* forebears, could clearly be thought of as having African roots.

19. Animation historians who have investigated the presence of stereotypes in cartoons have recorded some of the common rationalizations used to defend them—for instance, the critic Charles Solomon's claim that "At the time, most people considered this style of humor both good fun and good taste" (quoted in Terry Lindvall and Ben Fraser, "Darker Shades of Animation: African-American Images in the Warner Bros. Cartoon," in *Reading the Rabbit: Explorations in Warner Bros. Animation*, edited by Kevin Sandler [New Brunswick: Rutgers University Press, 1998], 123). Solomon does not explain who "most people" might be.

20. Sampson, *That's Enough, Folks*, v. See also Bogle, *Toms, Coons, Mulattoes, Mammies, and Bucks*.

21. Erno Rapée, *Encyclopedia of Music for Pictures* (New York: Belwin, 1925; reprint, New York: Arno Press, 1970), 64. In the category titled "American (Southern)," Rapée includes songs such as "The Darkville Dance" and "From the Cotton Field," as well as "Turkey in the Straw" and Septimus Winner's "Listen to the Mocking Bird." The cue sheet for the Fleischer cartoon *Bimbo's Initiation*

(1932) lists "Old Zip Coon," but that title might have referred to "Turkey in the Straw," the song into which "Old Zip Coon" had eventually mutated at the turn of the century (Charles Hamm, *Music in the New World* [New York: W. W. Norton, 1983], 259–60).

22. Of course, "Sweet Georgia Brown" has continued to serve as a racial marker in its role as the theme music for the Harlem Globetrotters, who provide a latter-day minstrel show on the basketball court.

23. Leslie Cabarga, *The Fleischer Story,* 2nd ed. (New York: Da Capo Press, 1988), 63–64.

24. Among the other performers who appeared in Fleischer cartoons were Arthur Tracy, Lillian Roth, Irene Bordoni, the Royal Samoans, Gus Edwards, the Three X Sisters, the Boswell Sisters, Borrah Minnevitch and His Harmonica Rascals, Vincent Lopez, Jimmy Dorsey, and even Colonel Stoopnagle and Budd; see Cabarga, *The Fleischer Story,* 212–13, for a complete list.

25. For more on the cultural life of New York in the Fleischers' time, see Ann Douglas, *Terrible Honesty: Mongrel Manhattan in the 1920s* (New York: Farrar, Straus, and Giroux, 1995).

26. Nathan Irvin Huggins, *Harlem Renaissance* (New York: Oxford University Press, 1971), 89.

27. Cabarga, *The Fleischer Story,* 63.

28. LeRoi Jones [Imamu Amiri Baraka], *Blues People: Negro Music in White America* (New York: Morrow Quill Paperbacks, 1963), 149.

29. Huggins, *Harlem Renaissance,* 300. In his examination of homosexuality and animation, Sean Griffin observes that a wide variety of subverted cultures flourished in 1920s New York: "The Prohibition era created in New York City a vast underground of speakeasies and gin joints that allowed individuals who had considered themselves law-abiding before Prohibition to mix with minorities and outcasts from society" (Griffin, "Pronoun Trouble: The 'Queerness' of Animation," *Spectator: USC Journal of Film and Television Criticism* 15.1 [Fall 1994]: 99).

30. Others in this series from Fleischer include Cab Calloway and his orchestra in *Minnie the Moocher* (1932), *Snow-White* (1933), and *The Old Man of the Mountain* (1933); the Mills Brothers in *I Ain't Got Nobody* (1932), *Dinah* (1933), and *When Yuba Plays the Rumba on the Tuba* (1933); and Don Redman and his orchestra in *I Heard* (1933).

31. The session players for the songs in this cartoon were Armstrong on trumpet and vocals; Zilmer Randolph, trumpet; Preston Jackson, trombone; George James and Lester Boone, alto saxophone; Al Washington, tenor saxophone; Charlie Alexander, piano; Mike McKendrick, banjo; Johnny Lindsay, bass; and Tubby Hall, drums (Tom Lord, *The Jazz Discography,* vol. 1 [West Vancouver, B.C.: Lord Music Reference, 1992], A334).

32. For more on the ubiquity of "Chinatown, My Chinatown" and other Asian-themed Tin Pan Alley songs, see Charles Garrett, "Chinatown, Whose Chinatown? Defining America's Borders with Musical Orientalism," *Journal of the American Musicological Society* 57.1 (Spring 2004): 119–73.

33. Paul Wells, *Understanding Animation* (London: Routledge, 1998), 217. Sean Griffin similarly describes Betty's descent into the cave in *Snow-White* as

"much like the entrance to a speakeasy, dark and secret" (Griffin, "Pronoun Trouble," 99).

34. Bogle, *Toms, Coons, Mulattoes, Mammies, and Bucks,* 13.

35. *I Heard,* featuring Don Redman and his orchestra, takes place at a mining camp. The first half of the cartoon occurs nearby in Betty's Tavern, but the song's chorus is heard only when Bimbo, mining deep underground, comes upon a cavern inhabited by a skeleton and several ghosts (or spooks), singing "I Heard."

36. Huggins, *Harlem Renaissance,* 90.

37. On the derivation of "tom" from "Uncle Tom," see Bogle, *Toms, Coons, Mulattoes, Mammies, and Bucks,* 4–7.

38. Gabbard, *Jammin' at the Margins,* 207.

39. Huggins, *Harlem Renaissance,* 255.

40. The title of the cartoon clearly plays on the common pronunciation of the South Pacific island Pago Pago with a nasalized *g* (see *Merriam Webster's Collegiate Dictionary,* 11th ed.).

41. Several elements of *Pingo-Pongo* appear in other cartoons. The Mills Brothers and Fats Waller combination had already been seen in *Clean Pastures* (Warner Bros.; Freleng, 1937; discussed in this chapter). Bob Clampett would use the exact same gag of a switch from refined dancing to hot jitterbugging in *Coal Black and the Sebben Dwarfs* (Warner Bros., 1943): So White and the Prince first dance a courtly tune (to the tune of the nineteenth-century ballad "Long, Long Ago" by T. H. Bayley) before switching quickly to a more contemporary song and style ("Nagasaki").

42. The conflation of ethnicities or cultural groups in film music is not limited to cartoons. For articles on the musical depictions of Native Americans and Asians in film and in Western music in general, see Michael Pisani, "'I'm an Indian Too': Creating Native American Identities in Nineteenth- and Early Twentieth-Century Music," in *The Exotic in Western Music,* edited by Jonathan Bellman (Boston: Northeastern University Press, 1998), 218–57; Claudia Gorbman, "Drums along the L.A. River: Scoring the Indian," in *Westerns: Films through History,* edited by Janet Walker (New York: Routledge, 2001), 177–95; and Anthony Sheppard, "An Exotic Enemy: Anti-Japanese Musical Propaganda in World War II Hollywood," *Journal of the American Musicological Society* 54.2 (Summer 2001): 303–57.

43. Sampson's chronicle of black images in cartoons, *That's Enough, Folks,* confirms the ubiquity of the jungle portrayal of jazz's origins.

44. An all-black vocal jazz/rhythm group similar to the Mills Brothers, known as the Four Blackbirds, recorded the backing vocals for many cartoon soundtracks, including *Clean Pastures* and *The Isle of Pingo-Pongo.* One member of this group—possibly Leroy Hurte—also did the imitations of the famous music personalities. My thanks to Keith Scott for providing this information.

45. Hank Sartin, "From Vaudeville to Hollywood, from Silence to Sound: Warner Bros. Cartoons of the Early Sound Era," in Sandler, ed., *Reading the Rabbit,* 75. Sartin makes some very compelling arguments about the similarities between Hollywood musicals and the early sound cartoon, as well as the great debt that the storytelling practices in cartoons owe to vaudeville conventions.

46. Gerald Bordman, *The Oxford Companion to American Theatre,* 2nd ed. (New York: Oxford University Press, 1992), 306–7.

47. "Swing for Sale" was originally featured in a 1930 Vitaphone short of the same name, sung by Hal LeRoy.

48. Hamm, *Music in the New World*, 129.

49. We can see a similar relationship between jazz and hell in the Disney short *Goddess of Spring* (Jackson, 1934), which tells the story of Hades and Persephone. A balladlike song introduces the "goddess of spring," featuring a high tenor voice. When Hades takes Persephone down to his kingdom, he sings to her, "With this crown, I make you queen of Hades. Hi-dey Hades!" The latter phrase clearly alludes to Cab Calloway and his catchphrase "hi-de-ho." Hades' little devil henchman, all red and black, with black faces, green eyes, and pitchforks, sing a song to "Hi-dey Hades" around a geyser spurting lava—this in stark contrast to the flowers, birds, and little wood elves that grace Persephone's domain. My thanks to Ray Knapp for bringing this short to my attention.

50. Bogle, *Toms, Coons, Mulattoes, Mammies, and Bucks*, 68.

51. Cohen, *Forbidden Animation*, 29.

52. Barrier, *Hollywood Cartoons*, 342.

53. Bogle, *Toms, Coons, Mulattoes, Mammies, and Bucks*, 68.

54. Grant, "Jungle Nights in Harlem," 8.

55. The "world" to which Fats travels is "Wackyland," the wonderful never-never land first seen in Clampett's 1938 cartoon *Porky in Wackyland*.

56. For another take on salvation vs. redemption in this and other Hollywood cartoons, see Richard J. Leskosky, "The Reforming Fantasy: Recurrent Theme and Structure in American Studio Cartoons," *Velvet Light Trap*, no. 24 (Fall 1989): 53–66.

57. Although the cartoon's racism has rendered it largely unseen for the past twenty-five years, many animation and film historians agree that its animation and timing make *Coal Black* among the best cartoons ever produced at Warner Bros.

58. Barrier, *Hollywood Cartoons*, 439. Barrier also points out that the studio management turned down Clampett's request *not* to have the Warner Bros. orchestra record the score, though a trumpet player from a black band did perform the solo for the cartoon's finale.

59. Keith Scott, communication with author, 27 April 2003.

60. Among the notable artists who released "The Five O'Clock Whistle" were Ella Fitzgerald, Glenn Miller, and Duke Ellington (all in 1940, for Decca, Bluebird, and Victor, respectively).

61. For further discussion of this idea of the trumpet, see Gabbard, *Jammin' at the Margins*, 138–59.

62. For a discussion of this cartoon, see Rogin, *Blackface, White Noise*, 3–4.

63. In *The Singing Kid*, Jolson introduces "I Love to Singa" by singing it on the balcony of his penthouse apartment. His accompanist is Cab Calloway and his orchestra, who just happen to be playing on an adjacent penthouse balcony, dressed to the nines. Even Calloway cannot manage to make Jolson's rendition more than tepid. All three of Calloway's shorts for the Fleischer studio, showing a very different image of the popular bandleader, had already been released (one in 1932, the others in 1933).

64. In the cartoon *Goldilocks and the Jivin' Bears* (Warner Bros.; Freleng,

1944), a trio of bears (clarinet, bass, and piano) are shown jamming in their home (on the Raymond Scott tune "Twilight in Turkey") until each instrument in turn catches fire, literalizing the idea of "hot jazz" and the notion of a player "burning up."

65. Fifteen years earlier, Walter Lantz produced a "Three Little Pigs do jazz" short titled *The Hams That Couldn't Be Cured*. It opens with Algernon Wolf about to be hanged for trying to kill the three little pigs. Pleading with a noose around his neck, he cries, "I'll tell you what *really* happened." In a flashback we see the wolf's life as a simple, law-abiding music teacher. The pigs arrive at his house to take lessons, walking in with a trumpet, trombone, and a clarinet and stating, "We want youse to learn us to play music." The speech of the uncouth pigs is rough, with a smattering of jive; the first commands the wolf, "Shoot the tune to us, goon!" After the wolf plays the opening arpeggio of the second Kreutzer etude on the piano, the pigs turn it into a boogie-woogie tune. They play on every instrument in the place, including tuba, drums, and piano. One pig plays clarinet in a fishbowl, making bubbles that float away while another plays a tune on them; as he hits the bubbles with mallets, they make the sound of a vibraphone. The pigs corner the wolf and continue to play until their music literally blows the roof off the place. As in *Three Little Bops,* the wolf cannot play the *right* kind of music: that is, the pigs cannot appreciate the sounds he is producing, and therefore reject him.

66. The wolf's ejection from the clubs in *Three Little Bops* reminds me of a story told by Charlie Haden, the bass player who played on most of Ornette Coleman's earliest (and most controversial) albums on Atlantic Records, about the first time he saw Coleman play: "This guy came up on stage and asked the musicians if he could play, and started to sit in. He played three or four phrases, and it was so brilliant, I couldn't believe it—I had never heard any sound like that before. Immediately the musicians told him to stop playing, and he packed up his horn" (quoted by John Litweiler, *Ornette Coleman: The Harmolodic Life* [London: Quartet Books, 1992], 44; Litweiler is quoted in the brochure notes for Ornette Coleman, *Beauty Is a Rare Thing: The Complete Atlantic Recordings* [Rhino Records 71410, 1993], 8). Others, David Ake points out, were not so taken with Coleman's music as Haden; he specifically mentions an incident in which the drummer Max Roach reacted to Coleman's playing with physical violence (Ake, *Jazz Cultures* [Berkeley: University of California Press, 2001], 63).

67. Hamm, *Music in the New World,* 363.

68. I am referring here not to films that used popular songs or jazz or big band tunes within the narrative or the film's underscore, but rather to films that consistently incorporated elements of the jazz style and sound into the score as a whole.

CHAPTER 4. CORNY CONCERTOS AND SILLY SYMPHONIES: CLASSICAL MUSIC AND CARTOONS

1. Timothy and Kevin Burke, *Saturday Morning Fever: Growing Up with Cartoon Culture* (New York: St. Martin's Griffin, 1999), 95.

2. This assessment of how frequently composers are appropriated relies on a survey of the Warner Bros., MGM, Iwerks, Terry, and Fleischer cartoons.

3. The opposite logic dominated the selection of music in the spate of Hollywood feature films released in the 1930s and '40s that fetishized life in the concert hall. They showcased the performance, mainly on the piano, of famous works of music, as featured soloists (from Ignace Paderewski to Gracie Allen) displayed their skills at the keyboard. The more bombastic or intense the piece, the better. Thus among the works found in these films are longer pieces by composers such as Beethoven and Rachmaninoff, as well as excerpts from operas by Mozart and Verdi. For a detailed discussion of this film subgenre, see Ivan Raykoff, "Dreams of Love: Mythologies of the 'Romantic' Pianist in Twentieth-Century Popular Culture" (Ph.D. diss., University of California, San Diego, 2001).

4. I recently saw the film *A Christmas Story* (1983), which uses "Wintermärchen" in a scene of comic and melodramatic pathos clearly modeled (in part) on similar scenes in cartoons.

5. Lawrence W. Levine, *Highbrow/Lowbrow: The Emergence of Cultural Hierarchy in America* (Cambridge, Mass.: Harvard University Press, 1988), 130–31.

6. Some examples of plots derived from the pieces named by Levine: the first half of *A Corny Concerto* (Warner Bros.; Clampett, 1943) is a *Fantasia*-spoofing setting of Strauss's *Blue Danube Waltz*, which is also the featured piece in *The Blue Danube* (MGM; Harman, 1939); several of Brahms's Hungarian Dances are the only music used in *Pigs in a Polka* (Warner Bros.; Freleng, 1943); and the second of Liszt's Hungarian Rhapsodies is the featured work in *Bars & Stripes* (Columbia, 1931), *Dipsy Gypsy* (Paramount; Pal, 1941), *Rhapsody in Rivets* (Warner Bros.; Freleng, 1941), *Rhapsody Rabbit* (Warner Bros.; Freleng, 1946), *The Cat Concerto* (MGM; Hanna and Barbera, 1947), and *Magic Fluke* (UPA; Hubley, 1949).

7. Friz Freleng with David Weber, *Animation: The Art of Friz Freleng* (Newport Beach, Calif.: Donovan Publishing, 1994), 127.

8. Jerry Beck and Will Friedwald, *Looney Tunes and Merrie Melodies: A Complete Illustrated Guide to the Warner Bros. Cartoons* (New York: Henry Holt, 1989), 268–69.

9. In his quest to employ modernist music in cartoons, Scott Bradley defied the unwritten rule for catchy tunes, often using twelve-tone scales much as Stalling might have used a phrase from Liszt or Rossini. Bradley's scales may be considered "gestures" in that they are short, unique phrases matched specifically with a particular action, but they lacked the cultural associations typical of the Romantic melodies that were more common in film scores and radio programs. Without this extramusical resonance, audiences probably did not identify the avantgarde phrases as anything other than unusually precise mickey-mousing.

10. Reginald M. Jones, Jr., *The Mystery of the Masked Man's Music: A Search for the Music Used on "The Lone Ranger" Radio Program, 1933–1954* (Metuchen, N.J.: Scarecrow Press, 1987), 5. Jones quotes James Jewell, the first director of *The Lone Ranger*, describing how the Rossini overture was chosen: "It was actually a tossup between *March of the Light Brigade* and the *William Tell* with its inspiring fanfare and ominous galloping movement suggested by the storm scene. Of course, Rossini won out and the rumbling, ever-increasing cadence and roar of the brewing storm became a gallop whether or not it was intended as

such." Jones believes that "March of the Light Brigade" was likely Jewell's misnomer for von Suppé's "Light Cavalry Overture."

11. Chuck Jones, "Music and the Animated Cartoon" (1946), in *The Cartoon Music Book*, edited by Daniel Goldmark and Yuval Taylor (Chicago: A Cappella Books, 2002), 96.

12. Joseph Horowitz, *Understanding Toscanini* (New York: Alfred A. Knopf, 1987), 231–32 (brackets his).

13. Horowitz, *Understanding Toscanini*, 232. Adorno elaborated on this notion in great detail in the book he coauthored (though initially without credit) with the composer Hanns Eisler, *Composing for the Films* (New York: Oxford University Press, 1947).

14. Chuck Jones, "Music and the Animated Cartoon," unpublished typescript, Music and Contemporary Life Papers (Box 3, Item 54), Special Collections Library, University of California, Los Angeles.

15. Among the cartoons that begin with Bugs singing are *Bugs Bunny Nips the Nips* (Freleng, 1944; "Someone's Rocking My Dreamboat"), *Hare Trigger* (Freleng, 1945; "Go Get the Ax"), *Gorilla My Dreams* (McKimson, 1948; "Trade Winds"), *Hare Splitter* (Freleng, 1948; "If I Could Be with You (One Hour Tonight)"), *A-Lad-In His Lamp* (McKimson, 1948; "Massa's in the Cold, Cold Ground"), and *Rabbit Every Monday* (Freleng, 1951; "It's Magic").

16. Other cartoons in this vein include *The Band Concert* and *Music Land* (both Disney, 1935), *I Love to Singa* (Warner Bros.; Avery, 1936), and *Dixieland Droopy* (MGM; Avery, 1954).

17. Levine, *Highbrow/Lowbrow*, 232.

18. Philip Brophy, "The Animation of Sound," in *The Illusion of Life: Essays on Animation*, edited by Alan Cholodenko (Sydney: Power Publications, 1991), 97.

19. Viewing the scene more closely, I noticed on the wall inside Giovanni Jones's home a reproduction (or the original—who knows what Chuck Jones intended?) of Henri Rousseau's 1897 painting *La Bohémienne endormie (The Sleeping Gypsy)*, demonstrating that Jones (both the singer and the cartoon's director) is firmly entrenched in the highbrow world.

20. Jane Feuer, *The Hollywood Musical*, 2nd ed. (Bloomington: Indiana University Press, 1993), 54–56. The most famous example of this plot is the assimilation of music of the New World presented in Al Jolson's film *The Jazz Singer* (1927)—the film that helped usher in the sound era. Cartoons that use this same story line include *The Oompahs* (UPA; Cannon, 1952), *Music Land*, and *I Love to Singa* (Warner Bros.; Avery, 1936), the animated version of *The Jazz Singer*. See also my discussion of *I Love to Singa* in chapter 3.

21. Hank Sartin, "From Vaudeville to Hollywood, from Silence to Sound: Warner Bros. Cartoons of the Early Sound Era," in *Reading the Rabbit: Explorations in Warner Bros. Animation*, edited by Kevin Sandler (New Brunswick, N.J.: Rutgers University Press, 1998), 67–85.

22. Levine, *Highbrow/Lowbrow*, 140.

23. Christopher Small, *Musicking: The Meanings of Performing and Listening* (Hanover, N.H.: Wesleyan University Press, 1998), 24.

24. Small, *Musicking*, 23.

25. Small, *Musicking,* 70.

26. Some examples of orchestra-driven cartoons are *A Car-Tune Portrait* (Fleischer: Fleischer, 1937), *The Mad Maestro* (MGM; Harman, 1939), and *Concerto in B Flat Minor* (Columbia; Tashlin, 1942), in addition to most of Walter Lantz's "Musical Miniatures" series, including *The Poet and Peasant* (1946), *Overture to William Tell* (1947), and *Kiddie Koncert* (1948), all directed by Dick Lundy.

27. Small, *Musicking,* 78.

28. Small, *Musicking,* 65–66; Michael Barrier, *Hollywood Cartoons: American Animation in Its Golden Age* (New York: Oxford University Press, 1999), 490. We know this must be the cartoon's finale, because Bugs cannot rise any higher in the hierarchy of concert hall culture (unless he pretends to be a composer).

29. Small, *Musicking,* 65.

30. Levine, *Highbrow/Lowbrow,* 139.

31. Theodor W. Adorno, *Introduction to the Sociology of Music,* translated by E. B. Ashton (New York: Continuum, 1976), 104–5.

32. Adorno did write on both animation (discussing Disney and Mickey Mouse) and film music (most significantly, with Eisler in *Composing for the Films*)—he just never put the two topics together. For more on his treatment of the first, see Miriam Hansen, "Of Mice and Ducks: Benjamin and Adorno on Disney," *South Atlantic Quarterly* 92.1 (Winter 1993): 34.

33. Preben Opperby, *Leopold Stokowski* (New York: Midas Books, 1982), 130.

34. Adorno, *Introduction to the Sociology of Music,* 106.

35. Barrier, *Hollywood Cartoons,* 490.

36. Adorno, *Introduction to the Sociology of Music,* 108.

37. Small, *Musicking,* 80.

38. Simon Frith, *Performing Rites: On the Value of Popular Music* (Cambridge, Mass.: Harvard University Press, 1996), 206.

39. The voice of Poochini was provided by Carlos Ramirez, a contract singer for MGM; the Mary Kaye Trio, among others, sang the parts of the magically transformed Poochini. My thanks to Keith Scott for providing this information.

40. Thomson, quoted in Horowitz, *Understanding Toscanini,* 245. Thomson's phrase first appeared in an article he wrote for the New York *Herald Tribune,* reprinted soon after in Virgil Thomson, *The State of Music* (New York: W. Morrow, 1939), 121–31.

41. Horowitz, *Understanding Toscanini,* 215.

42. Stephen Handzo, "Appendix: A Narrative Glossary of Film Sound Technology," in *Film Sound: Theory and Practice,* edited by Elisabeth Weis and John Belton (New York: Columbia University Press, 1985), 418–19.

43. Leonard Maltin, *Of Mice and Magic: A History of American Animated Cartoons,* rev. ed. (New York: New American Library, 1987), 63; quoted in Nicholas Cook, *Analysing Musical Multimedia* (Oxford: Clarendon Press, 1998), 175.

44. Robin Allan, *Walt Disney and Europe: European Influences on the Animated Feature Films of Walt Disney* (Bloomington: Indiana University Press, 1999), 93.

45. Barrier, *Hollywood Cartoons,* 247.

46. Harold Rawlinson, "Fitting a Film to Music," *Film Music Notes* 5.8 (April 1946): 8.

47. Disney had long been the dominant figure in cartoons, and particularly (beginning in the late 1930s) in animated films, though to that point he had produced only two feature-length productions (*Snow White,* 1938; *Pinocchio,* 1940); his sole competition in the latter field came from the Fleischer studio, whose *Gulliver's Travels* appeared the year before *Fantasia.*

48. "Short Subject Reviews: 'Cat Concerto,'" *Film Daily,* 1 May 1947, 7.

49. For a thorough investigation into critical responses to *Fantasia,* see Moya Luckett, "*Fantasia:* Cultural Constructions of Disney's 'Masterpiece,'" in *Disney Discourse: Producing the Magic Kingdom,* edited by Eric Smoodin (New York: Routledge, 1994), 214–36.

50. Harry M. Benshoff, "Heigh-Ho, Heigh-Ho, Is Disney High or Low? From Silly Cartoons to Postmodern Politics," *Animation Journal* 1.1 (Fall 1992): 64.

CHAPTER 5. *WHAT'S OPERA, DOC?* AND CARTOON OPERA

1. Chuck Jones, "What's Up, Down Under? Chuck Jones Talks at *The Illusion of Life* Conference," in *The Illusion of Life: Essays on Animation,* edited by Alan Cholodenko (Sydney: Power Publications, 1991), 39.

2. Chuck Jones, *Chuck Reducks: Drawing from the Fun Side of Life* (New York: Warner Books, 1996), 157. Jones made a similar comment regarding both *What's Opera, Doc?* and *The Rabbit of Seville* in a telephone interview by the author, 14 September 1994.

3. Jones, interview by author.

4. These rules are very similar to those he established for the Coyote and Road Runner; see Chuck Jones, *Chuck Amuck: The Life and Times of an Animated Cartoonist* (New York: Avon Books, 1990), 224–25.

5. Lawrence W. Levine, *Highbrow/Lowbrow: The Emergence of Cultural Hierarchy in America* (Cambridge, Mass.: Harvard University Press, 1988), 235. Levine cites in particular a moment in *A Night at the Opera* when Harpo and Chico hoodwink the pit orchestra into playing "Take Me Out to the Ball Game" during the overture to *Il Trovatore.* See also Lawrence Kramer's discussion, "The Singing Salami: Unsystematic Reflections on the Marx Brothers' *A Night at the Opera,*" in *A Night in at the Opera: Media Representations of Opera,* edited by Jeremy Tambling (London: John Libbey, 1994), 253–65.

6. Occasional references to specific stars of the opera world do occur in cartoons, the most frequent being an image of Enrico Caruso as Canio from *Pagliacci,* dressed in a white clown outfit with black tassels and pointed hat; the Warner Bros. cartoons usually complete this caricature by having the clown sing the refrain of "Laugh, Clown, Laugh," a song by Joseph Fiorito.

7. See Bill Hanna with Tom Ito, *A Cast of Friends* (Dallas: Taylor Publishing, 1996); Joe Barbera, *My Life in 'Toons* (Atlanta: Turner Publishing, 1994); Jones, *Chuck Amuck.*

8. Jeremy Tambling, *Opera, Ideology and Film* (New York: St. Martin's Press, 1987), 42.

9. Tambling, *Opera, Ideology and Film*, 47. Rossini's "Largo al Factotum" aria from *The Barber of Seville* shows up nine times in Warner Bros. cartoons, and Donizetti's sextet from *Lucia di Lammermoor* six times; the pieces also appear a few times each in the MGM cartoons. The Rossini is, by far, the piece meant to represent what opera sounds like in almost any circumstances. For example, when Daffy tries to show his prowess as an entertainer to the live-action producer Leon Schlesinger in *You Ought to Be in Pictures* (Warner Bros.; Freleng, 1940), he sings,

> I'll be famous on the screen
> the greatest ever seen
> I'll put my heart and soul
> in each and every role
> if it's grand opera I'll be singing
> la la-la-la la-la-la la-la-la LA laaah

He ends on the melody to "Largo al Factotum," which goes on for another fifteen seconds. The Donizetti, usually performed by an ensemble, generally leads to some kind of gag involving the singers; for instance, in *Back Alley Oproar* (Warner Bros.; Freleng, 1948), the cartoon ends with the death of caterwauling Sylvester, whose nine lives all ascend to heaven singing the sextet. The short is a remake of *Notes to You* (Warner Bros.; Freleng, 1941), which ends with the same gag.

10. David Huckvale, "The Composing Machine: Wagner and Popular Culture," in Tambling, ed., *A Night in at the Opera*, 134.

11. Joe Adamson, *The Walter Lantz Story* (New York: G. P. Putnam's Sons, 1985), 144.

12. Few cartoons take place entirely in an operatic narrative space. In the mid- to late 1940s, Paul Terry produced a series of cartoons performed with an operetta-style score.

13. Reading a plot summary, however detailed, is no substitute for examining the work itself. *What's Opera, Doc?* is included on a recently released DVD, *Looney Tunes: Golden Collection*, vol. 2 (Warner Home Video DVD31284, 2004). The complete original soundtrack can be found on the two-CD collection of songs from the Warner Bros. cartoons from Rhino Records, *That's All Folks! Cartoon Songs from Merrie Melodies and Looney Tunes* (R2 74271, 2001).

14. This image directly refers to the demon Tchernobog in the Mussorgsky "Night on Bald Mountain" sequence from *Fantasia* (Disney, 1940), one of the many allusions made by the Warner Bros. directors and animators to their competitors.

15. Joseph Horowitz, *Wagner Nights: An American History* (Berkeley: University of California Press, 1994), 39–41.

16. Kate Hevner Mueller, *Twenty-seven Major American Symphony Orchestras: A History and Analysis of Their Repertoires, Seasons 1842–43 through 1969–70* (Bloomington: Indiana University Press, 1973), 380; John H. Mueller, *The American Symphony Orchestra: A Social History of Musical Taste* (Bloomington: Indiana University Press, 1951), 188.

17. Horowitz, *Wagner Nights*, 301–2.

18. Charles Hamm, *Music in the New World* (New York: W. W. Norton, 1983), 294.

19. Horowitz, *Wagner Nights*, 302–3.

20. Erno Rapée, *Encyclopedia of Music for Pictures* (New York: Belwin, 1925; reprint, New York: Arno Press, 1970).

21. When synchronized sound took over Hollywood, Wagner's own music was heard less often, though his influence on soundtracks remained strong. For example, the film scores of the accomplished composer Erich Wolfgang Korngold (successful outside of Hollywood as well as within it) are known for their use of unifying motifs, an approach he derived from the Wagnerian leitmotif.

22. The tabulated information is drawn from cartoon cue sheets, USC Warner Bros. Archives, School of Cinema-Television, University of Southern California. This tally does not include the use of Wagner in the Pvt. Snafu series (shorts produced by Warner Bros. for the war effort from 1942 to 1945), although Wagner's music does appear regularly there as well—*Lohengrin*'s "Bridal Chorus" and several selections from *The Rhinegold*—as is hardly surprising, since those cartoons deal expressly with World War II. In contrast, Scott Bradley lists Wagner only once on a cue sheet: the 1944 cartoon MGM produced for the U.S. Army, provisionally titled *Weapon of War*. Among the pieces listed are "Magic Fire Music," "Hagen's Motive," "Excerpt *Gotterdammerung*," and "Excerpt *Siegfried.*" Given Bradley's history not as a film accompanist but as a bandleader, as well as his oft-stated aversion to using anything but original music in his scores, such a paucity of Wagner cues (or *any* classical cues) is not surprising.

23. An equally interesting collection of more than a dozen Wagner selections appears in the library of sheet music and band arrangements in Stalling's possession at the time of his death, practically all of which dates back to Stalling's days as a film accompanist in Kansas City. We are lucky that so much—perhaps all—of Stalling's accompanying library still exists as a single unit, as it provides us with a remarkably clear view of both his performing repertoire and the music to which audiences were exposed during that period. See the Carl W. Stalling Papers, American Heritage Center, University of Wyoming.

24. Robin Allan, *Walt Disney and Europe: European Influences on the Animated Feature Films of Walt Disney* (Bloomington: Indiana University Press, 1999), 264–65. The extant material on these unproduced sequences includes a basic list of possible works to animate in the future as well as inspirational sketches that went into early stages of production, among them Debussy's *Clair de Lune* and Sibelius's *The Swan of Tuonela* as well as the Wagner. Though Disney's plan never came to fruition, several of these pieces and artistic concepts found their way into *Fantasia 2000*. The inspirational sketches mentioned above can be found on a special DVD produced by Disney titled *Fantasia Legacy* (included in *The Fantasia Anthology*, Disney DVD 21269, 2000).

25. Warner Bros.' biggest contribution to this effort was a special series of shorts starring an inept Army private, Pvt. Snafu, who did everything wrong; their moral was "Whatever you do, *don't* do what Snafu does."

26. See chapter 1, note 62, and related text.

27. "Ach du lieber Augustin" appears in seven different Warner Bros. cartoons, each one featuring Germans in some way: *The Ducktators* (McCabe, 1942), *Daffy—The Commando* (Freleng, 1943), *The Fifth-Column Mouse* (Freleng, 1943; see the discussion in chapter 1), *Tokio Jokio* (McCabe, 1943), *Scrap Happy*

Daffy (Tashlin, 1943), *Russian Rhapsody* (Clampett, 1944), and *Dumb Patrol* (Harman and Ising, 1931). The "heroes" of *Dumb Patrol* are not Nazis but German soldiers in general, taking part in an unspecified war (by implication, World War I). That Frank Marsales, the original composer at Warner Bros., scored *Dumb Patrol* indicates that the association of "Ach du lieber Augustin" with Germans was not limited to Stalling; further evidence is the song's listing under "German" in Rapée's *Encyclopedia*.

28. As explained in chapter 4, Beethoven's "da-da-da-daaah," which rhythmically echoes the letter V in Morse code, came to signify victory; it plays this role in several Warner Bros. cartoons, including *The Fifth-Column Mouse, Ding Dog Daddy* (Freleng, 1942), and *Scrap Happy Daffy* (Tashlin, 1943).

29. Freleng's *Herr Meets Hare* cartoon clearly influenced *What's Opera, Doc?*, but Freleng himself apparently gleaned some visual inspiration for his cartoon from a 1943 Disney short, *Education for Death*, adapted loosely from Gregor Ziemer's 1941 text *Education for Death: The Making of a Nazi*. One sequence of the film describes the Nazis' version of the story of Sleeping Beauty, who is revealed to be a characterization of the German homeland (Germania), a rather large and quite amorous Brünnhilde, making fun (in part) of Hermann Göring. The prince in armor who rides to her rescue removes his helmet, revealing that he is actually Hitler. The music for this sequence relies largely on the Ride of the Valkyries; Germania's responses to Hitler's incoherent ravings are to screech "Heil Hitler" to the tune of the Valkyries' "Ho-yo-to-ho!"

30. Production notes, Chuck Jones Collection, Warner Bros. Corporate Archive, Warner Bros. Studios, Burbank, California.

31. Huckvale, *The Composing Machine*, 124.

32. Michael Barrier, *Hollywood Cartoons: American Animation in Its Golden Age* (New York: Oxford University Press, 1999), 542.

33. Leonard Maltin, *Of Mice and Magic: A History of American Animated Cartoons*, rev. ed. (New York: New American Library, 1987), 268. Noble is referring to the scene in which Elmer becomes infuriated with Bugs and calls the elements of nature down upon his enemy; as he yells out "I'll KILL the wabbit," the normally colored scene is suddenly flushed with bright magenta on Elmer and deep purple in the background, a startling and dramatic change.

34. Barrier, *Hollywood Cartoons*, 543. Jones told Barrier that he "was so familiar with the characters" that he could "lay out a Road-Runner in two weeks or less."

35. Jerry Beck, ed., *The 50 Greatest Cartoons: As Selected by 1,000 Animation Professionals* (Atlanta: Turner Publishing, 1994), 31.

36. Barrier, *Hollywood Cartoons*, 542. *Looney Tunes: Golden Collection*, vol. 2, which contains *What's Opera, Doc?*, includes an audio channel dedicated to the voice artists in that cartoon—Mel Blanc and Arthur Q. Bryan—including some retakes and outtakes from the recording session.

37. Jones, *Chuck Reducks*, 159.

38. The rotoscope was a device invented by Max Fleischer. It projects film onto a surface one frame at a time, allowing the animator to trace the outline of a figure in each image and thus to give the animation a seemingly natural effect.

39. Jones had actually planned an elaborate gag for this short sequence that

was not included in the final film. "Elmer's skirt is made of short metal slats, and when he is jabbing the hole, his head is at one point lower than his feet, causing the skirt to turn over one slat at a time. I envisaged the slats making a metallic musical scale as they flipped over, slat by slat—do, re, mi, fa, so, la—but we never recorded it, and I miss that sound every time" (Jones, *Chuck Reducks,* 162).

40. Tambling, *Opera, Ideology and Film,* 105.

41. Martin Miller Marks, *Music and the Silent Film: Contexts and Case Studies, 1895–1924* (New York: Oxford University Press, 1997), 198–206; Rapée, *Encyclopedia of Music for Pictures,* 387. The accounting of how many times *Rienzi* and other Wagner pieces appear is drawn from my research on the cue sheets for these cartoons.

42. Chuck Jones, "Music and the Animated Cartoon" (1946), in *The Cartoon Music Book,* edited by Daniel Goldmark and Yuval Taylor (Chicago: A Cappella Books, 2002), 98.

43. Jones, *Chuck Reducks,* 159; Jones, interview by author. According to the animation historian Greg Ford, for years Jones had no idea that the music that accompanied his Road Runner and Coyote cartoons to such great success was actually "The Dance of the Comedians" from Smetana's *The Bartered Bride,* not an original Stalling composition (Ford, communication with author, 2002).

I call the aphorism a "misquotation" because what Jones attributes to Twain is actually Twain quoting another humorist, Edgar Wilson "Bill" Nye: "The late Bill Nye once said, 'I have been told that Wagner's music is better than it sounds'" (Mark Twain, *Mark Twain's Autobiography,* edited by Albert Bigelow Paine [New York: Harper and Brothers, 1924], 1:338).

44. Huckvale, "The Composing Machine," 130.

45. Jones, *Chuck Reducks,* 157.

46. Jaime Weinman, "What's Up, Chuck?" *Salon.com,* 6 June 2000 http://dir.salon.com/ent/feature/2000/06/06/chuck_jones/index.html?sid=806031 (accessed 22 October 2004).

47. David Schroeder, *Cinema's Illusions, Opera's Allure: The Operatic Impulse in Film* (New York: Continuum, 2002), 227.

48. Philip Brophy, "The Animation of Sound," in Cholodenko, ed., *The Illusion of Life,* 99.

49. "The Ride of the Valkyries" also appeared as music accompanying death and warfare in *Music Land* (Jackson, 1935), one of Disney's Silly Symphonies. When the strings (classical music) go to war with the brass and reeds (jazz and swing), the queen of the strings fires her cannon at the enemy by playing "The Ride" on the pipe organ.

50. Christopher Small, *Musicking: The Meanings of Performing and Listening* (Hanover, N.H.: Wesleyan University Press, 1998), 101.

51. Jones, *Chuck Reducks,* 157.

52. Barrier, *Hollywood Cartoons,* 542.

53. According to Greg Ford (communication with author, 2000), Arthur Q. Bryan, who created and who alone voiced the character of Elmer until his death in 1958, performed all his role in *What's Opera, Doc?*—except for the word "smog," which was shouted by Mel Blanc (who also performed Bugs's voice).

54. Maurice Noble, interview by Greg Ford and Margaret Selby, in "Chuck Jones: Extremes and Inbetweens—A Life in Animation," *Great Performances,* Public Broadcasting System, 22 November 2000.

55. Chuck Jones, interview by Greg Ford and Margaret Selby, in "Chuck Jones: Extremes and Inbetweens—A Life in Animation"; Jones, interview by author.

56. Jones, "What's Up, Down Under?" 64.

57. For more on Bugs Bunny and drag, see Sean Griffin's "Pronoun Trouble: The 'Queerness' of Animation," *Spectator: USC Journal of Film and Television Criticism* 15.1 (Fall 1994): 95–109; and Kevin Sandler, "Gendered Evasion: Bugs Bunny in Drag," in *Reading the Rabbit: Explorations in Warner Bros. Animation,* edited by Kevin Sandler (New Brunswick, N.J.: Rutgers University Press, 1998), 154–71.

58. Jones, *Chuck Amuck,* 207; Jones, *Chuck Reducks,* 165.

59. Small, *Musicking,* 101.

60. Horowitz, *Wagner Nights,* 304–19.

61. The remainder of this scene is quite telling as well. In response to Bill's claim that opera without Bugs and Elmer is boring, Andre says, "Boring? Bizet's *Carmen* has a knife fight. Puccini's *Butterfly* commits hari-kari. Strauss's *Salome* kisses a head that is not attached to a body. And she's naked." My thanks to the writer of this episode, Susan Dickes, and to Renee Kurtz and Erika Weinstein at the William Morris Agency, for providing me with an excerpt from the original script to this episode (#221) of *The Jeff Foxworthy Show* (NBC, 28 April 1997).

62. Jones, "Music and the Animated Cartoon," 97.

A BRIEF CONCLUSION

1. For more on rock cartoons, see Jake Austen, "Rock 'n' Roll Cartoons," in *The Cartoon Music Book,* edited by Daniel Goldmark and Yuval Taylor (Chicago: A Cappella Books, 2001), 173–91; see also Kim Cooper and David Smay, eds., *Bubblegum Music Is the Naked Truth: The Dark History of Prepubescent Pop, from the Banana Splits to Britney Spears* (Los Angeles: Feral House, 2001).

2. Trey Parker and Matt Stone, "Cartman Gets an Anal Probe," *South Park,* Comedy Central, 13 August 1997. On *I Love to Singa* (Warner Bros.; Avery, 1936), see the discussion in chapter 3.

BIBLIOGRAPHY

Adamson, Joe. *Bugs Bunny: Fifty Years and Only One Grey Hare*. New York: Henry Holt, 1991.

———. "Chuck Jones Interviewed." In *The American Animated Cartoon*, edited by Gerald and Danny Peary, 128–41. New York: E. P. Dutton, 1980.

———. *Tex Avery: King of Cartoons*. New York: Popular Library, 1975. Reprint, New York: Da Capo Press, 1985.

———. *The Walter Lantz Story*. New York: G. P. Putnam's Sons, 1985.

Adorno, Theodor W. *Introduction to the Sociology of Music*. Translated by E. B. Ashton. New York: Continuum, 1976.

———. "On Popular Music." In *On Record: Rock, Pop, and the Written Word*, edited by Simon Frith and Andrew Goodwin, 301–14. New York: Pantheon Books, 1990.

Ake, David. *Jazz Cultures*. Berkeley: University of California Press, 2001.

Allan, Robin. *Walt Disney and Europe: European Influences on the Animated Feature Films of Walt Disney*. Bloomington: Indiana University Press, 1999.

Altman, Rick. *The American Film Musical*. Bloomington: Indiana University Press, 1987.

———. *Film/Genre*. London: BFI Publishing, 1999.

———. "The Silence of the Silents." *Musical Quarterly* 80.4 (1997): 648–718.

———. "The Sound of Sound: A Brief History of the Reproduction of Sound in Movie Theaters." *Cineaste* 21.1–2 (1995): 68–71.

———, ed. *Genre: The Musical*. London: Routledge and Kegan Paul, 1981.

———. *Sound Theory, Sound Practice*. New York: Routledge, 1992.

Anderson, Gillian B. *Music for Silent Films, 1894–1929*. Washington, D.C.: Library of Congress, 1988.

Anderson, Jervis. *This Was Harlem*. New York: Farrar Straus Giroux, 1982.

Anderson, Tim. "Reforming 'Jackass Music': The Problematic Aesthetics of Early American Film Music Accompaniment." *Cinema Journal* 37.1 (Fall 1997): 3–22.

Austen, Jake. "Rock 'n' Roll Cartoons." In *The Cartoon Music Book*, edited by Daniel Goldmark and Yuval Taylor, 173–91. Chicago: A Cappella Books, 2002.

Baker, Margaret P. "The Rabbit as Trickster." *Journal of Popular Culture* 28.2 (Fall 1994): 149–58.

Barbera, Joe. *My Life in 'Toons*. Atlanta: Turner Publishing, 1994.

Barrier, Michael. *Hollywood Cartoons: American Animation in Its Golden Age*. New York: Oxford University Press, 1999.

Barrier, Michael, and Milton Gray. "Bob Clampett: An Interview." *Funnyworld*, no. 12 (Summer 1970): 13–37.

Barrier, Michael, Milton Gray, and Bill Spicer. "An Interview with Carl Stalling." In *The Cartoon Music Book*, edited by Daniel Goldmark and Yuval Taylor, 37–60. Chicago: A Cappella Books, 2002. Originally published in *Funnyworld*, no. 13 (Spring 1971): 21–29. All citations are to the reprint.

Bashe, Philip, and Mel Blanc. *That's Not All Folks!* New York: Warner Books, 1988.

Beck, Jerry. *"I Tawt I Taw A Putty Tat": Fifty Years of Sylvester and Tweety*. New York: Henry Holt, 1991.

———, ed. *The 50 Greatest Cartoons: As Selected by 1,000 Animation Professionals*. Atlanta: Turner Publishing, 1994.

Beck, Jerry, and Will Friedwald. *Looney Tunes and Merrie Melodies: A Complete Illustrated Guide to the Warner Bros. Cartoons*. New York: Henry Holt, 1989.

Behlmer, Rudy. "Come On Along and Listen To . . ." Brochure notes for *Warner Bros. 75 Years of Film Music*. Rhino Records 75287, 1998.

Bell, Elizabeth, Lynda Haas, and Laura Sells, eds. *From Mouse to Mermaid: The Politics of Film, Gender, and Culture*. Bloomington: Indiana University Press, 1995.

Bendazzi, Giannalberto, Manuele Cerconello, and Guido Michelone. *Coloriture: Voci, rumori, musiche nel cinema d'animazione*. Bologna: Edizioni Pendragon, 1995.

Benshoff, Harry M. "Heigh-Ho, Heigh-Ho, Is Disney High or Low? From Silly Cartoons to Postmodern Politics." *Animation Journal* 1.1 (Fall 1992): 62–85.

Berg, Charles Merrell. "Cinema Sings the Blues." *Cinema Journal* 17.2 (1978): 1–12.

———. *An Investigation of the Motives for and Realization of Music to Accompany the American Silent Film*. New York: Arno Press, 1976.

Bogle, Donald. *Toms, Coons, Mulattoes, Mammies, and Bucks: An Interpretive History of Blacks in American Films*. New York: Continuum, 1994.

Bordman, Gerald. *American Musical Theatre: A Chronicle*. 2nd ed. New York: Oxford University Press, 1992.

———. *The Oxford Companion to American Theatre*, 2nd ed. New York: Oxford University Press, 1992.

Bordwell, David, Janet Staiger, and Kristin Thompson. *The Classical Hollywood Cinema: Film Style and Mode of Production to 1960*. New York: Columbia University Press, 1985.

Bowers, Q. David. *Nickelodeon Theatres and Their Music*. New York: Vestal Press, 1986.

Bradley, Scott. "Cartoon Music of the Future." *Pacific Coast Musician* 30.12 (21 June 1941): 28.

———. "The Evolution of Music in Cartoons." Unpublished typescript, 1947.

———. "Evoluzione della musica nei disegni animati." In *Musica e film*, edited by S. G. Biamonte, 217–21. Rome: Edizioni dell'Ateneo, 1959.

———. Interview by Michael Barrier and Milton Gray, 11 March 1977.

———. "'Music in Cartoons,' Excerpts from a talk given at The Music Forum October 28, 1944." In *The Cartoon Music Book*, edited by Daniel Goldmark and Yuval Taylor, 115–20. Chicago: A Cappella Books, 2002. Originally published in *Film Music Notes* 3.4 (December 1944): n.p. All citations are to the reprint.

———. "Open Forum." *Hollywood Reporter,* 28 October 1946, 10.

———. "Personality on the Sound Track: A Glimpse behind the Scenes and Sequences in Filmland." *Music Educators Journal* 33.3 (January 1947): 28–30.

———. Scott Bradley Collection. American Heritage Center, University of Wyoming.

———. Scott Bradley Collection. MGM Collection. USC Cinema-Television Library, University of Southern California.

Brion, Patrick. *Tom and Jerry.* New York: Harmony Books, 1990.

Brophy, Philip. "The Animation of Sound." In *The Illusion of Life: Essays on Animation,* edited by Alan Cholodenko, 67–112. Sydney: Power Publications, 1991.

Burke, Timothy, and Kevin Burke. *Saturday Morning Fever: Growing Up with Cartoon Culture.* New York: St. Martin's Griffin, 1999.

Burlingame, Jon. *TV's Biggest Hits: The Story of Television Themes from "Dragnet" to "Friends."* New York: Schirmer Books, 1996.

Cabarga, Leslie. *The Fleischer Story.* 2nd ed. New York: Da Capo Press, 1988.

Canemaker, John. *Felix: The Twisted Tale of the World's Most Famous Cat.* New York: Pantheon Books, 1991.

———. *Tex Avery.* Atlanta: Turner Publishing, 1996.

Care, Ross B. "The Film Music of Leigh Harline." *Film Music Notebook* 3.2 (1977): 32–48.

———. "Symphonists for the Sillies: The Composers for Disney's Shorts." *Funnyworld,* no. 18 (Summer 1978): 38–48.

———. "Threads of Melody: The Evolution of a Major Film Score—Walt Disney's *Bambi.*" In *Wonderful Inventions: Motion Pictures, Broadcasting, and Recorded Sound at the Library of Congress,* edited by Iris Newsom, 81–115. Washington, D.C.: Library of Congress, 1985.

"Carl Stalling." *Exposure Sheet* 2.7 (15 April 1940): n.p.

Carroll, Joe. "Sound Strategies." *Animatrix* 7 (1993): 31–36.

Carroll, Noël. "Notes on the Sight Gag." In *Comedy/Cinema/Theory,* edited by Andrew Horton, 25–42. Berkeley: University of California Press, 1991.

"Cartoons." *Film Music Notes* 1.3 (December 1941): 6.

Chion, Michel. *Audio-Vision: Sound on Screen.* Edited and translated by Claudia Gorbman. New York: Columbia University Press, 1994.

———. *The Voice in Cinema.* Translated by Claudia Gorbman. New York: Columbia University Press, 1999.

Christlieb, Anthony, and Carolyn Beck, eds. *Recollections of a First Chair Bassoonist: 52 Years in the Hollywood Studio Orchestras.* Sherman Oaks, Calif.: Christlieb Products, 1996.

Chusid, Irwin. Brochure notes for Raymond Scott, *Reckless Nights and Turkish Twilights: The Music of Raymond Scott.* The Raymond Scott Quintette. Sony 53028, 1992.

———. "Carl Stalling: Music to Toon By." *Animation Magazine,* no. 31 (October/ November 1994): 74–75.

————. "50 Years of Musical Mayhem." *Animation Magazine,* no. 24 (Summer 1993): 43–47.

————. "Raymond Scott: Accidental Music for Animated Mayhem." In *The Cartoon Music Book,* edited by Daniel Goldmark and Yuval Taylor, 151–60. Chicago: A Cappella Books, 2002.

Chute, David. "Keeping Up with the Jones." *Film Comment* 21.6 (November–December 1985): 14–19.

Citron, Marcia J. *Opera on Screen.* New Haven: Yale University Press, 2000.

Clark, Frances Elliott. *Music Appreciation for Children.* Camden, N.J.: RCA Manufacturing Company, 1939.

Classified Catalogue of Sam Fox Publishing Co. Motion Picture Music. Cleveland: Sam Fox Publishing, 1929.

Cockrell, Dale. *Demons of Disorder: Early Blackface Minstrels and Their World.* Cambridge: Cambridge University Press, 1997.

Cohen, Karl F. *Forbidden Animation: Censored Cartoons and Blacklisted Animators in America.* Jefferson, N.C.: McFarland, 1997.

Cohen, Mitchell S. "Looney Tunes and Merrie Melodies." *Velvet Light Trap,* no. 15 (Fall 1975): 33–37.

Cook, Nicholas. *Analysing Musical Multimedia.* Oxford: Clarendon Press, 1998.

Cooper, Kim, and David Smay, eds. *Bubblegum Music Is the Naked Truth: The Dark History of Prepubescent Pop, from the Banana Splits to Britney Spears.* Los Angeles: Feral House, 2001.

Corliss, Richard. "Warnervana." *Film Comment* 21.6 (November–December 1985): 11–13.

Costello, Eric O. *The Warner Bros. Cartoon Companion.* http://members.aol .com/EOCostello/, 1998 (accessed 22 October 2004).

Crafton, Donald. *Before Mickey: The Animated Film, 1898–1928.* Chicago: University of Chicago Press, 1982.

————. "Pie and Chase: Gag, Spectacle and Narrative in Slapstick Comedy." In *Classical Hollywood Comedy,* edited by Kristine Brunovska Karnick and Henry Jenkins, 106–19. New York: Routledge, 1995.

————. *The Talkies: American Cinema's Transition to Sound, 1926–1931.* Berkeley: University of California Press, 1997.

————. "The View from Termite Terrace: Caricature and Parody in Warner Bros. Animation." *Film History* 5 (1993): 204–30.

Culhane, John. *Fantasia 2000: Visions of Hope.* New York: Disney Editions, 1999.

————. *Walt Disney's "Fantasia."* New York: H. N. Abrams, 1983.

Culhane, Shamus. *Animation: From Script to Screen.* New York: St. Martin's Press, 1988.

————. *Talking Animals and Other People.* New York: St. Martin's Press, 1986.

Culshaw, John. "Violence and the Cartoon." *Fortnightly,* no. 1020 (December 1951): 830–35.

Curtis, Scott. "The Sound of the Early Warner Bros. Cartoons." In *Sound Theory, Sound Practice,* edited by Rick Altman, 191–203. New York: Routledge, 1992.

Dahl, Ingolf. "Notes on Cartoon Music." *Film Music Notes* 8.5 (May–June 1949): 3–13.

Daniel, Oliver. *Stokowski: A Counterpoint of View.* New York: Dodd, Mead, 1982.

Darby, William, and Jack Du Bois. *American Film Music: Major Composers, Techniques, Trends, 1915–1990.* Jefferson, N.C.: McFarland, 1990.

Dickinson, Roger, Ramaswami Harindranath, and Olga Linné, eds. *Approaches to Audiences: A Reader.* London: Arnold, 1998.

Douglas, Ann. *Terrible Honesty: Mongrel Manhattan in the 1920s.* New York: Farrar, Straus, and Giroux, 1995.

Durgnat, Raymond. *The Crazy Mirror: Hollywood Comedy and the American Image.* London: Faber and Faber, 1969.

Eisenstein, Sergei M. *Film Form and the Film Sense.* Cleveland: Meridian Books, 1957.

Eisler, Hanns. *Composing for the Films.* New York: Oxford University Press, 1947.

Ernst, Hugh C. "The Man Who Made a Lady out of Jazz (Paul Whiteman)." In *Keeping Time: Readings in Jazz History,* edited by Robert Walser, 39–40. New York: Oxford University Press, 1999.

Evans, Mark. *Soundtrack: The Music of the Movies.* New York: Hopkinson and Blake, [1975]. Reprint, New York: Da Capo Press, 1979.

Faulkner, Anne Shaw. *What We Hear in Music.* 4th rev. ed. Camden, N.J.: Victor Talking Machine Company, 1921.

Feisst, Sabine M. "Arnold Schoenberg and the Cinematic Art." *Musical Quarterly* 83.1 (Spring 1999): 93–113.

Feuer, Jane. *The Hollywood Musical.* 2nd ed. Bloomington: Indiana University Press, 1993.

Fink, Robert. "Elvis Everywhere: Musicology and Popular Music Studies at the Twilight of the Canon." *Popular Music* 16.2 (Summer 1998): 135–79.

Flinn, Caryl. *Strains of Utopia: Gender, Nostalgia, and Hollywood Film Music.* Princeton: Princeton University Press, 1992.

Floyd, Samuel A., Jr. *The Power of Black Music: Interpreting Its History from Africa to the United States.* New York: Oxford University Press, 1995.

———, ed. *Black Music in the Harlem Renaissance.* Knoxville: University of Tennessee Press, 1990.

Ford, Greg. Brochure notes for Carl Stalling, *The Carl Stalling Project: Music from Warner Bros. Cartoons, 1936–1958.* Warner Bros. Records 26027, 1990.

Ford, Greg, and Richard Thompson. "Chuck Jones." *Film Comment* 11.1 (January–February 1975): 21–38.

Freleng, Friz, with David Weber. *Animation: The Art of Friz Freleng.* Newport Beach, Calif.: Donovan Publishing, 1994.

Friedwald, Will. "Winston Sharples: Cat and Mouse Melodies and Haunting Refrains." In *The Harvey Cartoon History,* edited by Jerry Beck, n.p. New York: Harvey Comics, 1997.

Friedwald, Will, and Jerry Beck. *The Warner Brothers Cartoons.* Metuchen, N.J.: Scarecrow Press, 1981.

Frith, Simon. *Performing Rites: On the Value of Popular Music.* Cambridge, Mass.: Harvard University Press, 1996.

Furniss, Maureen. *Art in Motion: Animation Aesthetics.* London: John Libbey, 1998.

Gabbard, Krin. *Jammin' at the Margins: Jazz and the American Cinema.* Chicago: University of Chicago Press, 1996.

Gaines, Jane. "The Showgirl and the Wolf." *Cinema Journal* 20.1 (Fall 1980): 53–67.

Garcia, Roger, and Bernard Eisenschitz, eds. *Frank Tashlin.* London: British Film Institute, 1994.

Garrett, Charles. "Chinatown, Whose Chinatown? Defining America's Borders with Musical Orientalism." *Journal of the American Musicological Society* 57.1 (Spring 2004): 119–73.

Giddings, Thaddeus P., et al. *Music Appreciation in the Schoolroom.* Boston: Ginn, 1926.

Giroux, Henry A. *Fugitive Cultures: Race, Violence, and Youth.* New York: Routledge, 1993.

Goldmark, Daniel. ". . . And That's Not All Folks!" Brochure notes for *Warner Bros. 75 Years of Film Music.* Rhino Records 75287, 1998.

———. "Carl Stalling and Humor in Cartoons." *Animation World Magazine,* 1 April 1997. http://mag.awn.com/index.php?ltype=search&sval=goldmark &article_no=786 (accessed 22 October 2004).

Goldmark, Daniel, and Yuval Taylor, eds. *The Cartoon Music Book.* Chicago: A Cappella Books, 2002.

Gorbman, Claudia. "Drums along the L.A. River: Scoring the Indian." In *Westerns: Films through History,* edited by Janet Walker, 177–95. New York: Routledge, 2001.

———. *Unheard Melodies: Narrative Film Music.* London: BFI Publishing; Bloomington: Indiana University Press, 1987.

Grandinetti, Fred M. *Popeye: An Illustrated History.* Jefferson, N.C.: McFarland, 1994.

Grant, Barry Keith. "'Jungle Nights in Harlem': Jazz, Ideology and the Animated Cartoon." *University of Hartford Studies in Literature* 21.3 (1989): 3–12.

Gray, Milton. *Cartoon Animation: Introduction to a Career.* Northridge, Calif.: Lion's Den Publications, 1991.

Griffin, Sean. "Pronoun Trouble: The 'Queerness' of Animation." *Spectator: USC Journal of Film and Television Criticism* 15.1 (Fall 1994): 95–109.

———. *Tinker Belles and Evil Queens: The Walt Disney Company from the Inside Out.* New York: New York University Press, 2000.

Guernsey, Otis L., Jr. "The Movie Cartoon Is Coming of Age." *Film Music Notes* 13.2 (November–December 1953): 21–22.

Gunning, Tom. "'Animated Pictures': Tales of Cinema's Forgotten Future." *Michigan Quarterly Review* 34.4 (Fall 1995): 465–85.

———. "The Cinema of Attractions: Early Film, Its Spectator and the Avant-Garde." In *Early Cinema: Space, Frame, Narrative,* edited by Thomas Elsaesser and Adam Barker, 56–62. London: BFI Publishing, 1990.

———. "Crazy Machines in the Garden of Forking Paths: Mischief Gags and the Origins of American Film Comedy." In *Classical Hollywood Comedy,* edited by Kristine Brunovska Karnick and Henry Jenkins, 87–105. New York: Routledge, 1995.

———. "Response to 'Pie and Chase.'" In *Classical Hollywood Comedy,* edited

by Kristine Brunovska Karnick and Henry Jenkins, 120–22. New York: Routledge, 1995.

Habermeyer, Sharlene. *Good Music, Brighter Children.* Rocklin, Calif.: Prima
Publishing, 1999.

Hagen, Earl. *Scoring for Films.* New York: EDJ Music, 1971.

Hall, Mary Harrington. "The Fantasy Makers: A Conversation with Ray Brad-
bury and Chuck Jones." *Psychology Today,* April 1968, 28–37, 70.

Hamilton, Marie L. "Music and Theatrical Shorts." *Film Music Notes* 6.2 (November 1946): 20.

Hamm, Charles. *Music in the New World.* New York: W. W. Norton, 1983.

Handzo, Stephen. "Appendix: A Narrative Glossary of Film Sound Technology."
In *Film Sound: Theory and Practice,* edited by Elisabeth Weis and John Belton, 383–426. New York: Columbia University Press, 1985.

Hanna, Bill, with Tom Ito. *A Cast of Friends.* Dallas: Taylor Publishing, 1996.

Hansen, Miriam. "Of Mice and Ducks: Benjamin and Adorno on Disney." *South
Atlantic Quarterly* 92.1 (Winter 1993): 27–61.

Heinle, Lothar. *Vom Konzertsaal zur Soundstage: Wege zur symphonischen Film-
musik.* 2nd ed. Heilbronn: Stadtbücherei Heilbronn, 1995.

Henderson, Brian. "Cartoon and Narrative in the Films of Frank Tashlin and
Preston Sturges." In *Comedy/Cinema/Theory,* edited by Andrew Horton,
153–73. Berkeley: University of California Press, 1991.

Heraldson, Donald. *Creators of Life: A History of Animation.* New York: Drake
Publishers, 1975.

Hickey, Dave. *Air Guitar: Essays on Art and Democracy.* Los Angeles: Art issues.
Press, 1997.

Hoffer, Thomas W. *Animation—A Reference Guide.* Westport, Conn.: Green-
wood Press, 1981.

Horowitz, Joseph. "'Sermons in Tones': Sacralization as a Theme in American
Classical Music." *American Music* 16.3 (Fall 1998): 311–39.

———. *Understanding Toscanini.* New York: Alfred A. Knopf, 1987.

———. *Wagner Nights: An American History.* Berkeley: University of California
Press, 1994.

Huckvale, David. "The Composing Machine; Wagner and Popular Culture." In
A Night in at the Opera: Media Representations of Opera, edited by Jeremy
Tambling, 113–43. London: John Libbey, 1994.

Huggins, Nathan Irvin. *Harlem Renaissance.* New York: Oxford University Press,
1971.

Irving, Ernest. "Music in Films." *Music and Letters* 24.4 (1943): 223–35.

"Jazz and 'Aesop's Film Fables' Good Mixers." *Motion Picture News,* 2 June
1923, 2651.

Jenkins, Henry. *What Made Pistachio Nuts? Early Sound Comedy and the Vaudeville Aesthetic.* New York: Columbia University Press, 1992.

Jones, Chuck. *Chuck Amuck: The Life and Times of an Animated Cartoonist.*
New York: Avon Books, 1990.

———. *Chuck Reducks: Drawing from the Fun Side of Life.* New York: Warner
Books, 1996.

———. Interview by author. Tape recording. 14 September 1994.

————. Interview by Greg Ford and Margaret Selby. In "Chuck Jones: Extremes and Inbetweens—A Life in Animation." *Great Performances*. Public Broadcasting System, 22 November 2000.

————. "Music and the Animated Cartoon." In *The Cartoon Music Book*, edited by Daniel Goldmark and Yuval Taylor, 93–102. Chicago: A Cappella Books, 2002. Originally published in *Hollywood Quarterly* 1.4 (July 1946): 363–70. All citations are to the reprint.

————. "132 Takes/Th-Th-That's All Folks." *Film Comment* 25.2 (March–April 1989): 2–3.

————. "What's Up, Down Under? Chuck Jones Talks at *The Illusion of Life* Conference." In *The Illusion of Life: Essays on Animation*, edited by Alan Cholodenko, 37–66. Sydney: Power Publications, 1991.

Jones, LeRoi [Imamu Amiri Baraka]. *Blues People: Negro Music in White America*. New York: Morrow Quill Paperbacks, 1963.

Jones, Reginald M., Jr. *The Mystery of the Masked Man's Music: A Search for the Music Used on "The Lone Ranger" Radio Program, 1933–1954*. Metuchen, N.J.: Scarecrow Press, 1987.

Kahn, Douglas. *Noise, Water, Meat: A History of Sound in the Arts*. Cambridge, Mass.: MIT Press, 1999.

Kalinak, Kathryn. *Settling the Score: Music and the Classical Hollywood Film*. Madison: University of Wisconsin Press, 1992.

Karlin, Fred. *Listening to Movies: The Film Lover's Guide to Film Music*. New York: Schirmer Books, 1994.

Karlin, Fred, and Rayburn Wright. *On the Track: A Guide to Contemporary Film Scoring*. New York: Schirmer/Macmillan, 1990.

Kassabian, Anahid. *Hearing Film: Tracking Identifications in Contemporary Hollywood Film Music*. New York: Routledge, 2001.

Kaufman, J. B. "Who's Afraid of ASCAP? Popular Songs in the Silly Symphonies." *Animation World Magazine*, 1 April 1999. http://mag.awn.com/index.php?ltype=search&sval=j.b.+kaufman&article_no=789 (accessed 22 October 2004).

Kennicott, Philip. "What's Opera Doc? Bugs Bunny Meets the Musical Masters." *Classical* 3.1 (January 1991): 18–24.

Kinder, Marsha. *Playing with Power in Movies, Television, and Video Games*. Berkeley: University of California Press, 1991.

Kingsley, Walter. "Whence Comes Jass? Facts from the Great Authority on the Subject." In *Keeping Time: Readings in Jazz History*, edited by Robert Walser, 5–7. New York: Oxford University Press, 1999. Originally published in the *New York Sun*, 5 August 1917, 3. All citations are to the reprint.

Klein, Norman M. *7 Minutes: The Life and Death of the American Animated Cartoon*. New York: Verso, 1993.

Kramer, Lawrence. "The Singing Salami: Unsystematic Reflections on the Marx Brothers' *A Night at the Opera*." In *A Night in at the Opera: Media Representations of Opera*, edited by Jeremy Tambling, 253–65. London: John Libbey, 1994.

Krausz, Michael, ed. *The Interpretation of Music: Philosophical Essays*. Oxford: Clarendon Press, 1993.

Lahee, Henry C. *Annals of Music in America*. Boston: Marshall Jones, 1922.
Lakoff, George, and Mark Johnson. *Metaphors We Live By*. Chicago: University of Chicago Press, 1980.
Lang, Edith, and George West. *Musical Accompaniment of Moving Pictures*. Boston: Boston Music Company, 1920. Reprint, New York: Arno Press, 1970.
LaPrade, Ernest. *NBC Music Appreciation Hour, Sixth Year—1933–34: Instructor's Manual*. New York: National Broadcasting Company, 1933.
Lenburg, Jeff. *The Great Cartoon Directors*. Jefferson, N.C.: McFarland, 1983.
Leskosky, Richard J. "The Reforming Fantasy: Recurrent Theme and Structure in American Studio Cartoons." *Velvet Light Trap*, no. 24 (Fall 1989): 53–66.
Levine, Lawrence. *Highbrow/Lowbrow: The Emergence of Cultural Hierarchy in America*. Cambridge, Mass.: Harvard University Press, 1988.
Lewis, David Levering. *When Harlem Was in Vogue*. New York: Alfred A. Knopf, 1981.
Leyda, Jay. *Eisenstein on Disney*. Calcutta: Seagull Books, 1986.
Liebman, Roy. *Vitaphone Films: A Catalogue of the Features and Shorts*. Jefferson, N.C.: McFarland, 2003.
Limbacher, James L. *Film Music: From Violins to Video*. Metuchen, N.J.: Scarecrow Press, 1974.
———. *Keeping Score: Film Music, 1972–1979*. Metuchen, N.J.: Scarecrow Press, 1981.
Lindvall, Terry, and Ben Fraser. "Darker Shades of Animation: African-American Images in the Warner Bros. Cartoon." In *Reading the Rabbit: Explorations in Warner Bros. Animation*, edited by Kevin Sandler, 121–36. New Brunswick, N.J.: Rutgers University Press, 1998.
Litweiler, John. *Ornette Coleman: The Harmolodic Life*. London: Quartet Books, 1992.
London, Kurt. *Film Music*. [Translated by Eric S. Bensinger.] London: Faber and Faber, 1936. Reprint, New York: Arno Press, 1970.
Looney Tunes: Golden Collection. Vol. 2. Warner Home Video DVD31284, 2004.
Lord, Tom. *The Jazz Discography*. Vol. 1. West Vancouver, B.C.: Lord Music Reference, 1992.
Lott, Eric. *Love and Theft: Blackface Minstrelsy and the American Working Class*. New York: Oxford University Press, 1993.
Lowan, Lester, ed. *Recording Sound for Motion Pictures*. New York: McGraw-Hill, 1931.
Luckett, Moya. "*Fantasia*: Cultural Constructions of Disney's 'Masterpiece.'" In *Disney Discourse: Producing the Magic Kingdom*, edited by Eric Smoodin, 214–36. New York: Routledge, 1994.
Lutz, E. G. *Animated Cartoons: How They Are Made, Their Origin and Development*. New York: C. Scribner's Sons, 1920. Reprint, Bedford, Mass.: Applewood Books, 1998.
Malotte, Albert Hay. "Film Cartoon Music." In *Music and Dance in California*, edited by José Rodriguez, 128–32. Hollywood: Bureau of Musical Research, 1940.
Maltin, Leonard. *Of Mice and Magic: A History of American Animated Cartoons*. Rev. ed. New York: New American Library, 1987.

Manvell, Roger, and John Huntley. *The Technique of Film Music*. New York: Hastings House, 1975.

Marks, Martin Miller. *Music and the Silent Film: Contexts and Case Studies, 1895–1924*. New York: Oxford University Press, 1997.

Martin, Donald. "Two Outstanding Films with Music." *Etude* 58.12 (December 1940): 805, 846.

Mast, Gerald, Marshall Cohen, and Leo Braudy, eds. *Film Theory and Criticism: Introductory Readings*. 4th ed. New York: Oxford University Press, 1992.

Mayerson, Mark. "The Lion Began with a Frog." *Velvet Light Trap*, no. 18 (Spring 1978): 39–45.

McCarty, Clifford. *Film Composers in America: A Filmography, 1911–1970*. 2nd ed. New York: Oxford University Press, 2000.

———, ed. *Film Music I*. New York: Garland, 1989.

McClary, Susan. *Conventional Wisdom: The Content of Musical Form*. Berkeley: University of California Press, 2000.

———. *Feminine Endings: Music, Gender, and Sexuality*. Minneapolis: University of Minnesota Press, 1991.

McClary, Susan, and Robert Walser. "Start Making Sense! Musicology Wrestles with Rock." In *On Record: Rock, Pop, and the Written Word*, edited by Simon Frith and Andrew Goodwin, 277–92. New York: Pantheon Books, 1990.

Meeker, David. *Jazz in the Movies*. New enl. ed. New York: Da Capo Press, 1981.

Mellot, Albert. "*The Two Mouseketeers* with Score Excerpts." *Film Music Notes* 11.5 (May–June 1952): 9–11.

Merritt, Russell, and J. B. Kaufman. *Walt in Wonderland: The Silent Films of Walt Disney*. Perdenone, Italy: Le Giornate del Cinema Muto, 1992.

Meyer, Leonard B. *Emotion and Meaning in Music*. Chicago: University of Chicago Press, 1956.

Mosley, Leonard. *Disney's World*. New York: Stein and Day, 1985.

Mueller, John H. *The American Symphony Orchestra: A Social History of Musical Taste*. Bloomington: Indiana University Press, 1951.

Mueller, Kate Hevner. *Twenty-seven Major American Symphony Orchestras: A History and Analysis of Their Repertoires, Seasons 1842–43 through 1969–70*. Bloomington: Indiana University Press, 1973.

Neale, Steve, and Frank Krutnik. *Popular Film and Television Comedy*. London: Routledge, 1990.

Neumeyer, David, with Caryl Flinn and James Buhler. Introduction to *Music and Cinema*, edited by James Buhler, Caryl Flinn, and David Neumeyer, 1–29. Hanover, N.H.: Wesleyan University Press, 2000.

"News Items . . . Comments." *Film Music Notes* 3.3 (December 1943): n.p.

Newsom, Jon. "'A Sound Idea': Music for Animated Films." *Quarterly Journal of the Library of Congress* 37.3–4 (Summer–Fall 1980): 279–309.

Noble, Maurice. Interview by Greg Ford and Margaret Selby. In "Chuck Jones: Extremes and Inbetweens—A Life in Animation." *Great Performances*. Public Broadcasting Service, 22 November 2000.

O'Connell, Charles. *The Victor Book of Overtures, Tone Poems and Other Orchestral Works*. New York: Simon and Schuster, 1950.

Onosko, Tim. "Bob Clampett: Cartoonist." *Velvet Light Trap,* no. 15 (Fall 1975): 38–41.

"Open Forum." *Hollywood Reporter,* 28 October 1946, 10.

Opperby, Preben. *Leopold Stokowski.* New York: Midas Books, 1982.

"Oratorio Society Gives Fine Dual Performance." *Pacific Coast Musician* 23.12 (24 March 1934): 5.

Palmer, Charles. "Cartoon in the Classroom." *Hollywood Quarterly* 3.1 (Fall 1947): 26–33.

Paulin, Scott. "Richard Wagner and the Fantasy of Cinematic Unity: The Idea of the *Gesamtkunstwerk* in the History and Theory of Film Music." In *Music and Cinema,* edited by James Buhler, Caryl Flinn, and David Neumeyer, 58–84. Hanover, N.H.: Wesleyan University Press, 2000.

Peary, Gerald, and Danny Peary. *The American Animated Cartoon.* New York: E. P. Dutton, 1980.

PianOrgan Film Books of Incidental Music, Extracted from the World Famous "Berg" and "Cinema" Incidental Series. 7 vols. New York: Baldwin, n.d.

Pilling, Jayne, ed. *A Reader in Animation Studies.* Bloomington: Indiana University Press, 1997.

Pisani, Michael. "'I'm an Indian Too': Creating Native American Identities in Nineteenth- and Early Twentieth-Century Music." In *The Exotic in Western Music,* edited by Jonathan Bellman, 218–57. Boston: Northeastern University Press, 1998.

Prendergast, Roy M. *Film Music: A Neglected Art.* New York: W. W. Norton, 1977.

"Questions Answered—Suggestions Offered." *Moving Picture World,* 23 March 1918, 1662.

Rapée, Erno. *Encyclopedia of Music for Pictures.* New York: Belwin, 1925 (as *Erno Rapee's Encyclopædia of Music for Pictures*). Reprint, New York: Arno Press, 1970.

———. *Motion Picture Moods for Pianists and Organists.* New York: Schirmer, 1924. Reprint, New York: Arno Press, 1974.

Rawlinson, Harold. "Fitting a Film to Music." *Film Music Notes* 5.8 (April 1946): 8.

Raykoff, Ivan. "Dreams of Love: Mythologies of the 'Romantic' Pianist in Twentieth-Century Popular Culture." Ph.D. diss., University of California, San Diego, 2001.

Redewill, Helena Munn. "Laugh and the World Laughs (An Interview)." *Triangle,* February 1932, 91–94.

Richmond, Ray, and Antonia Coffman, eds. *The Simpsons: A Complete Guide to Our Favorite Family.* New York: Harper Perennial, 1997.

Rogin, Michael. *Blackface, White Noise: Jewish Immigrants in the Hollywood Melting Pot.* Berkeley: University of California Press, 1996.

Rosen, Philip, ed. *Narrative, Apparatus, Ideology.* New York: Columbia University Press, 1986.

Rosenberg, Neil V. *Bluegrass: A History.* Urbana: University of Illinois Press, 1992.

Rózsa, Miklós. *Double Life.* New York: Wynwood Press, 1989.

Sabaneev, Leonid. *Music for the Films.* Translated by S. W. Pring. London: Sir I. Pitman and Sons, 1935. Reprint, New York: Arno Press, 1978.

Sam Fox Incidental Music for News Reels, Cartoons, Pictorial Reviews, Scenics, Travelogues, etc. 4 vols. Cleveland: Sam Fox Publishing, 1931.

Sam Fox Loose Leaf Collection of Ring-Hager Novelties for Orchestra. Vol. 1. Cleveland: Sam Fox Publishing, 1926.

Sam Fox Moving Picture Music. Vol. 4. Cleveland: Sam Fox Publishing, 1924.

Sampson, Henry T. *That's Enough, Folks: Black Images in Animated Cartoons, 1900–1960.* Lanham, Md.: Scarecrow Press, 1998.

Sandler, Kevin. "Gendered Evasion: Bugs Bunny in Drag." In *Reading the Rabbit: Explorations in Warner Bros. Animation,* edited by Kevin Sandler, 154–71. New Brunswick, N.J.: Rutgers University Press, 1998.

———, ed. *Reading the Rabbit: Explorations in Warner Bros. Animation.* New Brunswick, N.J.: Rutgers University Press, 1998.

Sanjek, David. "No More Mickey-Mousing Around." In *Kaboom! Explosive Animation from America and Japan,* 30–41. Sydney: Power Publications, 1994.

Sanjek, Russell. *Pennies from Heaven: The American Popular Music Business in the Twentieth Century.* New York: Da Capo Press, 1996.

Sapoznik, Henry. *Klezmer! Jewish Music from Old World to Our World.* New York: Schirmer Books, 1999.

Sartin, Hank. "Drawing on Hollywood: Warner Bros. Cartoons and Hollywood, 1930–1960." Ph.D. diss., University of Chicago, 1998.

———. "From Vaudeville to Hollywood, from Silence to Sound: Warner Bros. Cartoons of the Early Sound Era." In *Reading the Rabbit: Explorations in Warner Bros. Animation,* edited by Kevin Sandler, 67–85. New Brunswick, N.J.: Rutgers University Press, 1998.

Schneider, Steve. *That's All Folks! The Art of Warner Bros. Animation.* New York: Henry Holt, 1988.

Scholes, Percy A. *Music Appreciation: Its History and Technics.* New York: M. Witmark and Sons, 1935.

Schroeder, David. *Cinema's Illusions, Opera's Allure: The Operatic Impulse in Film.* New York: Continuum, 2002.

Sheppard, Anthony. "An Exotic Enemy: Anti-Japanese Musical Propaganda in World War II Hollywood." *Journal of the American Musicological Society* 54.2 (Summer 2001): 303–57.

Shilkret, Nathaniel. "Condensed from 'Some Predictions for the Future of Film Music' in *Music Publishers' Journal*—Jan., Feb. 1946." *Film Music Notes* 5.8 (April 1946): 14.

"Short Subject Reviews: 'Cat Concerto.'" *Film Daily,* 1 May 1947, 7.

Shull, Michael S., and David E. Wilt. *Doing Their Bit: Wartime American Animated Short Films, 1939–1945.* Jefferson, N.C.: McFarland, 1987.

Sikov, Ed. *Laughing Hysterically: American Screen Comedy of the 1950s.* New York: Columbia University Press, 1994.

Slafer, Eugene. "A Conversation with Bill Hanna." In *The American Animated Cartoon,* edited by Gerald and Danny Peary, 255–60. New York: E. P. Dutton, 1980.

Small, Christopher. *Musicking: The Meanings of Performing and Listening.* Hanover, N.H.: Wesleyan University Press, 1998.

Smith, Jeff. "Popular Songs and Comic Allusion in Contemporary Cinema." In *Soundtrack Available,* edited by Pamela Robertson Wojcik and Arthur Knight, 407–30. Durham, N.C.: Duke University Press, 2001.

———. *The Sounds of Commerce: Marketing Popular Film Music.* New York: Columbia University Press, 1998.

Smith, Paul J. "The Music of the Walt Disney Cartoons: A Conference with Paul J. Smith." *Etude* 58.7 (July 1940): 438, 494.

Smith, William Ander. *The Mystery of Leopold Stokowski.* Rutherford, N.J.: Fairleigh Dickinson University Press, 1990.

Smoodin, Eric. *Animating Culture: Hollywood Cartoons from the Sound Era.* New Brunswick, N.J.: Rutgers University Press, 1993.

Solomon, Charles. *The Art of the Animated Image: An Anthology.* Los Angeles: American Film Institute, 1987.

Stalling, Carl W. Carl W. Stalling Papers. American Heritage Center, University of Wyoming.

Stam, Robert, et al. *New Vocabularies in Film Semiotics.* London: Routledge, 1992.

Steele, R. Vernon. "'Fairyland Goes to Hollywood': An Interview with Leigh Harline." *Pacific Coast Musician* 26.22 (20 November 1937): 10.

———. "'Scoring for Cartoons': An Interview with Scott Bradley." *Pacific Coast Musician* 26.10 (15 May 1937): 12–13.

Stilwell, Robynn J. "Music in Films: A Critical Review of Literature, 1980–1996." *Journal of Film Music* 1.1 (Summer 2002): 19–61.

Strauss, Neil. "Animated Rhythms: Tunes for Toons." *Ear Magazine* 3 (July–August 1989): 14–15.

Tambling, Jeremy. *Opera, Ideology and Film.* New York: St. Martin's Press, 1987.

———, ed. *A Night in at the Opera: Media Representations of Opera.* London: John Libbey, 1994.

Tebbel, John R. "Looney Tunester." *Film Comment* 28.5 (September–October 1992): 64–66.

Thompson, Kristin. "Implications of the Cel Animation Technique." In *The Cinematic Apparatus,* edited by Teresa de Lauretis and Stephen Heath, 106–20. New York: St. Martin's Press, 1980.

Thomson, Virgil. *The State of Music.* New York: W. Morrow, 1939.

Tietyen, David. *The Musical World of Walt Disney.* Milwaukee: Hal Leonard Publishing, 1990.

Tootell, George. *How to Play the Cinema Organ: A Practical Book by a Practical Player.* London: W. Paxton, n.d.

Torgovnick, Marianna. *Gone Primitive: Savage Intellects, Modern Lives.* Chicago: University of Chicago Press, 1990.

Tucker, Mark. *Ellington: The Early Years.* Urbana: University of Illinois Press, 1991.

Twain, Mark [Samuel Clemens]. *Mark Twain's Autobiography.* Edited by Albert Bigelow Paine. 2 vols. New York: Harper and Brothers, 1924.

Twenty-five Hebrew Songs and Dances. Arranged by Maurice Gould, compiled by Julius Fleischmann. New York: Fischer, 1912.

Vincentelli, Elisabeth. "Merrie Melodies: Cartoon Music's Contemporary Resurgence." *Village Voice,* 3 March 1998, 59.

Walser, Robert. *Running with the Devil: Power, Gender, and Madness in Heavy Metal Music.* Hanover, N.H.: Wesleyan University Press, 1993.

———, ed. *Keeping Time: Readings in Jazz History.* New York: Oxford University Press, 1999.

Weinman, Jaime. "What's Up, Chuck?" *Salon.com,* 6 June 2000. http://dir.salon .com/ent/feature/2000/06/06/chuck_jones/index.html?sid=806031 (accessed 22 October 2004).

Weis, Elisabeth, and John Belton, eds. *Film Sound: Theory and Practice.* New York: Columbia University Press, 1985.

Wells, Paul. *Understanding Animation.* New York: Routledge, 1998.

Westby, James. "Castelnuovo-Tedesco in America: The Film Music." Ph.D. diss., University of California, Los Angeles, 1995.

Whitburn, Joel. *Joel Whitburn's Top Pop Albums, 1955–1996.* Menomonee Falls, Wis.: Record Research, 1996.

———. *Pop Memories, 1890–1954: The History of American Popular Music.* Menomonee Falls, Wis.: Record Research, 1986.

White, Timothy R. "From Disney to Warner Bros.: The Critical Shift." *Film Criticism* 16.3 (Spring 1992): 3–16.

Winge, John H. "Cartoons and Modern Music." *Sight and Sound* 17.67 (Autumn 1948): 136–37.

Zorn, John. "Carl Stalling: An Appreciation." Brochure notes for Carl Stalling, *The Carl Stalling Project: Music from Warner Bros. Cartoons, 1936–1958.* Warner Bros. Records 26027, 1990.

INDEX

Page numbers in italic refer to figures.

"The Aba Daba Honeymoon," 81
Abie's Irish Rose (Fleming), 15
"Ach du lieber Augustin," 33, 143, 194n27
Adamson, Joe, 135
Adorno, Theodor, 113, 124–25, 191n32
Advanced (publishing house), 17
Aesop's Fables, 4–5, 12, 17
Ake, David, 188n66
A-Lad-In His Lamp (McKimson), 190n15
"Alice in Cartoonland" (series), 12
Alice in Wonderland (McLeod), 179n10
Allan, Robin, 128, 142
Allen, Gracie, 189n3
"All God's Chillun Got Rhythm," 67
Allied forces, 23, 143. *See also* World War II
"Aloha Oe," 92
Along Came Daffy (Freleng), 25
"Am I Blue," 22, 27
Anderson, Tim, 14–15, 24
"Angel in Disguise," 27, 28, 32
Angel Puss (Jones), 27
Animaniacs, 3, 76, 161
Animated cartoons: animals in, 60; censorship of, 96–97; and classical music, 8, 107–31, 162; as comedy, 3, 5; construction of, 43, 154; critical discourse on, 3; critical perception of, 2–3; cross-dressing in, 138, 143–45, 151–53, 155, 156–57; dancing in, 91–92, 143–45, 147–48, 157, 186n41; extreme physical takes, 58–61; female characters in, 156; film studies concerning, 3–4; generic elements, 24, 30–34, 36–39, 60, 129; as genre, 2–3, 7; homosexuality, issues in, 185n29; "lifelessness" of, 7; lifelike movement in, 148; metanarratives in, 153–54; musicologists concerning, 3; 1980s renaissance, 161–62; and opera, 133–36, 145; performances in, 93; production costs, 179n9; production process, 9, 15–21, 120, 145–46; as popular culture, 113–14; relation to 1930s musicals, 116; religion in, 94–99; rock bands in, 161; stereotypes in, 30–34, 134–35, 183n2, 184n19, 186n42 (*see also* Stereotypes); storytelling styles, 35–39, 50–51, 59–61, 118–19, 151, 162; syndication of, 161; on television, 67, 76, 161; used for publicity, 86; violence in, 58–61
Animation industry in Hollywood, 6, 75, 161–162
Anime, reception in the United States, 3
"April Showers," 28
Armstrong, Louis, 81, 84, 86–91, 94–96; portrayal in films and cartoons, 89–90; voice of, 90
Armstrong, Sam, 142
ASCAP (American Society of Composers, Authors and Publishers), 14–15, 45
Avery, Tex, 18–19, 43, 59–60, 103; at MGM, 73–75
Axis powers, 34, 143. *See also* World War II

Bach, Johann Sebastian, 159
Back Alley Oproar (Freleng), 153, 193n9
Ballet, 56–57, 144, 147–48, 157
Ballet Russe de Monte Carlo, 148
The Band Concert (Jackson), 116–17, 190n16
Baraka, Amiri, 85
Barbera, Joe, 51–52, 58, 60–62, 134
Barber of Seville (Culhane), 135
The Barber of Seville (Rossini), 107. *See also* "Largo al Factotum"
Barney Bear, 55, 69
Barrier, Michael, 16, 19, 39, 59, 73, 74, 97, 122, 125, 128, 146, 155, 178n2, 179n9, 180n23
Bars & Stripes, 189n6
Bar sheets, 20–21, 52, 64
The Bartered Bride (Smetana), 26, 39, 196n43
Bartók, Béla, 45
Batman, 161
Baton Bunny (Jones), 35, 120, 121, 123, 127
Bayley, T. H., 186n41
Bayreuth, 155. *See also* Wagner, Richard
Beautiful Galatea (von Suppé), 109
Bebop. *See* Jazz: bebop
The Bee-Deviled Bruin (Jones), 175n39
Beethoven, Ludwig van, 41, 109–10, 128, 140, 143, 159, 189n3, 195n28; Fifth symphony and World War II, 109, 143, 195n28; Sixth symphony, "Pastoral," 130, 157
Bel canto. *See* Opera: bel canto
Bellini, Vincenzo, 135
Belwin (publishing house), 110
"Be My Little Baby Bumble Bee," 175n39
"Be My Love," 74
Benshoff, Harry, 130
Berg, Charles, 15–16
Bernie, Ben, 84
Bernstein, Leonard, 49
Betty Boop, 86–90, 99; interactions with black men, 88; and stereotypical plotlines, 87–88
Betty Boop's Big Boss (Fleischer), 31–32
Big band music, 8, 81, 93, 99. *See also* Jazz
Billboard (periodical), 10
Bill Haley and His Comets, 54
Bimbo's Initiation (Fleischer), 184n21
The Birth of a Nation (Griffith), 142, 150
Bishop, Henry Rowley, 55
Bisociation, 22–23, 26
Blackboard Jungle (Brooks), 54
Blackface minstrelsy: characteristics of,

83–84, 86, 94, 105–6; songs of, 83–84, 96, 105–6
"Blackout" gags, 37, 74
Blanc, Mel, 196n53
Bland, James, 96
Blimele (Mogulesko and Lateiner), 32
Blue Danube Waltz (Strauss), 189n6
Blues, 79
"Blues in the Night," 27, 100
Bogle, Donald, 88, 96–97, 102
Booby Hatched (Tashlin), 27
Boogie woogie. *See* Jazz: boogie woogie
Boogie Woogie Bugle Boy of Company "B" (Lantz), 102
Boogie Woogie Man (Culhane), 102
Boogie Woogie Sioux (Lovy), 102
Bosko: at MGM, 55, 184n18; at Warner Bros., 83, 105
Bosko the Talk-Ink Kid, 31–32
Boulevardier from the Bronx (Freleng), 35
Bowery Theatre, 140
Bradley, Scott, 46; approach to humor, 53; biography, 45–47, 75–76, 178nn1,5, 180n23; and chase music, 54–55; compared to Carl Stalling, 17, 47–55, 57; compositional style, 51–55, 162, 174n33; concert music, 50, 57; feature film scores, 47, 49–50, 54; illustrative scoring style, 44, 63–67; at MGM, 44, 179n20; and mickey-mousing, 63–64, 69, 72, 189n9; and modern music, 8, 49–50, 70–73, 182nn62,63, 189n9; orchestration style, 48–49, 53–54, 55; possibly at Iwerks, 45–46; preference for original music, 44; reputation, 44, 178n1, 180n21; salary, 180n21; scoring process, 51–54, 62; theories on cartoon music, 47–50, 55–56, 62–67, 167–69, 179n17, 180n33; use of MGM-owned songs, 67; use of popular music, 52–53, 55, 67–68, 181n54; use of string instruments, 54; use of themes, 68–69; use of Wagner's music, 194n22; and violence, 44, 61; work with Hanna and Barbera, 52–55, 61–62, 73; work with Tex Avery, 73–75
Brahms, Johannes, 2, 45, 107, 109–10, 140, 189n6
Breen, Joseph I., 97
Breil, J. C., 142, 176n58
"Bridal March," 150, 194n22. *See also* Lohengrin
"British Grenadiers," 74

Britten, Benjamin, 49
Brophy, Philip, 115, 152
Brown, Bernard, 6, 177n64
Bruckner, Anton, 110
Brünnhilde, 143–45, 151, 156–57,
    195n29
Bryan, Arthur Q., 196n53
Buck, as defined by Bogle, 88
Buddy's Pony Express (Hardaway),
    177n64
Bugs Bunny, 28, 39–42, 111, 114–26,
    136–40, 143–45, 147–57, 159,
    184n17; as anti-aesthete, 117;
    cartoons with Elmer Fudd, 152–
    54; in drag, 138, 143–45, 151–53,
    155, 156–57; as performer, 41, 125;
    singing, 114–17
Bugs Bunny Nips the Nips (Freleng),
    176n62, 190n15
Bugs Bunny Rides Again (Freleng),
    39–42
Burke, Timothy and Kevin, 107

Cage, John, 73
Calker, Darrell, 6, 102–3
Calloway, Cab, 84–85, 87–89, 94–96,
    98, 187nn49,63
"The Campbells are Coming," 81
"De Camptown Races," 33
The Captain and the Kids, 174n30
Captain Hareblower (Freleng), 142
The Carl Stalling Project, 10, 24, 161–
    62, 172n1
Carmen Get It! (Deitch), 127, 156
Carnegie Hall, 111–12, 114, 118, 127
Cartman, Eric, 162
"Cartman Gets an Anal Probe," 162
Cartoonia, 50, 57, 180n23
Cartoon music: and exoticism, 87,
    186n42; characteristics of, 109,
    112; common perceptions of,
    6; contemporary characteristics,
    162; early, 4–5, 174n33; and
    genre, 7; humor in, 21–30; mickey-
    mousing, 6, 63–64, 72; modernist
    approach, 70–73; orchestrating,
    136, 174n35; prescored, 56, 82,
    146, 180n33; roles of, 7, 30; scor-
    ing process, 16, 20–21, 48–49,
    50–55, 146; sing-along cartoons
    (*see* Fleischer studio: Song Car-
    Tunes); singing, 22–23, 55, 93,
    114–17, 121, 135–36, 148–49;
    special scores, 5; stock music in,
    161; synchronization, 19–20, 52–
    53, 63–66, 82, 98, 155, 162; in
    television cartoons, 161; use of

avant-garde music, 111; use of clas-
    sical music, 107–31, 150; use of
    jazz idiom, 77–78, 99, 105–6, 130;
    use of opera, 132–36, 141–42, 145;
    use of public domain music, 21,
    108, 162
"Cartoon Music of the Future" (Bradley),
    48, 167–68
Cartoon Network, 25
A Car-Tune Portrait (Fleischer), 191n26
Caruso, Enrico, 192n5
Casey, Kenneth, 84
Castelnuovo-Tedesco, Mario, 49, 179n20
Catch as Cats Can (Davis), 26
The Cat Concerto (Hanna and Barbera),
    116, 129, 189n6
Céleste, Bernadette, 69–70
Censorship. *See* Animated cartoons:
    censorship of
Central Avenue. *See* Nightclubs: Los
    Angeles
"The Charleston," 104
Chase cartoons, 36–39, 52–53, 54–55,
    58–61, 153–54
"Cheyenne," 31, 39
Chili Con Carmen, 156
"Chinatown, My Chinatown," 33, 87,
    176n58, 185n32
Chion, Michel, 62–66, 69–70
Chopin, Frédéric, 34, 107, 109, 176n58
Christlieb, Anthony, 49
Chuck Amuck (Jones), 157. *See also*
    Jones, Chuck: autobiographies
Chuck Reducks (Jones), 157. *See also*
    Jones, Chuck: autobiographies
"Cinema of attractions," 30
Ciro's, 123
Clair de Lune (Debussy), 194n24
Clampett, Robert, 18–19, 39, 43, 100–
    101, 153, 186n41, 187n55
Classical music: audiences for, 125; attire
    of, 121–23, 126; canon, 108–10,
    159; class issues of, 115–17, 119,
    123, 127, 128–31, 135; conductors,
    114, 121–27; in conflict with pop-
    ular music, 91, 114–18, 127, 130;
    culture of, 114, 117–27; and early
    film scores, 110; light classics, 109–
    10, 150; musicians, 120–21, 125;
    nineteenth-century music, 108–
    13, 132; orchestras, 120–21, 140;
    performance spaces for, 114, 116,
    117–23; sacralization of, 117, 119,
    127–31; singing, 114–16, 121, 135–
    36. *See also* Opera
Clausen, Alf, 76
Clean Pastures (Freleng), 93–99, 102

Click track, 48–49
Club Alabam, 100
Clydesdale horses, 143
Coal Black and de Sebben Dwarfs (Clampett), 99–101, 186n41
Cohen, Karl, 96–97
Coleman, Ornette, 104–5, 188n66
Columbia cartoons, 121, 180n25
Comedy shorts, 24
Como, Perry, 118
Concert halls, 111–12, 189n3. *See also* Classical music: performance spaces for
Concerto in B-Flat Minor (Tashlin), 191n26
Conductors. *See* Classical music: conductors
Congo Jazz (Harman and Ising), 77
Cooper, Gary, 41
Copland, Aaron, 49
Corbett, Horton, 45
A Corny Concerto (Clampett), 127, 189n6
Cotton Club, 85
The Courage of Lassie (Wilcox), 54
Crosby, Bing, 81
Cubby's Picnic (Donnelly and Muffati), 31
Cue sheets, 4–5, 34, 45–46
Culshaw, John, 60
"A Cup of Coffee, A Sandwich and You," 22, 25
Curtin, Hoyt, 6
Czibulka, Alphons, 150

Daffy Duck, 19, 193n9
Daffy—The Commando (Freleng), 194n27
Dahl, Ingolf, 45, 51, 180n21
Damrosch, Walter, 113
Dance music, electronic, 162
"The Dance of the Comedians," 26, 196n43
"The Dance of the Hours," 129
Dance of the Weed (Ising), 50, 56–58, 180n33
Dancing. *See* Animated cartoons: dancing in
Dandridge, Ruby, 100
Dandridge, Vivian, 100
Dangerous When Wet (Walters), 54
"The Darkville Dance," 184n21
Davis, Arthur, 19
Debussy, Claude, 48, 194n24
DeFrancesco, L. E., 5
Delalande, François, 69–70
de Nat, Joe, 6, 174n33

Dessau, Paul, 179n12
DeSylva, Brown & Henderson (publishing house), 17, 173n21
Detail sheets. *See* Bar sheets
Dexter's Laboratory, 3
Dialogue, 43, 49, 51
DIC (studio), 161
Diegetic music, 4, 63
Dietrich, James, 6, 174n33
Ding Dong Daddy (Freleng), 195n28
"Dinner Music for a Pack of Hungry Cannibals," 29
Dipsy Gypsy (Pal), 189n6
The Discontented Canary (Ising), 47, 55
Disney, Walt, 128, 165
Disney studio, 9, 192n47; characters, 83, 101; classical music, attitude toward, 127–31, 158, 162; output, 180n25; production costs, 179n9; role of music in, 19, 21, 57, 127–31, 142, 184n12, 187n49; Silly Symphonies, 48, 55, 57, 165; style, 24, 35–36, 55, 60; use of Wagner's music, 142, 195n29; and World War II, 143, 195n29
"Dixie," 33, 74, 100, 176n58
Dixieland Droopy (Avery), 190n16
Dixieland jazz, 8. *See also* Jazz
Donald Duck, 116–17
Donizetti, Gaetano, 118, 135, 157, 193n9
Dopey, 101
Doug, 161
Drag, 31
Drumming, jungle, 87
The Ducktators (McCabe), 176n62, 194n27
Dumb Patrol (Harman and Ising), 195n27

Early to Bet (McKimson), 27, 30
Eddy, Nelson, 130
Education for Death (Geronimi), 195n29
Education for Death: The Making of a Nazi (Ziemer), 195n29
Egghead, 91
Eisenstein, Sergei, 7
Eisler, Hanns, 182n62
Ellington, Duke, 81, 85
Elmer Fudd, 91, 119–20, 123, 136–40, 144–45, 148–49, 151–57; cartoons with Bugs Bunny, 152–54
Emmett, Daniel Decatur, 33, 176n58
Encyclopedia of Music for Pictures (Rapée), 4, 31, 141, 150, 184n21, 195n27
"Die Erlkönig," 1, 31

Etude (periodical), 129
"Evenings on the Roof" (concert series), 50
"Evening Star," 110
Exposure sheets, 174n33

Fairly OddParents, 3
Famous Studios, 99
Fantasia (Sharpsteen), 123, 127–31, 132, 142, 157, 158, 189n6, 192n47; initial failure of, 128; "Night on Bald Mountain" sequence, 193n14; reviews of, 128–29; "The Ride of the Valkyries" sequence, 142
Fantasia 2000, 130–31, 194n24
Fantasound, 128
Farnon, Dennis, 75
Fast and Furryous (Jones), 25–26, 27
Feature films, conventions of, 24
Fechit, Stepin, 94
Felix the cat, 4, 12, 17
Feuer, Jane, 116
The Fifth-Column Mouse (Freleng), 23, 33–34, 194n27, 195n28
Fifth Symphony (Beethoven), 109, 143, 195n28. *See also* Beethoven, Ludwig van
Filmation (studio), 161
Film funners, 15–16, 22
Film music: accompanying methods and manuals, 5, 13–16, 24, 30, 78–80, 108, 110, 141, 159, 176n58; ethnic stereotypes in, 186n42; generic, 30–34, 177n64; modern music in, 72, 182n62; mood music, 14, 161; popular music in, 14–16, 173n17; Romantic style, 54, 112; theme songs, 14–15; use of classical music, 110, 132, 159; use of jazz, 106; use of opera, 134–35, 141; use of public domain music, 21, 108, 162
Film Music (London), 5
Film Music: A Neglected Art (Prendergast), 6
Film musicals, 2, 67, 93, 96, 116, 162; "opera *vs* swing" narrative, 116
Film music criticism, 3
Film Music Forum (conference), 56
Film Music Notes, 6, 48
Film music terminology, 4
Film sound technology, 7, 184n14
"Fingal's Cave," 22, 175n39, 177n70
Fiorito, Joseph, 192n6
"The Five O'Clock Whistle," 100, 187n60
Flappers, 87
Die Fledermaus (Strauss), 143

Fleischer, Dave, 6
Fleischer, Lou, 6, 85
Fleischer studio: cartoons, 9, 84–91, 158; famous performers, 84–85, 185nn24,30; gag style, 89; history, 99; and Jewish identity issues, 85; and Paramount Pictures, 84–85, 90–91; production process, 84–85; Song Car-Tunes, 48, 84–85
Flinn, Caryl, 72
Floyd, Samuel, 184n17
The Flying Dutchman (Wagner), 28, 136, 138, 142, 150, 151
Foghorn Leghorn, 19
Forbstein, Leo, 166
Ford, Greg, 10, 196n43
42nd Street (Bacon), 93
Foster, Stephen, 2, 33, 84, 105, 108, 176n58
Foxworthy, Jeff, 158–59
Franklyn, Milt, 6–7, 21, 150, 174n35
"Frat," 31
Freberg, Stan, 104
Free jazz. *See* Jazz: free
Freleng, Isadore "Friz," 18, 20, 145, 153, 174n30; on Carl Stalling, 20, 22; on Frank Marsales, 19; at MGM, 174n30; on music, 110; storytelling style, 39–42, 177n71
Friedhofer, Hugo, 50, 73
Friedwald, Will, 24, 111
Frith, Simon, 125
Frog, Michigan J., 135
"From Nippon Bridge," 176n62
"From Spirituals to Swing," 127
"From the Cotton Field," 184n21
"Furioso #2," 35
Futurama, 3

Gabbard, Krin, 80–81, 89
Gallopin' Gaucho (Disney), 12, 166
Gershwin, George, 81, 130
Gesamtkunstwerk. See Wagner, Richard: and *Gesamtkunstwerk*
"Gimme That Old Time Religion," 98–99
Goddess of Spring (Jackson), 187n49
"Go Get the Ax," 190n15
Gold Diggers of 1933 (LeRoy), 93
Gold Diggers of 1935 (Berkeley), 93
Golden age of Hollywood animation, 2
Goldilocks and the Jivin' Bears (Freleng), 187n64
Goldsmith, Jerry, 49
Gorbman, Claudia, 30, 63
Gorilla My Dreams (McKimson), 190n15

Göring, Hermann, 143–45, 195n29
Grant, Barry Keith, 78, 83
Gray, Milt, 26
Greatest Man in Siam (Culhane), 102
The Great Train Robbery (Porter), 12, 165
The Green Pastures (Connelly), 93–94
The Green Pastures (Keighley and Connelly), 93–94, 96–97
Griffin, Sean, 185n29
Griffith, D. W., 142
Gulliver's Travels (Fleischer), 192n47
Gunning, Tom, 17, 30

Haden, Charlie, 188n66
Hall, Tubby, 87, 90–91
Hamilton, Marie L., 107
The Hams that Couldn't Be Cured (Lantz), 102, 188n65
Hanna, Bill, 51, 58–62, 134
Hanna-Barbera (studio), 161
Hansel and Gretel (Humperdinck), 69
Happy Harmonies (series), 47, 50, 55–58, 68
Hardaway, Ben "Bugs," 13
Hardaway, Ben, and Cal Dalton, 19
Hare Ribbin' (Clampett), 153
Hare Splitter (Freleng), 190n15
Hare Trigger (Freleng), 19, 177n73, 190n15
Hare We Go (Freleng), 27
Harlem, 80, 88–89, 93, 96, 102
Harlem Renaissance, 85
Harman, Hugh, 18
Harman-Ising, 179n10; at Disney, 20; at MGM, 18, 45, 47, 50–51, 55–58, 184n18; production costs, 179n9; at Warner Bros., 20, 47, 179n9, 184n18. *See also* Harman, Hugh; Ising, Rudy
Harms (publishing house), 17
Hawaii, 92
"The Headless Horseman," 45
Henderson, Fletcher, 85
Hérold, Louis, 150
Herr Meets Hare (Freleng), 143–45, 148, 152, 157, 195n29
Hickey, Dave, 61
High culture/low culture conflict, 115–17, 134, 154–55, 162
High Diving Hare (Freleng), 28, 166
Hindemith, Paul, 45, 54, 179n12
Hitler, Adolf, 23, 143, 145, 195n29
Hollywood Bowl, 114, 118, 121
Hollywood Bowl (Perkins), 118
Hollywood Canine Canteen (McKimson), 123

Hollywood Hills, 114
Hollywood Production Code, 31, 97
Hollywood Steps Out (Avery), 123
"Home! Sweet Home!" 34, 74
Honegger, Arthur, 45
The Horn Blows at Midnight (Walsh), 54
Horowitz, Joseph, 113, 128, 140–41, 158
How to Play the Cinema Organ (Tootell), 4
Huckvale, David, 135, 150
Huggins, Nathan Irvin, 85, 89, 90
Humperdinck, Engelbert, 69
Humor and music, 22
Hungarian Dances (Brahms), 110, 189n6
Hungarian Rhapsodies (Liszt), 110
Hungarian Rhapsody No. 2 (Liszt), 8, 110–13, 116, 126, 129, 162, 189n6
"Hurry No. 2," 14

Iconic music, 4
"If I Could Be with You (One Hour Tonight)," 190n15
I Heard (Fleischer), 88, 186n35
"I'll Be Glad When You're Dead, You Rascal You," 86–87, 90
I'll Be Glad When You're Dead, You Rascal You (Fleischer), 86–91
"I Love to Singa," 94, 97, 162
I Love to Singa (Avery), 103, 162, 190nn16,20
"I'm a Busy Little Bumble Bee," 22
"I'm Forever Blowing Bubbles," 26
"I'm Looking Over a Four Leaf Clover," 25–26
Impressionist music, 56
"In an Eighteenth Century Drawing Room," 1, 29
Independence, MO, 12
"Indian Dawn," 14
"Inflammatus," 41
Inki, 177n70
Interstate highways, 26
"In the Stirrups," 14, 31
Irving, Washington, 45
Irwin, Charles, 82
Ising, Rudy, 18, 174n29. *See also* Harman-Ising
The Isle of Pingo-Pongo (Avery), 35, 91–93
Isomorphic music, 4, 70
"Is You Is or Is You Ain't My Baby?" 62, 67
"It Had to Be You," 32
"It's Magic," 190n15
Iwerks, Ub, 12

Jabberjaw, 161
Jackson, Wilfred, 172n6
"Japanese Sandman," 34
Jazz: bebop, 8, 103; and black culture,
    77–78, 80, 83–84, 88–89, 95–103;
    and the body, 80, 85–86, 100;
    boogie woogie, 8, 77, 99, 102–3,
    116, 126; in cartoons, 5, 8, 33,
    77–106 (see also Cartoon music:
    use of jazz idiom); early jazz, 78–
    84; in Fleischer cartoons, 84–91;
    free, 8, 103–5; "hot," 96, 103–4,
    188n64; in Lantz cartoons, 99,
    101–3; message of, 79–80; modal,
    103; primitivism and, 80, 81–92,
    105–6; public perception of, 8,
    78–80, 103, 105–6; rhythm of,
    80, 96, 100, 102–3, 106; songs,
    famous, 84; stereotypes of, 77–80,
    83–84, 99–103, 104–5; supposed
    African origins of, 80–83; swing
    music in cartoons, 8, 99–103;
    trumpet, 98, 101; in Warner Bros.
    cartoons, 93–101, 103–5; West
    Coast, 104–5
The Jazz Fool (Disney), 77
Jazz Mad, 77
Jazzmania, 90
Jazz musicians, representations of in
    film, 8
The Jazz Singer (Crosland), 93, 103, 106,
    190n20
The Jeff Foxworthy Show, 158–59
Jenkins, Henry, 30–31
Jewell, James, 189n10
Jews in cartoons. See Fleischer studio:
    and Jewish identity issues;
    Stereotypes, Jewish
"Jim Crow," 84
Jive, 99–100
Jolson, Al, 94, 103, 104, 162, 187n63,
    190n20
Jones, Chuck, 18, 58; autobiographies,
    150, 157; on Carl Stalling, 11, 22;
    on classical music and opera, 113–
    14, 120, 124–25, 132–33, 134–35,
    150, 151–57, 159; directorial style,
    25–26, 35–39, 146, 153; influence
    by Disney, 35–36; at MGM, 172n9;
    on Twain, 150; at Warner Bros., 18,
    19, 35–39, 145–146
Jones, Quincy, 130
Jones, Spike, and His City Slickers, 32
"Jonny's Got a Nickel," 74
Josie and the Pussycats, 161
"Jubilo (Kingdom Coming)," 33
Jump Start (comic strip), 159

Jungle Jazz (Bailey and Foster), 77
Jungle Jive (Culhane), 77, 103
Jungle Rhythm (Disney), 77, 183n12
Jungle settings, 80–84, 86–92

Kansas City, MO, 12
Kansas City Star, 12
Keaton, Buster, 17
"Khosn, Kale Mazl Tov," 32, 176n60
Kiddie Koncert (Lundy), 191n26
Kilenyi, Edward, 5
Kilfeather, Eddie, 6
"Kimygayo," 176n62
"King David," 45
King of Jazz (Anderson), 80–84, 103,
    184n13
King of the Hill, 3
The Kissing Bandit (Benedek), 54
Klein, Norman, 75
Knapp, Ray, 187n49
Kodály, Zoltán, 49
Koestler, Arthur, 22–23
Korngold, Erich Wolfgang, 194n21
Krazy Kat, 17
Kreutzer, Rodolphe, 188n65
Kubik, Gail, 6, 75
Ku Klux Klan, 142, 150

Ladies Home Journal, 129
"The Lady in Red," 22, 32, 175n39
Lampe, J. B., 176n58
Lang, Edith, 4, 13–15, 78–80
Lantz, Walter, 101–3, 135; cartoons, 9,
    121, 143, 158, 180n25; and King
    of Jazz, 81–83, 184n14; Musical
    Miniatures series, 191n26; Swing
    Symphonies series, 99, 101–3,
    188n65
"Largo al Factotum," 114, 126–27,
    135, 193n9. See also The Barber
    of Seville
Lateiner, Joseph, 32
"Laugh, Clown, Laugh," 192n6
Laundry Blues (Davis and Foster), 31–32
Laura, 171n11
Lava, William, 6
Layout artist, role of, 146
"The Legend of Sleepy Hollow," 45
Leitmotif. See Wagner, Richard:
    leitmotifs
"(Lena is the Queen of) Palesteena," 32
Lerner, Neil, 180n21
Levine, Lawrence, 109–10, 115, 117,
    123, 134
Lexington, MO, 12
Lichine, David, 148
Light Cavalry (von Suppé), 109, 189n10

"Listen to the Mocking Bird," 27, 55, 184n21
Liszt, Franz, 2, 109–11, 113, 116, 162, 189n9
Little Cheeser, 69
Little Red Rodent Hood (Freleng), 28
Lohengrin (Wagner), 112, 150, 194n22
London, Kurt, 5
The Lone Ranger (radio series), 112–13, 189n10
Long-Haired Hare (Jones), 114–27, 134, 156
"Long, Long Ago," 186n41
Looney Tunes, 16–17, 174n29, 175n50, 189n8, 193n13, 195n36
Los Angeles Oratorio Society, 45
Los Angeles Philharmonic Auditorium, 45
Low culture/high culture conflict, 115–17, 134, 154–55, 162
Lucia di Lammermoor, 118, 193n9
Lutz, E. G., 58–59
Luz, Ernst, 176n58
Lyman, Abe, 174n29

The Mad Maestro (Harman), 127, 191n26
Magical Maestro (Avery), 125–27, 135–36
Magic Fluke (Hubley), 189n6
Mahler, Gustav, 110
Make Mine Music (Grant), 130
Maltese, Michael, 19, 58, 133, 145, 146, 150, 152–53, 157
Maltin, Leonard, 146, 180n27
"Mama yo quiero," 127
"Manhattan Serenade," 67
"The Man on the Flying Trapeze," 55
The Man with the Golden Arm (Preminger), 106
"Marche Funèbre," 109, 176n58
Marks, Martin, 150
Marsales, Frank, 6, 17, 19, 174n33, 176n64, 179n10, 195n27
"La Marseillaise," 55
Martin, Steve, 130
Marx Brothers, 134
"Massa's in de Cold, Cold Ground," 33, 190n15
The Mastersingers of Nuremberg (Wagner), 145
McCabe, Norman, 19
McKimson, Robert, 19
McLaren, Norman, 6
Melody Time (Sharpsteen), 130
Mendelssohn, Felix, 109, 159, 175n39, 177n70

Merman, Ethel, 84
Merrie Melodies, 16, 174n29; early requirement to use songs, 17, 19, 21; theme song, 34–35. See also Warner Bros. cartoons
"Merrily We Roll Along," 34–35
"The Merry-Go-Round Broke Down," 136
MGM: musical films, 67; music publishing, 67; studio, 49, 53–54, 75
MGM cartoons, 6, 18, 143, 158; gags in, 68; music in, 44–76; output, 180n25; physicality of, 63; production costs, 179n9, 180n21; and sound effects, 64–66; timing in, 52; use of bar sheets, 52; use of dialogue, 50–51, 57–58; use of MGM-owned songs, 53; violence in, 52, 58–61; writing style of, 50–51, 58–61, 121
Mickey Mouse, 83, 84, 105, 116–17, 130, 183n12
Mickey-mousing. See Bradley, Scott: and mickey-mousing; Cartoon music: mickey-mousing
Midler, Bette, 130
Military bands, 141
Milk and Money (Avery), 34
Mills Brothers, 84, 92, 94–95, 186n41
"Minnie's Yoo Hoo," 165
Minnie the Moocher (Fleischer), 88
Minstrelsy: characteristics of, 83–84, 86, 94, 105–6; songs of, 83–84, 96, 105–6
Miranda, Carmen, 127
Modal jazz. See Jazz: modal
Modernist music, 72. See also Bradley, Scott: and modern music
Mogulesko, Sigmund, 32
Monteux, Pierre, 50
Morning, Noon, and Night in Vienna (von Suppé), 109, 121
Motion Picture Moods for Pianists and Organists (Rapée), 14, 31
The Mouse Catcher, 5
Mouse Warming (Jones), 36–38, 177n68
Mouse Wreckers (Jones), 27
Moving Picture World (periodical), 79
Mozart, Wolfgang Amadeus, 140, 189n3
Musical Accompaniment of Moving Pictures (Lang and West), 13–15
Musicals. See Film musicals
Music appreciation, 107–8, 158
"Music Hath Charms," 81
Music Land (Jackson), 190nn16,20, 196n49
Mussorgsky, Modest, 128, 193n9
Mutiny on the Bunny (Freleng), 27

"My Darlin' Clementine," 127
"My Gal," 114
"My Little Buckaroo," 39
"My Old Kentucky Home," 21
Mythology, German, 142
Mythology, Norse, 142, 143, 151

"Nagasaki," 33, 94, 98, 100, 186n41
"Navajo," 39
Nazis, 143, 145; music used to depict, 33–34, 143, 195n27
NBC Music Appreciation Hour, 113
The New Car (Iwerks), 32
Newman, Alfred, 73
Newsom, John, 6
Newsreels, 24, 84
"New Year's Eve in a Haunted House," 29
A Night at the Opera (Wood), 134, 192n5
A Night on Bald Mountain (Mussorgsky), 128
Nightclubs: Los Angeles, 100, 102, 104–5, 123–24; New York, 86, 88–89, 93, 96, 102
Noble, Maurice, 146, 155
Notes to You (Freleng), 193n9
Novochord, 54
Nye, Edgar Wilson "Bill," 196n43

"Oh! Dem Golden Slippers," 96, 98
Ohrwurm, 1
"Oh, You Beautiful Doll," 32, 42
"Old Folks at Home (Swanee River)," 33, 94, 101–2, 176n58
"The Old Gray Mare," 175n40
"Old King Cole," 100
The Old Man of the Mountain (Fleischer), 88
One Froggy Evening (Jones), 35, 135–36
"On the Atchison, Topeka, and Santa Fe," 67
The Oompahs (Cannon), 190n20
Opera: bel canto, 135, 149; in cartoons, 8, 132–36; conventions of, 120, 121, 148, 151, 154; costumes, 156–57; fans of, 154; language used for cartoons, 135–36, 156; overtures, 140; popular culture and, 132–33; satire of, 133–36, 140, 159; singers, 136, 148; stereotypes of, 132–35, 136, 148, 154, 158; stereotypes of women in, 156–57
Opera house, 155
Operation: Rabbit (Jones), 26
opera versus swing, 8, 116
Opium den, reference to, 87

The Opry House (Disney), 32
Orchestras. See Classical music: orchestras
Organists, theater and film, 4, 13–16
Original Dixieland Jazz Band, 32
Oswald the Rabbit, 83, 105, 184n17
"Our Gang" (shorts), 12, 17
Out-foxed (Avery), 74
"Over the Rainbow," 67
Overture to William Tell (Lundy), 191n26

Pacific Coast Musician, 45
Paderewski, Ignace, 189n3
Pagliacci (Leoncavallo), 192n6
Pantomime, 35–37, 177n71
Paramount Pictures, 84–85, 90, 99, 179n10
Parlor songs, 2
Pastoral stories, 55
Pathé, 5
Patterson, Prof. William Morrison, 80, 85
Payne, John Howard, 55
Pearl Harbor, attack on, 23
Pebbles and Bamm-Bamm, 161
Pelléas et Mélisande (Debussy), 62
Penn and Teller, 130
Peter and the Wolf (Prokofiev), 130
Photoplay music, 5
Piano playing, 148
Piano sonata in C major, K. 545 (Mozart), 1
Pied Piper of Basin Street (Culhane), 102
Pigs in a Polka (Freleng), 127, 177n71, 189n6
"Pilgrims' Chorus," 110, 138, 140, 143, 149, 151. See also Tannhäuser
Pinkard, Maceo, 84
Pinky & The Brain, 161
Pinocchio (Sharpsteen and Luske), 192n47
Pizzicato Pussycat (Freleng), 111, 118
Plane Crazy (Disney), 12
"Plugging" (Adorno), 113
Poddany, Eugene, 6, 172n9
The Poet and Peasant (Lundy), 191n26
The Poet and Peasant (von Suppé), 109
Popeye, 99
Porky at the Crocadero (Tashlin), 123
Porky in Wackyland (Clampett), 187n55
Porky Pig, 19
Porky's Duck Hunt (Avery), 27
Porky's Moving Day (King), 34, 177n64
Porky's Poultry Plant (Tashlin), 34
"Powerhouse," 29–30
The Powerpuff Girls, 3, 162

"Pre-Festival Music for the Coming
    Merger of Two Professional
    Marriage Brokers," 29
"Prelude to the Afternoon of a Faun," 48
Prendergast, Roy, 6
Prescoring. *See* Cartoon music: prescored
Previn, André, 49
Prokofiev, Sergey, 49, 130
"The Punch" (Chion terminology),
    65–66
Puss Gets the Boot (Hanna and Barbera),
    61
"Put 'Em in a Box, Tie 'Em with a
    Ribbon (and Throw 'Em in the
    Deep Blue Sea)," 27
Puttin' on the Dog (Hanna and Barbera),
    53, 62, 69–72
Pvt. Snafu (series), 194nn22,25

Quimby, Fred, 47, 58

Rabbit Every Monday (Freleng), 190n15
The Rabbit of Seville (Jones), 119–20,
    156
Rachmaninoff, Sergey, 189n3
Ragtime, 80
"A Rainy Night in Rio," 114
Raksin, David, 6, 50, 73
Rap, 106
Rapée, Erno, 4, 13, 14–15, 41, 150,
    176n58
Ravel, Maurice, 50, 57; *Daphnis and
    Chloé,* 50, 57
Rawlinson, Harold, 128
Raye, Martha, 137
Raymond Scott Quintette, 28–29
Read, Harry, 5
Rebecca of Sunnybrook Farm (Dwan),
    29
"Reckless Night on Board an Ocean
    Liner," 29
Red Hot Riding Hood (Avery), 99
Redman, Don, 88, 186n35
Religion. *See* Animated cartoons: religion in
Remick, Jerome (publishing house), 17,
    84, 173n21
Ren & Stimpy, 3, 161
Rendering, 62–63
A Rhapsody in Black and Blue (Scotto),
    90–91
Rhapsody in Blue (Gershwin), 81, 130,
    183n11
Rhapsody in Rivets (Freleng), 111, 119,
    177n71, 189n6
Rhapsody Rabbit (Freleng), 111, 118,
    126, 148, 177n71, 189n6
The Rhinegold (Wagner), 194n22

Rhinemaidens, 151, 156
Rhythm Boys, 81. *See also* Whiteman,
    Paul
Riabachinska, Titania, 148
Riddle, Nelson, 49
"The Ride of the Valkyries," 142, 150,
    196n49
Riefenstahl, Leni, 145
Rienzi (Wagner), 109, 137, 150, 151
The Ring of the Niebelungen (Wagner),
    133, 151, 155
Roach, Max, 188n66
Road Runner and Coyote (series), 19,
    25–27, 36–39, 52, 58, 146
Robinson, Bill "Bojangles," 94
"Rock around the Clock," 54
Rock 'n' roll, 106
Rodemich, Eugene, 6, 32
Rodeo Dough, 31
Rogers, Shorty, 104–5
Rogin, Michael, 80–81
"Rosemary," 15
Rossini, Gioacchino, 1, 39, 109, 112–
    14, 135, 156, 189nn9,10, 193n9
Rotoscoping, 148, 195n38
Rousseau, Henri, 190n19
Ruby-Spears (studio), 161
Rugrats, 161
"Running Wild," 68
Russian Rhapsody (Clampett), 195n27

Sally, Irene and Mary (Seiter), 29
Salvation Army, 98
Sam Fox (publishing house), 5, 34, 110
Sampson, Henry, 83
Sanjek, Russell, 81
Sapoznik, Henry, 32
Sartin, Hank, 16, 93, 116, 186n45
"Save Me Sister," 94
Scheib, Philip, 6, 174n33
Schlesinger, Leon, 13, 17–19, 21, 47, 97,
    179n9, 193n9
Schneider, Steve, 16
Schnittke, Alfred, 179n12
Schoenberg, Arnold, 70–73, 182n63
Schroeder, David, 151
Schubert, Franz, 1, 41, 109
Schumann, Robert, 109
Scott, Keith, 186n44, 191n39
Scott, Raymond (Harry Warnow), 1,
    28–30, 188n64
Scotto, Aubrey, 90
Scrap Happy Daffy (Tashlin), 194n27,
    195n28
Scrub Me Mama with a Boogie Beat
    (Lantz), 101–2
Seinfeld, 108

Selznick, David O., 6
Sharples, Winston, 6
"The Sheik of Araby," 32
"She'll Be Comin' 'round the Moutain,"
91
She Was an Acrobat's Daughter (Freleng),
123
"Shine," 86, 90
Shock chords. See Stinger chords
Short subjects, 24
Shostakovich, Dimitri, 49, 179n12
Sibelius, Jean, 194n24
Siegfried (Wagner), 149, 150, 151
Silly Symphonies, 48, 55, 57, 165
The Simpsons, 3, 76
Sinatra, Frank, 118
Singing: popular, 114–17; operatic, 114–
17, 135–36, 148–49
The Singing Kid (Keighley), 94, 103
The Skeleton Dance (Disney), 165
Slapstick, 51, 67–68, 144
The Sliphorn King of Polaroo (Lundy),
102
Small, Christopher, 119–20, 122–23,
154, 157
Smetana, Bedrich, 26, 39, 196n43
Smith, Jeff, 22–24, 26
Snow White, 100
Snow-White (Fleischer), 185n33
Snow White and the Seven Dwarfs
(Hand), 100, 128, 192n47
Solid Serenade (Hanna and Barbera),
62–69, 72
"Someone's Rocking My Dreamboat,"
190n15
Song Car-Tunes. See Fleischer studio
Song plugging, 15–16
Sound editor, role of, 49
Sound effects, 49, 51, 64–66, 161
Source music, 4
Sousa, John Philip, 141
South Park, 162
Spielberg, Steven, 161
SpongeBob SquarePants, 3
Spooks, 5
Stage Door Cartoon (Freleng), 123
Stalling, Carl, 11; approach to humor,
6–9, 24–25, 74; as arranger, 13,
177n65; biography, 10, 12–13,
19, 165–66, 172nn3,9; colleagues'
perception of, 11, 22; compared
to Scott Bradley, 17, 47–55, 63;
compositional style, 11, 16, 22,
31, 34–42; at Disney, 7, 10, 12–13,
21, 43, 165, 177n65; on Disney,
21; feature film score, 54; as film
accompanist, 12–16, 31, 142,

194n23; at Iwerks, 7, 10, 13, 43,
46, 165, 177n65; as postmodernist,
43, 108, 177n74; and Raymond
Scott, 28–30; recent fame of, 10,
44; scoring process, 53; scoring
style, 10–43, 161–62, 177n65; use
of popular music, 7, 10–43, 53,
84, 100, 174n38; use of Wagner's
music, 141–42; at Van Beuren, 13;
at Warner Bros., 10, 165; work with
Milt Franklyn, 7, 174n35; work with
Tex Avery, 74
Steamboat Willie (Disney), 12, 172n6,
183n12
Steiner, Max, 6
Stereotypes: African American, 31–32,
78–103, 183n2; Africans, 82–84,
86–89; American South, 176n58;
Asian, 33–34, 87, 127, 176nn58,62;
Chinese, 176n58; gender, 31–32,
84, 156–157; German, 33–34, 142,
143, 145, 195n27; Japanese, 33–34,
143; Jewish, 31–32; Native Ameri-
can, 87, 91; Pacific Islander, 92,
127; race, 32–33, 78–86, 105–6;
religion, 31
Stinger chords, 53, 63–65, 72, 75
Stokowski, Leopold, 111, 121–26,
128–30, 180n23; idiosyncrasies
of, 124–25
Stone, Richard, 76, 162
Storyboard, in Stalling's composing pro-
cess, 20
Strauss, Johann, 109–10, 140, 143, 189n6
Stravinsky, Igor, 45, 54; "The Rite of
Spring," 50
The Swan of Tuonela (Sibelius), 194n24
"Sweet and Lovely," 74
"Sweet Dreams, Sweetheart," 27
"Sweet Georgia Brown," 33, 84, 92, 97,
185n22
"Swing for Sale," 33, 94–95, 97
Swing music. See Jazz: swing music in
cartoons
Swing Social (Hanna and Barbera), 99
The Swooner Crooner (Tashlin), 29–30
Sylvester, 174n31
Symphonic poems, 48
Synchronization. See Cartoon music:
synchronization

"Take Me Out to the Ball Game," 192n5
Tambling, Jeremy, 134–35, 149
Tannhäuser (Wagner), 138, 140, 150,
151, 152; ballet in, 147–48; Venus-
berg music, 147–48, 151. See also
"Pilgrims' Chorus"

Tashlin, Frank, 19, 35
Taylor, Cecil, 111
Taylor, Deems, 130
T. B. Harms (publishing house), 17
Tchaikovsky, Pytor Il'yich, 109, 140
Teagarden, Jack, 103
Tebbel, John, 25
Television, cartoons produced for: music
    in, 67, 76, 161–62; relation to the-
    atrical cartoons, 162; time-saving
    production techniques, 161
Terry cartoons, 121
"Thanatopsis," 45, 47, 178n3
"That Old Feeling," 69
Three Little Bops (Freleng), 104–5, 188n66
Three Little Pigs (Gillett), 13, 31
Thompson, Kristin, 2–3
Thomson, Virgil, 127
Timberg, Sammy, 6
Timing, 20
Tin Pan Alley, 2, 15, 28, 35, 81–82,
    85, 117, 173n21; relationship with
    Hollywood film studios, 14–15,
    17–18
Tin Pan Alley Cats (Clampett), 98–99
Tiny Toon Adventures, 161
"A Tiskit, A Tasket," 127
Tokio Jokio (McCabe), 176n62, 194n27
"Tom" (Bogle), 89
Tom and Jerry (series), 36, 50–53, 58–
    62, 73, 129; musical themes, 69
Tom and Jerry in the Hollywood Bowl
    (Hanna and Barbera), 118, 127
Tootell, George, 4
Toy Town Hall (Freleng), 34
"Trade Winds," 190n15
Tristan and Isolde (Wagner), 69
Triumph of the Will (Riefenstahl), 145
"The Trolley Song," 67
Trumpet, jazz. See Jazz: trumpet
"The Turkey in the Straw," 117, 183n12,
    184n21. See also "Zip Coon"
Turkisher, Art, 6
Twain, Mark, 150, 196n43
Tweety, 19, 174n31
Twelve-tone music, 70–73, 182n62. See
    also Bradley, Scott: and modern
    music
"Twilight in Turkey," 188n64

UCLA, 113
Underscore music, 4
United Productions of America (UPA),
    6, 9, 75
Universal Pictures, 83
UPA (United Productions of America),
    6, 9, 75

Valkyrie leitmotif, 149, 150, 151, 152,
    155. See also Wagner, Richard:
    leitmotifs
The Valkyries (Wagner), 151, 155,
    195n29
Vallee, Rudy, 84
"The Valley of the White Poppies," 45
Van Beuren studio, 13
Vaudeville, 30, 32, 51, 67, 69, 83, 85,
    123, 154
Venusberg. See Tannhäuser
Verdi, Giuseppe, 110, 189n3
"Vienna Life," 143
Viennese opera, 2
Violence in cartoons. See MGM cartoons:
    violence
"Vision of Salome," 176n58
Vitaphone, 173n24
Von Suppé, Franz, 2, 34, 109, 121, 150,
    190n10

Wagner, Richard, 48, 69, 109–10, 112,
    149–50, 155; associated with Nazi
    Germany, 145; Bayreuth, 155; and
    Gesamtkunstwerk, 48, 132, 151,
    155; leitmotifs, 136, 142, 148, 149,
    151, 152, 155, 194n21; melodic
    style, 135, 149, 150, 152; music
    in cartoons, 132–33, 136, 141–42,
    149–50, 194n22; music in films,
    132, 149–50, 194n21; operas,
    stereotypes of, 132–33, 136, 151,
    153–54, 157–58; orchestration,
    136; popularity in the United States,
    140–42
Waller, Fats, 92, 94, 98–99, 186n41
Walton, William, 49
Waltz, 143
Warner Bros.: film musicals, 93–94, 96;
    music publishing, 11, 17–18, 34,
    173n21 (see also Stalling, Carl: use
    of popular music); studio, 18, 148;
    studio orchestra, 35, 53–54,
    174n29, 177n65
Warner Bros. cartoons: caricatures of
    famous persons, 91–99; characters
    of, 19, 83; death in, 152–54; gags
    in, 52, 154–55; influence of film
    musicals, 93, 96, 116; intertextual-
    ity of, 43, 155; jazz in, 93–101,
    103–5; musical instrumentation of,
    35; musical style of, 16–21; music
    requirements, 17–18, 174n29; popu-
    larity of, 161; primitivism stereo-
    types in, 91–92; production process,
    15–21, 145–46; singing in, 20, 22–
    23; topical humor in, 155; trave-

logue plots, 91–92; use of Warner
Bros.–owned songs, 17–21, 53, 84,
93–94, 97–99, 173n21, 174n38;
vaudeville influence on, 30, 154,
157; voice artists, 93; and World
War II, 143; writing style, 16–21,
35–42, 86, 121, 129, 145, 152,
153. *See also* Looney Tunes; Merrie
Melodies
Warnow, Mark, 29
Watson, Leo "Zoot," 100
Waxman, Franz, 73
"We Did It Before (And We Can Do It
Again)," 23
Weinman, Jaime, 151
Wells, Paul, 87
"We're Off to See the Wizard," 67
West, George, 4, 13–15, 78–80
Westby, James, 179n20
West Coast jazz. *See* Jazz: West Coast
Western films, 39–42
What's Opera, Doc? (Jones), 35, 132–59;
dancing in, 147–48; and *Gesamt-
kunstwerk*, 151; inspiration for,
143–45, 152, 157, 195n29; "Kill
the wabbit!" 136–37, 148, 149,
152–53, 155; as opera parody, 145;
plot synopsis, 136–40; production
issues, 145–46; "Return My Love,"
138, 149; role of music, 146–51;
soundtrack, 146; story construction,
151; unused gags, 145, 195n39
Wheeler, Clarence, 6
"When It's Sleepy Time Down South,"
89
"When Yuba Plays the Rhumba on the
Tuba," 114
Whiteman, Paul, 80–84, 183n12; style
of jazz, 81–83, 104, 184n13
Whitney, John, 6

Whole-tone music. *See* Bradley, Scott:
and modern music
Williams, Esther, 54
Williams, John, 49
William Tell overture (Rossini), 8, 31, 39,
112–13, 189n10
Willie the Whale, 130
Willner, Hal, 10
Winge, John, 54, 71
Winner, Septimus, 55, 184n21
"Wintermärchen," 109, 189n4
Witmark & Sons (publishing house), 17,
110, 173n21
Woody Woodpecker, 135
Work, Henry Clay, 33
World War I, 195n27
World War II, 23, 29, 33–34, 44, 60,
100–101, 109, 142–45, 194n22.
See also Allied forces; Axis powers;
Disney studio: and World War II;
Nazis

"Yankee Doodle," 183n12
The Yellow Cab Man (Donohue), 54
Yiddish theater, 32
Yodeling, 91
Yosemite Sam, 19, 177n73
"You and You," 143
You Ought to Be in Pictures (Freleng),
193n9
Your Hit Parade, 29

Zamecnik, John Stepan, 5, 34–35, 177n64
Zampa (Hérold), 150
Ziemer, Gregor, 195n29
"Zip Coon," 84, 185n21. *See also* "The
Turkey in the Straw"
Zoot Cat (Hanna and Barbera), 99
Zorn, John, 177n74
Zurke, Bob, 103

COMPOSITOR: *Integrated Composition Systems*

TEXT: *10/13 Sabon*

DISPLAY: *Triplex Bold and Light; Franklin Gothic Book*

PRINTER AND BINDER: *Thomson-Shore, Inc.*